"I found *Awakening* by Mary Rodwell to be a fascinating book. It is insightful, factual, detailed, and looks at the many different aspects of the alien abduction and Contact phenomenon. Those interested in this subject will undoubtedly hail this book as being a classic. It will take pride of place in countless libraries around the world and will be referred to by scholars of the subject for a long time to come. It will also comfort many of those who have experienced the abduction phenomenon on a first hand basis."

Philip Mantle
Former Director of Investigations for
BUFORA (British UFO Research Association)
Co–Author *Without Consent*

"This isn't just another research book, it is much, much, more as it is written by a lady who has *hands on* contact with the people she writes about. Mary is a trained counsellor who has made it her life's work to help those who are trying to cope with the many aspects of alien or extraterrestrial Contact.

Her professionalism shines through the pages, combined with her compassion and true concern for the people she is trying to help. Her approach to each case is totally non–sensationalist, looking at all possibilities and explanations, logical, rational and often irrational. Mary softly challenges the reader's perceptions and many will no doubt find themselves questioning their own views on the realities of this bizarre subject. "Someone once said, with regards to the UFO/Abduction phenomenon, *the absence of evidence is NOT evidence of absence* and how true that statement is! At last, we have a well written, well researched book which will be of tremendous help to so many, both now and in the future."

Ann Andrews – Author of *Abducted*

Readers' response to Awakening:

"Awakening is an excellent resource book that helps laymen and experiencers, and professionals attempt to gain an understanding of this world wide Phenomenon."

Dolores Cannon – *Author* (USA)

"Awakening helped me enormously. It thrilled me to learn people in Australia have experiences like myself. I found these connections because of one keen and courageous woman, a professional. Awakening is a big lantern book. "

Dana Redfield: *Author* USA

"Mary your book is fantastic, I think it is the first truly comprehensive and accurate thing in print and you cover all with clarity and grace. Bravo to you.

Ruth McKinley Hoover, PhD – *President ACCET* USA

"I have recently bought your brilliant book *Awakening*. You are to be congratulated in capturing just what an abductee feels, experiences and goes through, something not done by so many writers. I have a huge library of UFO and paranormal books and your approach is rare, if not unique. Your book has many truths in its pages. It's great to read THE TRUTH about the continuing Alien enigma. Thanks again for the beautiful book."

Ernie Sears – *Healer, Ufologist* UK

"Regarding your book I can best describe the benefit of your book is whenever I feel like I need a question answered, I open any page and that question is answered. I guess like speaking to you without calling. Another strong message your book also portrays is how experiencers have coped with the whole fear factor. I now feel in control and not so insecure."

Karen – Australia

"This isn't just a research book, it's much, much, more, and written by a lady who has hands on contact with the people she writes about. Her professionalism shines through the pages, combined with compassion and concern for the people she is trying to help. This is a book about experiencers. That is an experience in itself. Quality!"

Kate Miller – *UFO Magazine* UK

"Awakening has become one of my 'bibles' for witness support literature because of its unique focus on how to help oneself and other experiencers."

James Basil – UK

"When you read a book like this that really makes you sit up and think, it is often hard to convey in words how good it is. I do feel it should be on all serious researchers' shelves. Congratulations on quite a groundbreaking book."

Steve Rider – *UFO Group Southampton* UK

AWAKENING
How Extraterrestrial Contact Can
Transform Your Life

MARY RODWELL

NEW MIND
PUBLISHERS

First published in the U.K. by
Beyond Publications, Fortune Books 2002

Re-published by Avatar Publications 2005

Revised and Re-published by New Mind Publishers 2010

Copyright © Mary Rodwell 2010

New Mind Publishers
www.newmindpublishers.com

ISBN: 978-0-9807555-0-3

Edited by Heather Pedley
Cover Artwork/Design by Rob Townshend © Rob Townshend
Cover Layout Danielle Johnson

It may surprise you to know that many people around the world, from all walks of life, believe themselves to be in regular contact with beings from 'outer–space'. Seven years ago, Mary Rodwell, trained midwife, counsellor, and therapist, would have considered these stories to be the stuff of science fiction, but through a series of events, she began to counsel individuals who claimed to be having these remarkable experiences. Mary grew to understand that these claims were not the product of an over–active imagination. They were real, happening to normal, healthy people, and what's more, it was all going on in her neighbourhood!

Through word of mouth Mary became known as a confidant and 'trustee', validating, honouring and helping people work through these bizarre and unusual experiences.

As the number of people that came to see Mary escalated into the hundreds, she realised that some people were aware of their Contact experiences, some had felt a lifelong inkling, but others were completely in the dark, being driven to find a therapist to help calm their unexplained and 'irrational' fears. Mary says: "The process of 'waking up' to this is not always an easy ride, but in every case, the outcome is transformational, it can be positively life–changing if the person has the right help and support."

Are you ready to ask yourself: *"Am I Experiencing Alien Contact?"* Let this book help you take the first step – why not find out for yourself?

Heather Pedley

ABOUT THE AUTHOR

Mary Rodwell RN, mother of three adult children, was born in the UK but migrated to Australia in 1991. Former nurse, midwife and a health educator in the UK, Mary worked as a counsellor in both a medical practice and two professional counselling agencies in Perth, Australia before branching out into her own private practice. For the past 14 years she has been working as a counsellor, hypnotherapist, metaphysical teacher, intuitive healer, researcher and writer. Mary is co-director of New Mind Records and has produced a number of meditation/relaxation CD's see **www.newmindrecords.com**

Mary became involved in the UFO/Abduction phenomenon whilst studying for an advanced diploma in counselling. The lack of professional support for this experience was instrumental in her forming the first professional support network in Australia, *The Australian Close Encounter Resource Network (ACERN)*. As Principal of ACERN she offers counselling support, hypnotherapy and information to those who have *anomalous experiences,* particularly ET Abduction/Contact. Up to date, ACERN has been resourced by over 1600 individuals in Australia as from overseas, Japan, Europe, UK and North America. Mary lectures nationally and internationally and has produced 2 award-winning documentaries: *Expressions Of ET Contact, A Visual Blueprint.* & *Expressions of ET contact, a communication and healing blueprint?*

Through her work as Principal of ACERN she has written numerous articles on this subject, *Awakening* is her first book. Mary is a clinical member of *The Academy of Clinical Close Encounter Therapists (ACCET)* in America, formerly a committee member of the *Australasian Society Of Psychical Research (ASPR)* and *UFO research (UFORUM)* in Western Australia. Advisor for the Exo-political movement. Full profile in the Biographical Encyclopedia of People in Ufology & Extraterrestrial Research. 2008. Maximillien de Lafayette

Mary and her support group have appeared in an Australian documentary, *OZ Encounters UFOs* and she also acted as research consultant for a UFO exhibition Australia called *Phenomena.* For more information contact ACERN by email **starline@iinet.net.au** or visit **www.acern.com.au**

To my three wonderful, and very special adult
children, Christopher, Michaela and Tim,
thank you for your continuous loving support,
tolerance and generosity of spirit throughout
the writing of this book.
You have been my greatest teachers.
I love you more than I can say!

To my very special parents.
My mother, Iris Magdelene Sherry, now in spirit,
I still feel your love, laughter and enthusiasm and through you,
I truly believe that all is possible!
And to my father, Henry Michael Sherry,
thank you for your continued love, openness,
acceptance, and support.
I have been very blessed with you both.

And to my siblings, I love you all.

CONTENTS

CONTENTS

FOREWORD

The tropical forest is replete with dense vegetation. Light from the sun ripples a long the jungle floor illuminating a thick undergrowth. There's a gentle breeze producing shadows on the jungle floor that swing back and forth with the movement of vegetation. Life forms are in abundance and their movements are easily detected, both flying through the air and scurrying throughout foliage, thick on the ground. There is a heavy scent of jungle, the weight of the atmosphere squeezing all life forms like the tentacles of an octopus. Sounds of life crackle everywhere. The weather is warm and humid, as one would expect in such an environment. Someone has spilled a can of dense, blue paint onto the heavens above. Now and then a few white, billowy clouds float randomly in contrast, moving too and fro in time to the movements of the high altitude currents. The serene waters are calm, a slight wave action sweeps along in tune to the gentle breezes. Reflections of the sparse clouds play upon the waters like the twirling of ballet dancers upon the stage. Could this be planet earth millions of years ago?

Suddenly a creature is seen cavorting through the jungle. On first impression it looks like an upright being, naked, bipedal with long hair, possibly an ape of some sort. If we look closer, no, it's not an ape. The creature's hair is long and blond, with a pinkish–white skin that is smooth, without body hair. This creature appears to be human in all respects and it looks like a male. Upon closer inspection the being is more than ordinary; it shows perfection both in form and action. His legs are muscular and they ripple as he runs, with blue eyes that match the sky like liquid, limpid, pools. He is able to leap to great heights, plucking vegetation from the trees, latching on to low tree branches to propel himself forward. Every so often he stops to rest, on his haunches he props himself up against a tree as he devours the food he has so skilfully collected. His height is about five–foot six inches and his estimated weight in the region of 150 pounds. No other similar creatures can be seen.

The darkness of night creeps slowly over the land as all signs of life melt into blackness. The winds grow silent and the oceans display the reflected light of the night sky. Stars glint like mirrors.

Suddenly in the midst of the calm the air stirs and a breeze manifests. It has no direction, but makes the skin tingle like a pulsing, electric current. It is not a normal sensation, it feels artificial.

Far up in the blackness of the nocturnal sky a single star brightens and starts to shine with great magnitude. It becomes brighter and brighter as it descends towards earth, closer, closer, and closer. The electrical pulsations make the body hair stand on end. The whispering breeze suddenly whips up as a large multi–storied craft slowly makes itself apparent. A lighting array circles it displaying a rainbow of colours. There are windows. The circular craft is silent; it approaches slowly, floating freely in defiance of any gravitational force. The immensity of the craft is overwhelming; it's as big as two city blocks!

Without warning, a cone of intense blue–white light blinks from under the surface of the craft, as if scanning the area. The craft moves slowly, deliberately, inching its way along the thick, dense jungle as if it is looking for something. Then all at once it stops dead. The bright cone of light widens, it focuses on the ground, a particular area. The centre of the beam targets the form of the pink–skinned, blonde haired male, he is now asleep, caught in the light and eerily he floats up towards the craft. As he approaches the underside, an aperture opens and the ship swallows the humanoid figure. Just as suddenly as it came, the light beam switches off. The craft slowly starts to rise and increases in speed until all that can be seen is a fading, brilliant star that takes its place among its stellar cousins.

Conceptually only a short amount of time passes, perhaps just days, month's maybe, or even years. The period is uncertain. The scene is the same, the same stillness of the night and crystal black sky. Once again as the air stirs with electricity a star descends from the heavens. Only this time there are twin moons in the sky that shine their reflected light upon the planet. One has a bright white colour, the other glows a deep pink, illuminating both land and water. It is apparent now that there is only one landmass, a vast expanse surrounded by a mighty ocean that covers the surface of the planet.

As before, the ship descends slowly. As it reaches a height of several hundred feet above jungle terrain the strange cone–shaped light beams forth, falling upon the dense jungle below. Two humanoid beings can be seen floating in a foetal position. Slowly they descend, coming to rest on the cushioned floor of the jungle. Through the brightness of the light, it is evident that one of the beings is the same male who was taken previously; the other is without doubt a humanoid female. She is the epitome of beauty, well endowed with long blonde hair that drapes her shoulders like a shawl. Her legs are long and shaped to perfection, her proportions like an hourglass. Her facial features appear angelic, with blue eyes and a facial expression of utmost peace. Once on the ground below, the male stands before the female. Their eyes meet and arms entwine in a romantic embrace. As in the previous encounter, the light beam suddenly vanishes and the ship slowly begins to rise. Because of the brightness emerging from the twin moons much of the circular craft's under structure can be visualized. There is a noted complexity of construction which is far beyond our comprehension. One outstanding feature becomes apparent, a large insignia in bold type, *The United States Air Force – Non Terrestrial Unit 605.*

The aforementioned scenario is a fictitious event framed in the future but its theme is ancient and borrowed from the Bible. Perhaps these events did occur here on earth, and perhaps they are responsible for humankind? This of course, is all speculative, but the events occurring today regarding the field of Ufology and in particular the Alien Abduction phenomenon are real and difficult to understand.

Mary Rodwell is an investigator and author, who in the writing of *Awakening,* has captured the very essence of the subject. Never before in the history of Ufology has anyone succeeded in setting forth the amount of material referenced in this work. In her writing, she not only sights the individual experiences of abductees, but delves with great prowess into both the physical and psychological components of the phenomenon. She is careful to stay with the facts at hand and clearly lays out the commonalties of the experiences. I am sure the reader will be fascinated with the ultra–personal aspects concerning the medical and non–medical signs and symptoms.

Mary has also included the psychological aspects that often don't get the attention they deserve. She should be given an award for her ability to present a clear and concise in-depth perspective of the phenomenon, from both a personal and non personal standpoint. This will translate into one giant step regarding the much needed help for experiencers who require this kind of general support and trust.

Although Mary Rodwell is not a scientist or medical doctor, *Awakening* presents medical and scientific evidence pertaining to the reality of this phenomenon, which is so very important to the experiencers and the public at large. It is time for the mythological aspects of this subject to be erased forever. Mary also touches, in a very comprehensive fashion, on an aspect of abduction that is beginning to make itself more apparent. That is, the actual purpose. Why are these events happening all over the world to so many people? One possibility is that the human race is being genetically manipulated, and perhaps this process has been occurring throughout history. Mary has done a superb job in illustrating the fact that children of today may be different to those born fifty or so years ago. The facts of my own study prove this to be the case. I have used 17 functional growth characteristics and compared them over a forty year period from 1947 to 1987. I have found there has been an accelerated change in these statistics varying from 16 to 80%. Most will agree this is very specific data and can not be attributed to the evolutionary process or any other known global or environmental factors. It should also be understood that this process seems to involve the expansion of consciousness. Have you ever stood in awe and wondered about the statement your young child has just uttered, and then perhaps retorted by saying, "Where in the world did you get that from?" This gives solid evidence that the human race is being genetically manipulated. It is also felt in certain scientific circles that our understanding of modern genetics can be used to prove this beyond the shadow of a doubt. *Awakening* looks at this subject in a very objective manner and sites numerous references from relevant sources.

In this comprehensive work Mary Rodwell concerns herself with numerous other related subjects, such as the *Missing Pregnancy Syndrome*, and includes an encyclopaedia of PSI abilities as well as a very comprehensive chapter on alien implants.

The manner of this text is extremely clear. It will give the reader a concise review of the abduction phenomena, from the Contact experiences themselves, right through to understanding the coping process and looking at what Contact may mean.

"In my opinion this will become the bible of the Alien Abduction Phenomenon and will make itself apparent in every library the world over."

Dr. Roger Leir,
September 2002

AWAKENING

Do you have experiences that you cannot explain? Contact with non-human 'extraterrestrial beings' is such a bizarre and surreal event that many people experiencing it quite naturally think that they must be going crazy! Because most people believe this experience is nothing more than an 'X-Files' fantasy, they cannot accept that their experiences might be real. What's more, unlike the popular X-Files stories, many have found that instead of the truth being 'out there', the truth is in fact within them and this realisation can be far stranger than fiction. Contact reality is such a phenomenon. Over the past couple of years I have come to believe that lots of people are experiencing Contact, however most of them don't know it and the vast majority probably never will.

The Contact experiences are both extraordinary and highly personal as this book will show. It begs a pertinent question: How many people have actually had these experiences? At my last count well over 1600. We have no way of knowing, but this could well be the tip of the iceberg because through experience, I have found that most people won't talk about it because they are afraid people will think they're crazy. In recent years however, there have been numerous books about ET Contact written by courageous experiencers who have felt compelled to tell all. By far, the majority of these people are very credible, honest individuals, from all professions and walks of life and there is one thing that they all agree on – the simple fact that they didn't want, nor need this scenario to be real! Many of these experiencers did not believe in UFOs beforehand and the prospect of extraterrestrial life had not crossed their minds. It was their encounters with alien life forms that ultimately forced them to own up to what they experienced, to face up to their reality despite the uncomfortable reactions they would undoubtedly receive from their close friends and family.

I have since found that experiencers can be driven by a fierce determination to understand what is it that's happened to them, giving them the courage to explore it more and 'own' their reality. Many have had to challenge everything they believed in before they could begin and for some, their experiences make the most far-fetched sci-fi feature look tame in comparison. A person who is experiencing Contact with what is deemed to be extraterrestrial, non-human life is forced to push their fear to the farthest limits as they gain new awareness of themselves and their reality. Whether the experiences themselves have been traumatic, or of the more 'subtle kind', the ultimate effects are usually the same – that Contact is a trigger for change. What their stories ultimately reveal is that irrespective of the nature of their encounters (e.g. bright lights, strange beings, or a visit to a space ship), Contact is a catalyst, awakening the individual to a multi-dimensional awareness, showing them new human potential that is absolutely extraordinary.

This book is intended to act as your guide and will take you through the process of 'awakening' to Contact. Whether you believe YOU are having Contact yourself, or not, we will explore together the process of waking up to this reality, providing you with information and resources that will help you with your own journey. There are pointers from time to time, to help guide you. You will be able to find out for yourself and . . . face your own fears, the fear for your sanity, the fear of being judged, the fear of being different and of finding out who you are, or 'what' you think you are! Most importantly, there is the fear of fear itself. As you read on you will be asked many questions, which you may ask yourself out of mild curiosity or a more distinct 'need to know'. You will find out whether you are able to trust yourself and, using your own 'inner knowing' explore your new and exciting expanded awareness through your experiences. As you learn to trust yourself you will be guided towards a deeper understanding, which will help you to find the answers you seek. Reading this book will help you assess your personal reality. Is this awakening process meant for a small few or is it more than that? Could it be humanity's 'wake-up call' and if it is, what could that mean?

The stories in this book are true accounts shared by a brave few. They are meant to illustrate how Contact changes people, not only in their personal awareness, but inspirationally, providing new abilities in fascinating ways as lives are transformed. These stories are written by 'ordinary' people from all walks of life as the Contact phenomenon appears not to discriminate. We are all susceptible to it! With this sharing process you are able to find out where you are on your own journey, as you ask yourself the question: *"Am I having multi-dimensional experiences?"* In other words, are you in Contact with extraterrestrial, non-human beings? As you ask yourself that question I would expect from most of you a quick 'knee-jerk' answer, either "yes", or "no", one way or the other. My question to you therefore would be: *"So how do you know?"*

INTRODUCTION

Contact experiences with non-human extraterrestrial beings are most commonly called 'abduction' or 'encounter' experiences and the person in question is usually referred to as an 'abductee'. I prefer to use the term 'experiencer' here as it has less emotional baggage and is a more appropriate definition in my mind. 'Experience' is exactly what these individuals are having, unlike the term 'abduction', which automatically has a negative connotation - 'experiencer' carries no judgement of the experience itself. It is also true to say that many who undergo Contact experience do not believe they have been abducted at all, but believe that they have consented to it on some level.

I've included in this book information on both the 'classic abduction' scenarios and the less publicised subtle forms of Contact. My research suggests that the classic forms of Contact published in the popular media reflect only a small percentage of those who have had Contact experiences. More recently I have formed the conclusion that greater numbers of people may well have had a more gentle and subtle form of Contact and because these experiences are not as confronting or traumatic, they are less known about. Even though we have little information about this at the moment, I feel that in time it may well prove to be that the 'classic' abduction cases are just the tip of the iceberg and that there is a far greater number of people who are having Contact experiences of the more 'subtle kind'.

Even though the more subtle forms of Contact are less traumatic than the classic Contact experience, people having them can live in fear and confusion through lack of understanding. All such experiences are accompanied by a sense of isolation and alienation from society and even close friends. This more subtle form can incorporate some of the classic signs, but more often it manifests as a strong feeling or an awareness of being very different to everyone else, even siblings and parents. This is often accompanied by a profound sense of isolation, or feelings of 'not belonging', as if it's a struggle to exist in this earth environment. Dare I say it; life can feel almost *alien* to them! They are aware of having a kind of 'spontaneous knowledge' and that they possess certain unusual abilities, but also feel unable to share this with others. They are afraid even, because if they 'come clean' it might make them unacceptable within their family unit, friends, or society in general. Because many people in this situation do not understand these feelings it can often create a deep sense of loneliness inside, as well as feelings of isolation. These 'perceptions' can make them feel as if they are from another planet, something many struggle to cope with as 'human' society and it's materialistic focus will suddenly appear very gross and violent. There is often extreme sadness felt with regards to the ways in which our societies harm and destroy our planet and watching any living creature fall prey causes profound upset and distress.

This heightened sensitivity will only increase this sense of isolation and as a result, many are drawn to the creative, 'alternative' and complementary fields of work. Heightened senses are something used in the psychic fields as well, such as 'energy' work and healing. But most people don't immediately connect the two, namely the reason why they may be different is because of their Contact experience.

Contact can explain these feelings as the experiencer is opened up to their own multi-reality. The awareness of Contact can become a catalyst in understanding themselves as their experiences cause them to question all they have ever known, been conditioned to believe in, or been taught about. It can cause a great paradigm shift within, should they decide to honour these experiences and embrace this expanded reality, creating a 'reality' that ultimately makes far more sense. It can resonate on some deep 'inner' level as they begin to put the confused jigsaw pieces of their life together.

As more information is gained, they can move from the isolation they have felt and realise that they are not alone with this and that there are many 'others' out there who feel the same way. This knowledge of their expanded reality encourages them to seek more understanding and through their 'awakening' and increased awareness they can explore who and what they are. But before they do this they have to honour their expanded reality and be prepared to challenge their previous, limiting mind-sets. To explore the reality of the experience from all levels of human understanding means that they first of all need to convince themselves that what they are actually experiencing is real and that they are not crazy after all!

So what makes Contact real? For anyone seriously interested, there is an enormous amount of 'nuts and bolts' scientific evidence available regarding the reality of unidentified flying crafts in our skies (UFOs) and there are daily sightings all over the world by 'normal' and credible people. There are thousands of people who have conscious memories of interacting with many diverse kinds of non-human beings and should anyone wish to intelligently and open-mindedly explore this overwhelming evidence, they will quickly discover that the answers speak for themselves. In fact, with the quantity and quality of material available it is hard to understand why it is still such a topic of ridicule in many circles. The public has been encouraged to remain in ignorance, with governments around the world going to great lengths over the years to keep the whole subject under wraps. Without wishing to delve into the purported cover-ups regarding Contact phenomena and UFOs, it is my belief that Contact reality has been successfully hidden from most of society for a number of obvious reasons and this has been successfully implemented, through a smoke screen of disinformation and ridicule.

So the reality of unexplained craft in our skies, mysterious landings and mass sightings, despite large, credible quantities of photographic and video evidence, is still treated by a huge portion of society as being nothing more than amusing fantasy. It is this deliberate and subtle innuendo that has promoted the belief that, if you are to accept the reality of this extraordinary phenomena you have to be either (a) very gullible, (b) living in a dream-world, or (c) borderline crazy! But for those out there, who are drawn to the subject and start to treat it seriously, the evidence is there and it is highly convincing. Many credible researchers and scientist who come into the field of Ufology are initially very sceptical. Once in it though, they discover that the evidence for its reality is overwhelming and cannot be ignored.

There is a theory that is contrary to popular belief, which states that those individuals, who are most sceptical about this reality, are in fact experiencers themselves. Many of those who have had Contact will tell you that they had no previous beliefs in the extraterrestrial hypotheses until it personally affected them. In fact, many Contactees have been known to become more and more sceptical about their experiences as they dig deeper and question their sanity. Because of their need to prove they are not crazy, their research becomes far more analytical, thorough and focused.

Researchers and therapists who become involved in this controversial topic, personally or professionally, undergo the same analytical process. Budd Hopkins (author of "Missing Time") a UFO researcher said that he was far more sceptical than the most sceptic of sceptics! It must be said that society is just as cruel to those that believe in the reality of Contact with non-human beings as to those who say they experience it firsthand. Furthermore, it can be professional suicide to even talk about such phenomena and should you challenge popular mindsets you are setting yourself up for a rough ride! So to compensate for this you have to ask yourself the same questions the experiencers do – and then some more. After all, what sensible person would want to mislead themselves about this, let alone others?

And so I was exposed to this reality. Not because I consciously sought it, but because it literally came knocking on my front door. The individual who introduced me to the concept of Contact Phenomena had nowhere else to go. He was brave enough to speak to a friend about it, and then he approached me because he had heard I was open minded. He was brave enough to entrust me with his extraordinary life experiences that were terribly confusing for him and most certainly frightening. What's more, he was scared for his family.

At the time I would only offer a respectful listening ear, my personal philosophy being *you don't know what you don't know*. But I was left with no doubt in my mind that he was speaking *his* truth, that these experiences were very real for him.

Also at this time, I was working on an advanced counselling diploma, so I took his case to supervision hoping for more help and information – and of course, some answers. Much to my surprise, neither the supervisor, nor course participants could offer any, although interestingly, they did not suggest that my client was mentally ill. I had read a few books on the subject a couple of years previously, due to my innate curiosity and the dearth of traditional, psychological explanations aroused my determination for 'finding out'. So this was my catalyst for exploring the mystery.

It is still very surprising to me how much 'hard' evidence we personally need to have, before we can accept the possibility that there may be more to life than what we are consciously aware of. We are made up of old patterns and beliefs and Oh, how strongly we cling to what we 'think' we know. Even the experiencer, who has experiential proof, either with physical marks and scars on the body or the fierce arousal of unexplained emotions, will continually question. But we are also programmed into 'traditionally defined' reality mindsets, which are so incredibly powerful, that we would prefer to deny all that we see and experience rather than question our beliefs, even if they may be too limited, or faulty. Contact is an experience that challenges our mindset of reality in many ways and it presses all those 'reality buttons'. But some experiences become so tantalising they become too hard to dismiss. This kind of Contact is a loud and alarming 'wake-up call' and we just cannot ignore the drama of it.

A classic form of Contact, one that is easily recognised by many, is called 'The Night Visitor' . . .

"A humming sound, your body stiffens, paralysed, a creeping dread . . . panic . . . as your eyes carefully scan the room while your heart pounds. You want to call out but can make no sound and it becomes the inner scream *No, not again!* You have no control as you hear the familiar low buzzing sound . . . something is about to happen. Now you sense rather than see the bizarre shadows, feeling a presence close by, something, *someone* is close. Suffocating, misty shapes . . . strange, elusive, they edge closer. Panic fills you and your mind screams . . . your worst nightmare unfolds once again . . . please . . . *PLEASE,* don't touch me! And then the deep knowing . . .*this has been happening all my life!*"

Julia has experienced this form of Contact many times. "Phew!" she said, "the first bit sounds like an excerpt from 'Psycho'. Yes, yes, I know, my experience was Psycho! I had no idea what was going on with me, but whatever it was, it never left me and I was literally terrified witless on a regular basis, all my life. So that by the age of 40 I used to put it into the *too hard to deal with* basket and get on with life. I felt I had *phenomena* tattooed on my forehead! Things happened to me, like audio tapes playing back to front, I had earth disaster dreams, sleeping problems, eating disorders, strange rashes, violent nose bleeds, anxiety. I woke up with my night clothes on back to front or inside out, this constant *presence* would sit on my bed at night, or tap me on the shoulder. There were footsteps in the house, walking up the path and *they'd call my name.* The paralysis and strange smells. My animals would behave strangely, electric lights would flicker, flash. The old weatherboard house I lived in literally shook so violently sometimes I thought it would collapse. There were strange events with black dogs, it was an endless saga of the unexplainable and I had nowhere to put this all mentally! People around me also saw these things going on, so I had proof, but I couldn't put it down to a *night visitor* because I never knew what would happen next.

"I went to psychic development classes, I thought that would sort if out. Nope! But I learned to distinguish what was what and it gave me an interest in healing. It let the floodgates open for manifestations beyond my wildest nightmares and then *I knew it was ET.* And now my world collapses a thousand times *plus* – in the realisation and the fact that this was what I had been dealing with, alone, all my life.

"Then when I met my partner something began to stir again, more phenomena this time, but now we were both in it. He was having his own individual experiences on his way to work and in the house. It was beyond our ability to deal with it without help. Even the neighbours saw a UFO while driving in their car, they were amazed. It's all around us Mary; people just don't know it, that's all. What I'm trying to say is, *you* are going to have to give people other scenarios, not just the commonly known ones, *but the ones that will make people think!"*

Julia, with all her physical evidence, still struggled to believe that her experiences were happening even though they were so incredible for her and very real. So how much harder must it be for the experiencer that has a more gentle and subtle form of Contact? There may be little bits of quantifiable data that will manifest here and there in different ways, through feelings for example, or through the desire to vocalise strange languages, or perhaps with the production of symbolism in the form of sketches or artwork. The majority of people who have experiences like this are not traumatised by them, but they can still feel very isolated and confused. However, the outcome for all forms of Contact is unanimous; these experiences all create major life changes within the person affected.

Initially, I only focused on individuals with 'classic' Contact experiences. But as I researched, I found several individuals to have some (but not all) of the aspects of the classic form and then others who had many different, more subtle indicators. All of them nevertheless, still suggested that Contact had been taking place, so slowly, I expanded the criteria. As I did this, the number of people who felt they were having some form of Contact grew and I began to conclude from this point that the phenomena affected far more people than I had initially thought, or that had been proposed (by researchers such as Dr. John Mack). However, whatever the form of Contact, it still created confusion and isolation within the individuals, creating a desperate need for them to understand their experiences.

I am a therapist and as more and more clients came to see me I began to research the reality of this human experience. I started with the initial 'nuts and bolts' approach, collating physical and tangible data and then moved into more serious investigation. When I discovered the possibility of the different kinds of Contact (i.e. that which had little, 'tangible' data), this created a new challenge for me. How can we prove the reality of such experiences? It is a similar challenge to those who have researched other 'non-physical', human experiences, such as astral travel, or out-of body experiences. You begin to collate how the individual data matches with each person and look at the changes such an experience will make within the individual and you see if there are any patterns developing that suggest the same reality exists for all of them. Intangible as this may be to some, I did find that the evidence for this reality was not just in the experience itself, it was in how this experience changed their abilities and perceptions from that point on. This was most intriguing for me. Contact may not offer the scientific, 'concrete' data we would all prefer to have, but proof of this experience is in the face, mind and emotions of those who are in it.

How do we challenge our mindset of reality?

The experience we call 'Contact', despite its multitude of facets and tangible and non-tangible expressions, challenges all that we believe in and questions that which make our reality. It is no wonder most individuals who experience it are forced to contest what is real! Even the Contact experience, with the tangible 'physical' evidence will demonstrate how limited our present understanding of reality is.

Two thousand years ago, a well-known spiritual teacher may have suggested the possibility of such an expanded multi-reality when he said: "In my house there are many mansions" (Jesus of Nazareth).

So what are the many mansions this special, gentle and holy man spoke about? Naturally the interpretation of this statement reflects the beliefs of the individual, but for me I would say that Jesus was a man who was certainly more multi-dimensionally aware than most others. Interestingly, he demonstrated many of the transformative abilities those in Contact manifest, such as healing and spiritual awareness - and of course he experienced the expanded realities of the many spiritual masters we venerate today.

The spiritual masters have already challenged our third-dimensional mindset in the guise of religion. Some have manifested extraordinary behaviour, which has not been explained by modern science, even yet. For some, this belief is a matter of truth and this may be correct. Perhaps though, it's not faith so much as a deeper understanding of how our beliefs about our reality do limit us. The so-called 'primitive' tribal cultures have no difficulty accepting this multi-reality and some of their experiences certainly echo Contact experiences. They talk of 'sky beings', 'chariots in the skies' and how 'gods' have visited them for centuries and taught them new things. They do not see these experiences as being mental aberrations, on the contrary, they are honoured and 'assumed' by a respected senior person within the tribe, someone who would demonstrate the abilities of the Shaman. Knowledge of Contact experiences with 'beings from the stars' are ensconced in tribal culture, from Africa to North and South America, across to the Aborigines of Australia. They believe that their ancestors came from the stars and some show amazing and detailed knowledge of the galaxy and constellations. These people have no access to powerful telescopes from which most of our knowledge about the galaxy is gained. So this in itself is quite a mystery, unless what they are telling us is true and the fact is, their understanding does come from our galactic visitors after all.

For those interested in the 'mystical', there is research which suggests that Contact experience could be interpreted as a 'partly shamanic' kind of experience. For, like Shamanism, individuals develop amazing gifts, heightened awareness, healing abilities, telepathic abilities and changes in perception within awareness of information and knowledge that is not consciously learned.

Simon Harvey-Wilson, ufologist and MUFON Researcher (Mutual UFO Network) thesis: "Shamanism and Alien Abductions, A Comparative Study, Dec 2000". Within this paper he demonstrates many amazing parallels between the Shamanistic and Abduction/Contact phenomena. So it appears that there is a possibility that various cultures experience Contact, but they come in different guises. It draws more on the interpretation of the experience; for example, one person may see an angel, another maybe a demon, or perhaps a spirit guide, or even a departed, lost soul. It would seem that so-called 'modern man' has his primitive fears triggered by this unseen world because he has been programmed always to question what his senses are showing him and if he has no answers immediately on hand, then he believes that it's not real!

Modern man's obsession with science has meant that we have learned to dismiss any personal experiences that cannot be explained scientifically, even though (I believe) most of us have them. We are often ashamed to admit to having unusual experiences and relegate them into a private, inner world, believing that if science can't explain them, then they must be suspect. Meanwhile, our experiences will come to us unbidden and tantalise us, as we struggle to understand what they mean. They will nag at us and force us to question, but if we question too deeply then we might open our 'can of worms'. The fear is that once you question one aspect of your reality it ultimately causes you to question everything. Scary stuff, but what's the alternative? Should we decide to believe in our experiences then this could prompt even scarier thoughts, perhaps we are crazy after all?

But whether we like this challenge to our reality or not, it exists nevertheless and it is an experience that is global, affecting people of all ages, from the toddler to the grandparent. Its tangibility is in a form which can leave physical marks and scars and sometimes 'implanted' solid objects. It is an experience that can be shared by more than one person at the same time and it presents itself in all cultures, irrespective of religious orientation and scientific beliefs. It can leave emotional and psychological scars on the psyche, but it can also create transformative outcomes.

Psychiatrist, Professor Dr. John Mack (author of "Abduction" and "Passport to the Cosmos") stated: "The Abduction/Contact phenomena challenges the sacred barrier we have created between the unseen and material world. It undermines the fundamental world view of the Western mind." He continues: "In this culture there may be a very small group of scientific, governmental, religious and corporate elite that determine the prevailing bounds of reality. People know their experiences and what they have undergone does not fit with the prevailing mechanistic worldview.

Large percentages of people seem to know there is an unseen world, or hidden dimensions of reality."

Modern man will continually struggle to fit the multidimensional reality it experiences into the third dimensional, conventional one. When it doesn't fit, he will deny and ignore it. It is this denial which causes the conflict and trauma to our psyche and which creates our confusion as we continually question what is real. So how can we integrate, or at least understand our experiences, whilst our beliefs are still rooted in this present 'limited' one? Our confused psyche tries to enforce a paradigm that does not fit with our perceptions. Professor Dr. John Mack also says: "People know their experiences." I agree with him, I believe that they do and what's more, they want to understand them. Feeling trapped and confused, they go to seek help from the very people who are promoting these limited beliefs. We are all taught to believe that if we have faulty perceptions this is down to our own 'reality' programming. So how do professionals help with this confusion?

Often by suggesting one should limit their experiences through medication. Medication, which can further trap the individual into the denial of their experience and keeps them bound to the limited reality they have been conditioned to believe they should stay in. Of course this action will not stop the experiences; it will just limit the effects. Meanwhile, the deeper part of the psyche will continue to question as it tries to marry these experiences up to accepted reality. But if we are to become paradigm healthy, then we have to acknowledge that our present understanding is very limited and we should first re-evaluate what is reality. To begin this, we must honour our personal experiences because this is the best way of understanding what our reality really consists of.

The non-physical reality expresses itself in many ways, consciously and unconsciously, through scientific remote viewing and out of body experiences. Multi-reality is expressed by precognition, (i.e. the ability to see future events). Those who are able to see energy and heal with it, access multi-reality and some access this reality by seeing spirits that are invisible to others. Could these experiences be the psyche giving us major clues to our multi-dimensional nature?

Contact consciously opens us up to our multi-reality and in doing so it can create a 'reality crisis'. These extraterrestrial beings tap into our reality space and demonstrate multi-reality as they work with us, within it, travelling through space, time and sometimes solid matter. They continually stretch our reality paradigms and force us to take a 'quantum leap' into the unknown of our own psyche. Human nature wants to understand, despite the conflict of a longing to 'file' the bizarre in a deep hole somewhere within and forget the whole thing! But often these bizarre events are evidence that something incredible and strange is occurring. The awakening of healing abilities, telepathy and clairvoyance can all suddenly manifest after Contact experience. This is information and knowledge that the person has not consciously learned.

Many are able to effortlessly produce symbols, drawings and scripts, without any conscious thought, whereby it is almost 'automatic'. There are individuals who change from destructive life-time habits, such as drug abuse, to becoming ecologically minded, non-materialistic and more spiritually orientated. But getting there is quite a journey and most of us appreciate a helping hand as we explore our human experiences. So if this experience is real (and from whatever point in 'quantum reality' it stems), then we have to honour it. And the trauma resulting from such Contact experiences is another validation of its reality.

Frankly, it is honest to say that until we do acknowledge it, we may never know how many lives it has affected, from dysfunctional relationships to phobias, anxiety attacks and sexual abuse. Notwithstanding, there are other causes for dysfunction and I am not suggesting that therapists or society should rule them out, but in addition they should accept that the Contact phenomena can also be either a contributing factor or a root cause in some cases.

To provide a helping hand where necessary, means helping to access information conscious or otherwise by using a deeper and more holistic model of therapy. We need to provide resources that honour the 'inner awareness' of the individual and give them the tools they can use that will enable them to empower themselves. By doing so, we are also creating useful markers for those in the process of integration, which will help validate their expanded reality.

Finally, we can offer emotional support through meeting others and the sharing of experiences. This is why we founded ACERN (The Australian Close Encounter Resource Network).

ACERN became official in 1997 and in just over 14years have resourced over 1600 individuals. I wanted to highlight a professional attitude and honour all 'anomalous' experiences. It's an area that is generally considered to only house the 'weird and wonderful' and it has always been my view that until the image of Contact is changed significantly, professionals will be reluctant to get involved.

Aiming for professional credibility was a challenge, but I was joined by Elle, a therapist with a degree in social work and psychology counselling. As a colleague and friend, she has also experienced the Contact phenomena herself, so she joined me in this endeavour and together we have strived to offer credible support to those people in need. Despite the fact that Contact challenges her professional and personal credibility, Elle courageously wrote about her own experiences and I include several references to her story throughout the following chapters. She also became a professional healer, she 'walked her walk' so to speak, believing as I do, that these experiences have such huge implications for humanity that the phenomenon must be exposed in some way, so that pubic awareness is raised and we can reach those who are suffering in isolation and fear.

Through the umbrella of ACERN, people from overseas came to me for help. I began to realise that many people are trapped through their lack of awareness and many don't have a clue with regards to what their experiences may be. So the only way to reach some of them, at least, was by writing a book such as this. Many of the chapters that follow almost wrote themselves. Often, as I explored a topic, I would receive a telephone call, or a new client would find me and offer up the data and information that I needed. It was through their generosity of spirit and openness that I am able to give you a small part of the whole.

As stated, this book is intended to be a guide for you, to offer you a gentle helping hand and take you through the process of awakening. It asks many questions, explores some incredible hypotheses, but ultimately you will be left to decide for yourself and make up your own mind. But before you take this journey you must know that there is no going back and the answers may confound and wake you up to a reality that is truly beyond your wildest dreams. However, it may well be the reality that resonates perfectly within your soul!

This book is full of information and resources to help you decide if you are experiencing a form of Contact. It is written as a practical based resource, and with the belief that we all have within us the understanding and answers to our world and experiences. I honour all beliefs and human experience and it is my hope to incite more public debate and openness to the Contact possibility; because if it is a reality, it would have vast implications for humanity as a whole. That is something I for one, cannot ignore.

CHAPTER ONE
Contact – Is This Real?

Confused, terrified . . . what's your worst nightmare? This chapter contains passages from a letter sent to me from a mature, professional man, who I shall call David. He'd read a book about abduction phenomena and this spurred him on to write to me. I include parts of his letter with his kind permission. It's an account of his emotional reaction as he read this book, as well as a detailed account of some of his experiences. You will see how it graphically illustrates many of the varied and bizarre aspects of Contact and demonstrates how a book called "Abduction" acted as a catalyst for him, making him wake up and face his own Contact experiences.

David mentions in his letter that he had never heard of Abduction/Contact phenomena until he read about Jason's experiences, the young man mentioned in the book "Abduction" (written by his mother, Ann Andrews and co-author Jean Ritchie). One thing that struck me as being important is that many of the experiences mentioned in this book were not at all identical to David's story. In David's letter he describes many of his own personal experiences, things that were most definitely unique to him and this for me, added validity to his account. He was totally unaware of the fact that a lot of the things that happened to him were classic patterns of Contact and this lack of knowing is something I have found to be quite common in the cases that came to me afterwards.

Within David's letter there was a brief history of his background. He said he was assessed as a child and was told that he had an extremely high IQ. Later on in life, when he attended university he was able to complete several degrees simultaneously. David said he grew up in a small farming community, his father being in his late fifties and mother in her late thirties when he was born. He was the youngest of three and by all accounts he felt he had a loving home and caring parents. He spent most of his time playing alone as a child and was quite shy, but apart from that he considered that his early childhood and schooling were normal.

His difficulties began when he was about eight or nine, when he said he experienced many frightening dreams. One of his reoccurring dreams involved three figures, very tall, elongated and unnaturally thin. They did not really frighten him but he said, that they made him feel very uneasy. They were always in a group, one slightly taller than the other two. They had brownish coloured skin, he doesn't remember if they had hair or not and they were always looking at him, although not necessarily watching him directly. He got the feeling that they were examining him. He got the clear impression that they were probing into his mind! But again, he said that these three didn't frighten him, but there was another, a small being – and this one did. He recalls it as being greyish-white, unnatural, almost 'sickly' in colour and it had a large head with no hair, but huge eyes. The eyes were the dominant feature; they attracted all of his attention. David said he had many visits from these beings.

In another dream he had, he said that he woke up in the middle of it and saw himself lying in a room that was grey-silver, but dullish in colour. The ceiling was curved slightly, but not oval shaped. David felt that he had several visits to this room and each time he was aware of floating feelings and sensations.

David had begun to read "Abduction" out of pure curiosity, he thought, but it had acted as a catalyst for him in some way. Up to that time, he had not read anything on this kind of subject, except for when he had spotted bits of news as he flicked through newspaper and magazine articles. He said that the subject did not seem relevant to him, but surprisingly, when he began to read this book he found that he struggled to get through it and that he became increasingly uncomfortable and disturbed as he carried on, so much so that he was unable to complete it. He went back to the library with the intention of returning it, but at the last moment for no apparent reason he changed his mind. David did end up finishing the book and it had a profound effect on him, which resulted in the excerpts of his letter that follows.

His letter was over 33 pages long and full of highly personal and sensitive information that would be inappropriate to print. However, I enclose some unedited highlights, which I believe demonstrate the classic patterns of the Contact process.

DAVID'S LETTER

Dear Mary

Frankly, I was still rather concerned about contacting you and very nervous about it, but I know I need to talk to someone directly about what has been happening to me for most of my life. It scares the hell out of me, but I know I cannot avoid it anymore, even more than I knew that I could no longer avoid writing about it.

At first I denied that I had been abducted. This was wishful thinking. But now I know that it is just too hard to keep inside me and I need to talk to someone. It will be hard to broach the subject with anyone I know and I shall probably make a dreadful mess of it. If I seem to be getting rather mixed up, I am. In one way I want to talk to someone, but in another I am too scared to. Not just because of the fear of ridicule, though. I think that I do not want to face what I have to talk about. It is too unpleasant to face, but deep down I know I will have to at some time or other. I am concerned about privacy in this. I suppose that is also a cause of my reluctance, it is not just a question of ridicule, though that does come into it. I think it would seriously affect my career. I have a natural reluctance to reveal this to anyone as I think the friend I have told is having difficulties with my having told him.

I would like to give an account of something that happened when I was six or maybe seven. A bridge had broken in a bad flood. When they were repairing it, I fell off while crossing the narrow plank that was there to walk on. The water was in full flood, going very fast. I could not swim and was dressed in a thick tweed overcoat and I was panicking. Then I felt someone helping me and I was guided across the current until I was able to grab a cable that was supporting a crane. It was almost straight across from where I had fallen in. It was almost impossible to go against the current, which was very strong. But though unable to swim at all (I disliked the water), somehow I did it. I held onto the cable for dear life, watching the people nearby scramble down to get me, with my vague vision - having lost my thick glasses. I looked around to thank the person who saved me, but there was no one there. Nor had there been. In subsequent times of my life, during various crises, I have often felt some reassuring presence, as if someone was guiding me, helping me or protecting me. This continues today.

Sometimes I have been very frightened by some unknown fear, yet behind it there seems to be someone protecting me, or at least there. It's hard to understand and very hard to describe. I do not want to know. Fear again, nervousness, anger, frustration, sheer fury and glimmers of something that perhaps I do not want to know, fear again, understanding on a different level and maybe even some relief. I do not know if I will finish this letter, or if I finish it, whether I will post it. I am pausing as I write, not only because I have difficulty writing about the subject matter in question, but because for some reason that I do not understand. I am having trouble stringing my thoughts together in any semblance of real order in my mind, let alone in a way that will make any sense to you. I may not be able to write about some things. I have never been able to talk about these things at all to anyone. I have difficulty thinking about them, much less writing about them. I found that as I was reading the book ("Abducted") I was crying and I am now, and I am not sure why.

As I read, I found myself steadily getting more disturbed and more upset. As I said, at first I was just interested, more or less academically. As I read more, I began to get so agitated that I actually took the book back because it was just becoming too uncomfortable to handle. My feeling as I read the book was that I was coming to some personal realisation that maybe I do not want to know, or understand. I began to get a bit frightened, scared or whatever the word is, when I thought I was reading things that were a bit too close to the bone.

I was having dreams that were not dreams (more real than dreams) and woke up frightened. I was not often able to remember their content, nor can I now. Those dreams are just hovering under the surface of my consciousness, as they did then, but I knew that they contained fear. Frightening nightmares, especially the 'black one', where I couldn't move and couldn't see or hear anything at all, but only experience sheer terror. The feeling over the years that someone was playing with my mind.

As a boy I was slowly made aware that I was in some way different and the things that happened to me did not happen to other boys. Then there was the scary feeling that someone was there sometimes. Just there, feeling what I was feeling. I would look around but there was never anyone there. The 'watching' did not somehow seem to be in the physical sense at all, it was as if I was being watched from the inside. It was not that I felt I was in any danger; it was just that I could feel someone there. Someone who was somehow experiencing what I was experiencing, feeling what I was feeling. Some marks occasionally, sometimes a little painful. Some unexplained tenderness would occur from time to time . . . these things usually appeared overnight, many of them were on my head, sometimes around my temples.

I have totally realised that I have forgotten something, but first I would like to mention that I found a small cut above the top joint of my middle finger on the left hand this morning. Though not painful, it was tender. It was definitely not there yesterday. The easiest way to describe it is to say that it looks like a bit has been scooped out. I was surprisingly tired this morning. What I had forgotten completely was that I have quite often had similar cuts, scoops, whatever, on me, mostly around joints where I should have noticed them the day before.

As a child I would sometimes wake up the wrong way around in the bed, or sitting up, or trying to go somewhere, or trying to get back into bed. I have always had lots of dreams, frequently ones that made me uneasy, some were frightening and some were terrifying. Being out of bed and so on, coincides either with certain really nasty (and very frightening) nightmares, or when I've got some weird thoughts or information in my mind the next day. I feel someone is also reading my thoughts and it makes me feel scared. In these dreams I have, I seem to know that I am getting information now, it feels like something's being put into my mind.

I find it hard to write the next sentence. Sometimes I have woken up and this is as an adult too, to feel that there is someone else in the room, or a presence, or just *something*. I always felt that I was paralysed, could not move at all, but nothing was ever holding me, or tying me down. I would always be tired afterwards, as if I had not had a proper sleep. I was always too frightened to tell anyone about it and I think I was too self-conscious to talk about it anyway. I had completely forgotten another very frightening dream. It was quite simply one eye, first in the distance, then coming very slowly towards me, as if to envelope me. There was no sound. Again, I could not move at all. The eye was very big, even in the distance and black. The background was also black, but it was just space. The eye seemed to hang there, I was not aware of any dream before I saw it. The eye never reached me, but somehow it was always getting closer and bigger, yet it stayed just that little distance away, even though it gradually got closer. I know this seems a contradiction and I was aware of this in my dream. I got this dream only a few times in my mid teens.

I get premonitions in my dreams and also when I'm awake. I'm scared of the dark but only sometimes. What confuses me is that it seems so stupid to be thinking about it, let alone worrying and writing about it. The awful thing is that I am. These things tore me apart as a child and in my early youth, I lived in torment throughout these years for much of the time, either in direct fear of it happening, the fear of it coming again, or the teasing by my peers, by some of the teachers or the adults in my home town who joined in the general ribaldry.

From about the age of nine or ten when the problems began to surface, I endured a lot of bullying at school. Much of this was verbal. I was considered to be different, I actually did not realise how I was different though. It hurt and upset me very much and I prayed to be the same as everyone else, to be 'normal', even though I didn't know what I meant by that. I think that deep down I have always known there was a difference and try as I may I would never be like the others.

Another aspect that I will mention here is that sometimes as a child I frequently had quite long periods of time that I could not account for. It would usually be in the daytime and it still happens occasionally. I have always been a bit of a daydreamer and have always put it down to that. Or perhaps I just fell asleep, except that sometimes I do wake up walking. I invariably feel tired after these experiences, sometimes irritable. I go for long walks alone, away from people and try to find parks and remote areas in which to walk and it's during these walks that this occurs. I always felt strongly impelled to take these walks, a kind of compulsion and I almost feel that I have no choice in taking them, somehow it is more than just a need for solitude, or to 'work things out'. Somehow or other, it seems different from that.

I slept badly last night and I was also extremely upset and cannot quite account for that. One thing that really worries me is that I am concerned at what I am opening up to by thinking about this so much and indeed by writing this letter, which I said, may be more for me than to you. My first reaction this morning was to hit the delete button, forget the whole thing and try to erase everything. Somehow I knew that I couldn't and I think that I now know that I do not just want to write about this, I need to.

At times I was aware of knowledge being implanted in my mind from outside. That is how I feel many of these flashes. On occasions I do not just get an idea and search for information around it, I get all the information, complete with all the details already in my mind. Then sometimes I just get the essential facts, without much detail, there seems to be no pattern to this at all. I can also get warnings not to pursue certain courses of action and that I would be adversely affected if I did. On the few occasions I have ignored my intuition the result has been very bad for me. I could not tell anyone about it, because what would I tell them, that someone was playing with my mind, or taking out bits of information and putting it back again?

Sometimes I would panic if I 'lost' information, but somehow I knew I would always get it back. In tutorials, some lecturers were puzzled by my perception and often asked where I got my information from? I was not experienced then at working out which information I should be revealing as being legitimate or which to keep private for fear of revealing it, especially if it did not come from a recognised source. The headaches I put down to weak eyes. I feel now that there was a strong connection between the headaches and the information I was receiving. I feel that the information was directly responsible for them, as if my mind was being taxed beyond its natural limits and causing me to have the headaches.

I went to a course on "Silva Mind Control". I was quite pleased a first, I learned to relax and got the benefit from that. I began to go deeply within myself. Then my troubles began again, strongly. I was bringing up things I most definitely didn't want to see, I began to recall things I had hoped I'd forgotten.

I began to get much more information and those feelings of panic arose again for no apparent reason. I immediately stopped meditating as I could not cope with it. I knew that my aunt had cancer; I knew that she would die. When she did eventually get sick I nursed her until she died some years later. Her death was a terrible loss, made worse by my knowledge that she was going to die long before it had been diagnosed.

I do not consider myself to be an abductee; I merely know my mind has been interfered with. I think that deep down I have really known for a very long time from whence the source came, but I could not articulate it. Then when I began to suspect, I feared it and indeed feared for my own sanity for even thinking it. The realisation began to creep upon me somehow. Then when I read 'the book' I began to panic as I realised there was so much there that I did not want to know.

I have never had any problems with the concept of life from other sources outside our planet or solar system. I could never see why people would get so worked up about it. It is quite obvious to me that there is, and it has always been obvious. I had heard of people having contact with aliens, but this was always remote and it applied to other people. It is interesting, as I said earlier, that I almost consciously never read anything about this. It's almost as if I have been trying to avoid it, or someone has been trying to make me avoid reading about it. I read all sorts of books about all sorts of things, so why have I never sought to read about this? The subject of alien life does interest me and always has. In virtually every other area that I have interest or curiosity in, I have gone out of my way to read more about it. I have that type of mind, I am by nature curious, but I have never gone into this area at all - and not about abduction.

As I have said, I do not consider that I have been abducted, so there should have been no fear of reading about it. I wanted to know the source of my knowledge. I have been trying to pretend it's not happening and that I do not have such information implanted in my mind. Several times early in my life, puzzled adults have said to my parents that I seemed to know a lot about things that young children would not normally know about. I remember my dentist being a little surprised when as a ten or eleven year old I began to talk to him about my body being a unified whole and that the whole being is a reflection of the parts. As I got older I tried to pretend it was not happening, then there was a gradual, reluctant acceptance of it, but I said to myself it was just intuition. This was not too hard to cope with, then through various ways and a little self-knowledge I got short glimpses of where the information was actually coming from.

When I first began to suspect 'where' this information was coming from I could not accept it at all, this had no basis in fact for me, no logic. I rejected it out of hand as being something that could not have happened to me and I felt very uncomfortable about it and then angry. The veils were starting to lift, as if 'this time' I could not stop the revelations any more. I got a feeling of the inevitability of it all and I began to get very nervous, as if I knew the truth would be revealed to me. It is interesting, now as I look back. I realise that I was starting to know where the source of my information was coming from even before I read anything about it in 'the book'. As I said, I had avoided reading about the subject previously or even thinking about it. The reason I almost took the book back was because I knew instinctively it was somehow relevant to me, but it was not something I could accept. It was too strange, too frightening and too weird for me to accept.

When I got the book it hit me hard and upset me tremendously. It made me cry and that is not something I do easily. I am not ashamed to cry, but if I cry I want a reason for it and to understand why I am so upset and not that I'm just experiencing some unknown, irrational and uncontrollable fear. The book brought this fear into consciousness, and then quite suddenly I knew what was happening to me.

I have had a fair amount of information given to me recently, both before and after reading the book. Also my laptop computer was behaving very strangely all yesterday afternoon when I was writing this down. Suddenly numbers were appearing instead of the letters and bits of sentences just disappeared. Other bits of sentences moved and appeared in different paragraphs, well away from where I had written them and spaces appeared in the document for no reason. Another disturbing occurrence, I was surprisingly hungry just after 4 o'clock by my wristwatch, so I had a snack to tide me over until my usual evening meal about 6pm and thought no more about it. I kept on reading the book, interspersed with some typing of this. I am staying at a hostel, sharing a room with others and I was surprised when they came to bed at about 10pm (by my watch). I found out later that my watch was one and a half hours slow, which accounts for the odd timings I had mentioned. I worked out that my watch had somehow 'lost' one and a half hours between about 2pm and 5pm. Incidentally, my mobile phone battery went flat after about one day and it usually lasts three to four days and my battery/electric shaver lasted only one day when this usually lasts three to four days, sometimes longer.

Similar things to this have happened to me in the past and it always seems to be around the time I receive information. Other symptoms I have are sensitive ears and eyes. I can't take the grating noise of pop music or small radios that blare out and I am super sensitive to light. Any flashing light really hurts my eyes and I have to shield them. I went for a walk today as a break from the computer; I often get information while walking.

I have had some out of body experiences. Most of them are in my sleep; mostly I am just looking down at myself sleeping. Some I had as a child, some as an adult. I had another out of body once, in deep meditation. I sometimes have had electrical problems with cars, but most of them were old, so I put it down to that.

There are two aspects that I cannot understand about this. I cannot understand why I am so frightened about it. I am not an abductee, all I get is information put in and occasionally borrowed, so why am I so fearful of that and especially at night? Why do I stay up as long as possible and try to stay awake to avoid losing consciousness? Just exactly what am I afraid of (and I am, very much afraid)?

The other thing that disturbs me is that I know my mind is being probed. It was bad enough when I thought, or tried to tell myself that it was just some form of telepathy by someone who belonged here. But now I know that if they are able to put this information in and borrow it, then they can also know anything else I am thinking. I hate that. It was bad enough when I didn't know the source, it's much worse now that I know what they are. That not only scares me, it makes me furious, and it scares me when I wonder just what else they could do? I feel so absolutely powerless and that scares me very much, as much as anything else. I can cope with normal fears because I can understand them rationally. But this is completely different and I cannot understand it or control it.

There are some things I have not written down for various reasons; basically I am still trying to work them out. I am having trouble with them and I do not want to be considered paranoid, hysterical, hallucinating or whatever. I have just finished reading the Epilogue of the book and was fascinated to read about spirituality. One of the main reasons I took up with meditation was in a search for help spiritually, which I could not find in religion, or anywhere else. The subject is inherent in my writings and is the theme in the works I am writing now. One of my other main themes is that of the materialistic nature of society in the world now and a diminution of real value. Another theme is about what we are doing physically to our world in the way of pollution and the general mistreatment and poisoning of our planet. I see these issues as being inextricably interwoven and inherently as being part of the same problem, basically part of the selfish society we live in, one in which the goals are not orientated around beauty and good, but around materialism and the acquisition of money as a goal in itself, at the expense of the world (i.e. the environment).

I have views on alien intervention and abduction. I have views regarding the human soul, humanity and 'other' beings in the universe, including the sum total of universes that exist, our own and those outside our own. I know somehow that my mind has been interfered with by these sources. I seem to know with absolute certainty that I have understood the other many experiences that I have had. It is not just a thought, not just an idea and not just a vague possibility. I know it in the same way that I knew those awful premonitions were true. I so wish it were not so, very desperately, that I could be mistaken. I so wish I were wrong, but I am sure I know that I am not. The obvious question I have to sort out is why me? I wish it would go away, but I know it will not. I wish that it were not happening to me, that I could just have an ordinary life. Why me and for what purpose?

DAVID

David's letter contains immense details and is full of emotions and content that demonstrate many of the classic patterns to Contact. They include:

- Anxiety and denial about Contact
- Avoidance and reluctance to read Contact material
- Fear of ridicule
- Fears for privacy and confidentiality
- Positive ET assistance
- Anger, frustration, fear and confusion associated with experiences
- Emotional and teary when discussing it
- Disturbed and emotional when reading about Contact
- Realisation on a deep level, but with denial
- Dreams that feel more than dreams
- Feeling of someone 'playing with your mind'
- Feeling of being different to everyone else
- Feeling watched
- Unexplained marks and scars on the body
- Vague memories, recollections
- Sense of having thoughts monitored
- Sense of receiving information
- Dreaming of being paralysed

- Fear of 'eyes' and dreaming of eyes
- Premonitions
- Childhood trauma and confusion
- Missing time episodes
- Impelled to go to remote places
- Afraid to write about experiences
- Strong, intuitive 'flashes'
- Access to knowledge and information unusual for age group
- Meditation revealed aspects of the Contact experience
- Drawn to the spiritual
- Continual denial of the Contact experience
- Opening to the greater reality
- Knowing intuitively what's happening
- Out of body experiences
- Night terrors
- Electrical/battery disturbances (e.g. watches, cars, computers etc)
- Fear for sanity
- Continual questioning, such as "Why me?"

I have added a small story here that David also sent through because I think it demonstrates the possibility of ET interaction with animals. He wrote:

"One morning when I was about ten or so, my father found the horse lying down. Dad was sad, the old Clydesdale was dead. Quietly, without telling me, he got a shovel to dig a hole to bury him. He knew I loved the animal and that I would be upset, so he and my mother agreed not to mention it to me until I came home from school later that day.

"Dad had been brought up before tractors were prevalent and was a master reins man of a team, so he knew horses very well, having been brought up with them. He spent the morning digging a hole beside the horse, then went for his lunch. He then brought the tractor up to push the horse in the hole. He arrived at the right moment, just as a slightly wobbly and apparently drunken 16 year-old horse staggered to his feet. Mum and Dad said he looked as if he was drunk or had been given an anaesthetic."

On the surface, this story of the horse could be dismissed as being nothing more than an interesting and intriguing tale, but added to the possibility of David's Contact history it has new meaning. It does suggest that animals could also have Contact experiences and certainly given the background to David's experiences it is possible that this old horse may have had some form of Contact. There are accounts by experiencers who say they have seen their pet animals on the spacecrafts during their experiences. Given the fact that David included this story in his letter to me is, I feel, a strong indicator that he felt it very significant.

David's letter does demonstrate very clearly, part of the process behind Contact, e.g. confusion, then curiosity, the researching of information through to questioning your own sanity, to confirmation and finally realisation. As you read on, this process will unfold for you, as it is my belief through my professional experience, that Contact is indeed the chrysalis for change.

The mere process of writing this letter was very therapeutic for David as it enabled him to put parts of his own personal jigsaw together. It also opened up more doors leading to information contained within his psyche or inner awareness. Although he was very traumatised by many of his experiences, some of this trauma stemmed from his feelings of isolation and his lack of understanding. He was left to cope with this bewildering and confusing reality on his own with little, if any, support. It is important to recognise David's extraordinary psi abilities, from accurate psi skills, such as precognition (e.g. the ability to see or read future events), as well as the 'downloading' of knowledge and information and the awareness of multi-dimensional realities. He also experienced a move and desire towards spiritual growth and self-awareness, demonstrating ecological and planetary concerns with a non-materialistic focus. These are all parts, I believe, of the transformative aspects to Contact.

CHAPTER TWO
Are You Having Contact Experiences?

Come to the edge, she said,
They said: We are afraid.
Come to the edge, she said,
They came, she pushed them . . .
and they flew."

Guillaume Apollinaire

The Contact Jigsaw . . . putting the pieces together

Contact can occur in a variety of ways and this can make it very confusing, as it does not always involve the more 'tangible', physical contact. Sometimes it will occur with the non-physical, spirit energy, or astral body and so in this section I'd like to explore both.

The UFO Contact

Statistics indicate 11% of the population have seen unidentified flying objects (UFOs), but with many of these 'sightings' the individual has no obvious interaction with it, or its occupants. With close encounters of the fourth and fifth kind, the experiencer will have seen a UFO and also felt that they had some kind of Contact experience with the beings from it.

The two most common Contact/Encounter experiences are:

- The UFO sighting, with some form of Contact and
- The night/day visitor

Let's start with a brief explanation. UFO sightings are broken down into four categories:

- CE 1 . . . Close Encounters of the First Kind: you see a UFO but
- you have no Contact with it
- CE 2 . . . Close Encounters of the Second Kind: you see a UFO, there are changes in the environment, vegetation may be burned etc. animals frightened, there may be electrical disturbances
- CE 3 . . . Close Encounters of the Third Kind: you see occupants in or about a craft
- CE 4 and CE 5 . . . Close Encounters of the Fourth and Fifth Kind: you have Contact with the occupants of the craft. *J. Allen Hynek,*

Chairman (deceased) of the Dept. Of Astronomy at Northwestern University, USA, was the first to describe 'close encounter' experiences in this form.

Many individuals have seen a UFO and have not had any unusual experiences. But if you have seen a UFO and afterwards experienced some 'unusual' feelings about it, then it is possible that you may have had some form of Contact without necessarily realising it!

Have you seen a UFO?
Have you experienced the following…?

- Did you see bright, unexplained lights in the sky that did not seem like aircraft or stars and did they behave in an unusual way?
- Did the lights or bright object dazzle or frighten you?
- Did the UFO follow, or seem to chase you?
- If you were in a vehicle, did you notice electrical disturbances with the car radio or was there any mechanical or electrical interference (e.g. did the engine cut out on you suddenly)?
- Did you experience sleepiness?
- Did you feel disorientated after you saw the UFO?
- Did you experience an anomaly with time?
- If there were animals around, did they behave strangely?
- Afterwards, did you feel nauseous, notice any strange rashes, scars or marks on your body?
- If you were in your vehicle, did it have unusual marks or debris on it?
- Did you feel a desire not to talk about it afterwards, or that you wanted to block it out of your mind? Did you simply forget about it?

Many people have reported these kinds of experiences after seeing a UFO, but having said that, there are many others who have seen a UFO without witnessing anything else. But, if your experience encompasses several of the above, then it is possible you have had a close encounter of the fourth kind and that some form of Contact may have taken place.

How can you tell if something else happened?
Memories of your UFO sighting may leave you with feelings of anxiety, or panic about seeing the UFO or about the place where you saw the UFO.

You may experience vague, disturbing flashbacks or 'dreams' about beings, unusual craft, animals, or insects with large eyes.

Why can't you remember?

If the event has been difficult or traumatic for you, psychologically or emotionally, you may find that the memory of the event is sketchy or incomplete. The conscious mind sometimes does this to protect you from re-experiencing the trauma. Research shows that the difficulty in remembering may also be due to psychological blocks put in place to stop you remembering the event, possibly by those who interacted with you, or by your own psyche, to protect you from any feelings of trauma from the experience.

The day or night Contact experience

The 'night visitor' is a commonly known classic form of Contact, even though night time is not the only time it can happen. Contact can happen at any time of the day or night and you do not have to be resting or sleeping. It can occur whilst having a shower, driving your car, watching television, or out walking. For children, it has even been know to happen while at school in the playground. Sometimes people feel an urge to go to a particular place, or location and feel a need to be alone. These can all be precursors to Contact. The following dialogue is part of a regression session that I conducted with a client who had lifelong Contact experiences:

Client: *They can make you go to places and do things and you don't remember any of it.*
Mary: Is it like you're given instructions and you do them without conscious awareness?
Client: *Yes.*
Mary: Why do they do this?
Client: *You have to be in a place they can access you . . . and someone else at the same time, but you think you have done something else.*
Mary: So you would have no recall of this?
Client: *Yes.*
Mary: Why don't they want you to know?
Client: *The fear.*
Mary: So it's to stop you from getting frightened?
Client: *Yes.*

This form of Contact is a far less tangible experience, but it is as real as the classic form that is experienced from say a UFO sighting. There may, or may not be a conscious sighting, or a craft, or beings, but often the person will have a sense that something is about to happen, or they may feel unusually sleepy or just have a sense of 'knowing'. In addition:

- Animals around them may act oddly, or become sleepy too. There may be a form of paralysis in the body, like a feeling of being unable to move.
- There may be feelings of fear or panic. One or several beings may be sensed or seen.
- There may be a sense of knowing that something is going to happen.
- Strange lights in the room.
- Other people in the room fall deeply asleep and cannot be woken up.
- Sometimes the physical body is transported to a craft, but sometimes only the spiritual/energy body is taken.

I have found that there are some typical or more common experiences on board the craft and some that may or may not be remembered. If they are, it comes usually as a flashback, or through disturbing dreams. These flashbacks/dreams can take many forms, such as:

- Seeing many different types of beings, some working all together.
- Some appear as 'light' or golden energy forms, some are very human-like, many are beautiful with different shaped eyes and some can have hair.
- There are small ones, about child size in height, with little or no facial emotion.
- They are more commonly known as 'Greys'. Some can be very animal in appearance, reptilian looking, or resemble small trolls. People have also said that some can be very robotic and simply bizarre. Some of the beings may seem very familiar and may evoke feelings of love between you and them. There can often be a feeling of 'connection'. Other beings may evoke fear or terror.
- Medical procedures and monitoring can be sometimes performed.
- Healing can be performed on your body.
- Educational and spiritual information can be given to you.
- Spiritually uplifting experiences can manifest, leaving you with a tremendous sense of well being.
- You may see other humans, people you may not know, or those you do (e.g. members of your immediate family, cousins, friends etc).

- There can be a sense of being 'taken' inter-dimensionally.
- You may visit or see strange landscapes.
- There is often a memory of being returned to the bedroom. The majority of people with these experiences find themselves back in bed.
- Waking up feeling quite tired or lethargic.
- Parts of the body can feel sore sometimes, with bruises, marks, or rashes visible and there is no memory of how they got there.
- Nightwear is found in an odd placed (e.g. under the bed), or it's arranged differently on the body from when you went to sleep.
- You may find yourself outside the house, often with doors locked from the inside.

This account is only a broad overview of the night abduction scenario. The fact that these experiences often happen at night when people are at their most vulnerable, may leave them feeling fearful and the majority of people are likely to dismiss the experiences as being a product of their imagination, a dream or hallucination. But there is often a vague uneasiness or unanswered query in the back of the mind.

It is important to note that some of the experiences mentioned above are not just related to Contact. For example, there are 'out of body' experiences, (OBEs), apparently up to 20% of the population spontaneously have these and they are not necessarily related to Contact. Also if you wake up tired or lethargic in the morning this can be the result of physical illness, such as anaemia or a virus.

I have put together a comprehensive questionnaire that can guide you and help you put your own Contact jigsaw together. It may act as a trigger that will open your subconscious mind to any Contact you may have experienced. It can help you put together any supposedly 'unrelated' incidents that may have occurred throughout your life that may have been dismissed by you at the time as being unimportant.

If you find that you have positive responses to a majority of the questions, or you have a marked emotional response, for example: anxiety, confusion or fear, then this can indicate a possible Contact experience. However, the questionnaire *WILL NOT tell* you if you are having contact, it is intended as a guide only. After reading the first few questions, if you do find that you start to feel uncomfortable or anxious, then take time out and move onto the next chapter if you like. It is important to think carefully as to whether you wish to continue at this time and it could be that you need to read on a bit more beforehand.

The Questionnaire – Am I Having Contact?

What will the questionnaire tell me?

It outlines a list of some of the patterns of Contact experiences. It catalogues some of the common experiences and feelings triggered by Contact. Answer the following:

The Physical Effects
Do you . . .

- Sometimes become unusually sleepy, with an overwhelming desire to sleep?
- Ever wake up with scratches, bruises, scars, rashes, and tenderness in a particular body area that cannot be explained?
- Have any unusual lumps or bumps, scratches or bruises on your body?
- Have an extreme sensitivity to noise?
- Have back or neck problems?
- Have sinus problems?
- Have sensitivity to light?
- Wake up with nose bleeds?
- Have low vital signs, i.e. low blood pressure, heart rate or body temperature?
- Miss your monthly periods occasionally and sometimes feel as if you are pregnant?
- Have a pregnancy confirmed, only to find that later there is no foetus?
- Have any dietary problems?
- Have abnormal sleep patterns, or insomnia?
- Have bedwetting difficulties as a child?
- Experience paralysis from time to time when you are unable to move your body when resting.

Dreams and Flashbacks
Do you dream of . . .

- Travelling through walls or windows?
- Seeing children or babies that look ill or different in some way?
- Having sex with people you don't know, or sex with strange beings?
- Being pregnant, or giving birth?
- Having foetuses taken from you?

- Seeing strange children and feel some connection with them?
- Global catastrophes, environmental issues, warnings etc.
- Strange, barren landscapes?
- Owls, clowns, cats, spiders or wolves?
- Being pursued?
- Being smothered in a gooey, thick substance?
- Breathing underwater?
- Being medically examined, with unusual instruments?
- Hospitals or doctors?
- Alien spacecraft or strange beings?

Psychology and Beliefs, how can they affect you?
Do you . . .

- Need to sleep with the light on?
- Experience difficulties with sex or relationships?
- Change your place or residence often?
- Have gaps in your childhood memory?
- Consider yourself to be very open-minded?
- Believe in extraterrestrial life?
- Have difficulties with personal self-esteem?
- Consider animals and plants to be as important as humans?
- Have a compulsion to go to remote places, or be on your own?
- Have a fear of the dark, even as an adult?
- Have to have your bed away from the window, perhaps next to a wall?
- Fear cupboards, or are you claustrophobic?
- Get a sense of panic or anxiety, in corridors or passageways?
- Dislike doctors or dentists?
- Often suspect you are being watched or observed?
- Have a phobia of needles?
- Find it hard to trust people?
- Have large memory gaps in your childhood or teen years?
- Are you interested in alternative realities?
- Are you passionate about the environment?
- Are you a vegetarian, or interested in being one?
- Are you deeply interested in your spirituality?
- Are you afraid of owls, clowns, Father Christmas, cats, insects, spiders or wolves?

Intuitive Feelings
Do you . . .

- Feel different, or unlike one or both of your parents?
- Feel that you are different to everyone else?
- Have a sense of having a mission, or special purpose in your life?
- Feel that you do not belong here?
- Have extraordinary abilities, i.e. paranormal abilities?
- Have a sense of longing, or are you drawn to the night sky?
- Are you attracted to the ET phenomena and UFOs etc?
- Do you have a sense of receiving telepathic information or messages?
- Do you have any awareness of information, or do you have knowledge that you haven't consciously learned?
- Do you have a sense of urgency about the planet or society?
- Are you interested in materialistic values?
- Do you have a desire to live and eat healthily?
- Do you have a strong desire to leave, i.e. have suicidal feelings, or does it feel too hard for you to be human sometimes?
- Are you drawn towards a particular place without knowing why?
- Have you had some past sexual trauma, especially as a child or teenager?
- Are you upset when you see pictures of UFOs or extraterrestrials?
- Is there something you should not talk about, but don't know why?

Paranormal, the unusual and bizarre!
Have you . . .

- Experienced time anomalies, e.g. 'extra time', or 'missing time', or arrived earlier than expected or later at your destination or activity?
- Found that watches, lights and electrical equipment, such as TVs etc. switch themselves on or off independently, or malfunction around you?
- Found that you wake up in a different place to where you went to sleep?
- Woken up to find your clothes are wrongly buttoned, or your clothes are somewhere else altogether?
- Had out of body experiences (OBEs)?
- Discovered you are very intuitive, telepathic or psychic?
- Woken up without remembering actually going to sleep?

- Heard unusual buzzing or high-pitched sounds, which sometimes can be directional?
- Smelt strange odours, like sulphur, or rubber?
- Seen unusual balls of light, or flashes of light in your home or elsewhere?
- Seen unusual mists or fogs?
- Experienced unusual black helicopters in your district?
- Experienced unusual noises around the home?
- Seen strange shaped clouds?
- Observed animals around you sometimes behaving strangely, or erratically?
- Seen hooded or shadowy figures in your bedroom or house?
- Had unusual stains on your pillow, or bed, with no idea of how they got there?
- Become aware of information that you had not consciously learned?
- Felt you have been healed in some way by your Contact experiences?
- Felt energies of 'presences' around you?

Do you have any fears or phobias? What are they?

- Being in an elevator?
- Windows without curtains?
- Fear of the dark?
- Home security?
- Fear of a specific area?

Other phobias that can relate to this experience are fears of open spaces and sometimes fear of spiders.

Flashbacks of events that seem like memories, or dreams.
What are they?

These experiences may occur at anytime. For example, you may get a sudden vision of another event; it may seem very real and can evoke feelings of extreme fear and anxiety. Other examples are:

- You may be doing an activity and suddenly see in your mind's eye that you are projected into a spacecraft (in your mind), which evokes fear, or panic in you.
- You could be driving your car and then have a flashback to another stretch of road that causes anxiety or fear. Flashbacks can be vague and be of strange events that you have no recollection of. But they can leave you feeling very disturbed, without knowing why.

Elle, an experiencer, recalls several of her flashback experiences that were triggered when she dined out at a restaurant that had a very clinical appearance in its décor. She said:

"We approached the restaurant. It was average size and quite modern in décor, long tables with stools and a stainless steel bar. The ceiling was low and coloured blue/grey with recessed lighting. Immediately, I began to be overwhelmed by emotional distress. This modern, yet somehow clinical environment had triggered a memory of being aboard a spacecraft. Vividly, with clarity so sharp, I could see the procedures, the ETs and their eyes, the brilliant surgical equipment. It was more real than ever before and I was utterly overwhelmed."

When you read the questionnaire, did it upset you? And . .

- Did you discover that in reading the questions you began to feel very uncomfortable with a market emotional response, e.g. anxiety, confusion, fear etc?
- Did you find it difficult to read through the entire questionnaire?
- Did you discover that there was a positive answer to a high percentage of the questions?

If the answer is 'yes' to any of the previous three questions, then you may be having some form of Contact experience.

Okay, I think I may be having Contact. What should I do?

If the above information raises questions in your mind, or creates some emotional response within you, then you have a decision to make. The following statements and questions should help:

- This subject is too difficult, or threatening at the moment and
- I will look at this issue another time.
- I want to know more, but life is too difficult right now.
- The questionnaire has affected me deeply and I want to know more.
- Is this really a close encounter experience, or am I just delusional? (There is a chapter later on in the book that goes into this and will help you should you be feeling this way.) I think that I have been affected in a major way by this experience. I have panic attacks, I feel confused, isolated and sometimes I feel terrified. (See symptoms of Post Traumatic Stress Disorder, PTSD, page 297)
- My experience was very special to me; I would like to find out more about it and what it means.

Okay - before you go any further with this, I have a cautionary note to make:

If your life is going well, unless you have a real need to know, think very carefully of what further investigation into your personal experiences could mean. If you do decide to explore this more, it is helpful to have some emotional support available, such as a family member, friend, support group or a professional counsellor, or therapist.

"I cannot decide, I feel very confused"

- Then put this issue on hold for a time.
- Resource more information to help you make a decision. Find out more about this experience and/or seek specialist help. (There is a list of professional organisations that offer support at the back of this book, see page *.)
- Talk to someone close to you who you can trust.
- Take time out, go somewhere quiet and ask your 'inner self', by using relaxation/ meditation exercises (see Chapter 5 for helpful techniques).

It is important that you take your time and remember that this book will keep! If you are fearful, or in doubt, then I suggest that you read on, even if it's out of mild curiosity and come back to this section at a later date when you are ready and able. The following chapters are designed to help you work through any confusion and draw some truthful conclusions for yourself.

CHAPTER THREE
Am I Crazy, Or Am I Having Contact?

Am I crazy or multi-dimensionally aware, with Contact being the chrysalis for change?

"For me it wasn't the fear of menacing aliens, it was I think the inescapable shock of it all. Experiencing something that you are not prepared for, by religion, by science, by psychology, nothing prepares you for these experiences. There are so many know-it-alls around, who think they can fit it into some 'box', because it sounds to them like something they are familiar with. I was driven, compelled to try to describe it in a way people could hear, *this is not like any experience you know about!* Probably I didn't convert one know-it-all, but at least other experiencers would know that I knew."

Excerpt from a letter to me by Dana Redfield
Author of *Summoned* and *The ET-Human Link*

In this chapter we are going to explore the psychological paradigm and its traditional explanations of Contact phenomena. This section is designed to help you decide if your experiences fit within the conventional explanations, or whether or not you are experiencing a form of Contact.

It's a question of 'informed choice', leading to greater understanding. However, be aware that the explanations depend very much on where you look for them.

What follows is a brief look at the varied interpretations (from historical and religious viewpoints), which demonstrate how different these explanations can be, followed by a simple exploration of the more usual, conventional interpretations – from the psychological perspective. All this will (I hope) help you gain an understanding and make you aware of the fact that those people who claim to be 'qualified', who are 'informed' also have many conflicting viewpoints. Knowledge of these interpretations can help you to decide what explanation suits you and what ultimately resonates and feels right.

Explanations for Contact are numerous and the historic references are overwhelming, but it's the interpretations of them that can cause the confusion. One example of this, put into historical context is how the ancient manuscripts speak of 'gods' visiting us from the stars, the numerous drawings and paintings - from cave drawings to medieval art, which all depict flying craft of some sort. These are often explained away as being symbolic, mythological analogies, or 'flights of ancient fancy'. Historical references that lean towards extraterrestrial visitation are also interpreted by some fundamentalist religions as being some form of 'possession' by evil entities or demons.

The interpretation of Contact experiences varies again, when more open and seeking individuals of the religious fraternity subscribe to alternate viewpoints. Presbyterian Minister, Rev. Dr. Barry H. Downing, author of "The Bible and Flying Saucers", examines our ET visitors and their craft from references in the Bible. He feels they demonstrate humanity's many historical and religious links with these phenomena. This interpretation is echoed by Monsignor Corrado Balducci, of the "Congregation for the Evangelisation of Peoples and Propagation of the Faith", a representative attached to the Vatican. Monsignor Balducci, 'exorcist and demonologist' (expert in demons and entity attachment), declared on Italian National Television that in his opinion ET encounters are neither demonic, nor due to psychological impairment and these encounters deserve to be studied fully. But we know that many people in the religious fraternity still interpret these experiences as being demonic visitations and sadly individuals who seek answers from such religious bodies and who subscribe to the demonic interpretation of Contact, can often end up more terrified than before.

Monsignor Baldacci is quoted in Whitley Strieber's book "Confirmation", there is a reference to an interview by Michael Hesemann and Monsignor Balducci. Michael Hessemann, an anthropologist, historian and author of several UFO books, such as "UFOs A Secret History", was also Editor-in-Chief of *Magazin 2000* for many years. Michael asked Monsignor Balducci the question:

"Is there a conflict between the belief in extraterrestrial life and the Christian faith, or is it acceptable for a Catholic to believe in extraterrestrials?"

Monsignor Balducci replied: *"There is no conflict. Not at all. It is reasonable to believe and affirm that extraterrestrials exist. Their existence can no longer be denied, for there is too much evidence for the existence of extraterrestrials and flying saucers, as documents by UFO research."*

Similarly, in the psychological field, many professionals have, through ignorance of this phenomenon interpreted it as psychosis or hallucination and a high percentage of the public feel comfortable in believing this to be true. This interpretation however, is a very frightening explanation.

Dana Redfield (experiencer and author) wrote a letter to me explaining how she dealt with her 'fear of humans' as she called it. She said: "This is not a threat with a gun, or kidnap by a human, but ridicule, deceit and ostracism. This is 'alienation' to the extreme, because who can we trust to talk to about it? At one point, talking with my parents, very emotionally, I snapped because I realised they were thinking I might need hospitalisation! It was these kinds of 'wake-ups' that caused me to retreat and finally write a book. And there was power in that; once you go public you can't be side-swiped so easily. Speaking the truth is always considered to be healthy, *but can we always speak the truth and be safe among humans?*"

Those experiencers who explore the psychological route for understanding often find that speaking of their Contact has proved to be very traumatic to their psychological wellbeing. Confessing to your family and friends, let alone the public at large can have very devastating consequences as shown in Sandra's story in the next chapter. For Sandra, being able to speak her truth and tell of her experiences proved very damaging to her psychological health. Again, it seems that the explanations vary and they depend very much of the awareness of others and how open-minded and informed the individual you are talking to is. They are, after all, interpreting your experience in the best way that they can. If they have nothing to compare it to, other than what they have read or seen at the movies, then their perception of these experiences could lack in sufficient understanding. This is why it is even more vital that *you* understand and learn about it yourself and make up your own mind first. You decide what this experience means for you.

Fortunately, not everybody in the psychological field will interpret these experiences with traditional limits. Professor of Psychiatry at Harvard University, Dr. John Mack initially admitted that he had been sceptical about it until Budd Hopkins, another researcher and author of several books on the phenomenon invited him to study it more fully. He then evaluated hundreds of Contact/Abduction cases and psychological histories and after performing batteries of clinical tests and intensive interviews, his conclusions were that people with Contact experiences are authentic.

He documented these findings in his first book, "Abduction Human Encounters with Aliens". Not surprisingly, he was ridiculed by many of his colleagues, who even attempted to remove him from the University. Fortunately they were unsuccessful and he continues his invaluable research today. He became the founding President of PEER (Program for the Study of Extraordinary Experience Research) and published a second book,

"Passport to the Cosmos". In a speech he gave at the "International Association for New Science Conference", Fort Collins, Colorado (1995), he said:

"In this culture there may be a very small group of scientific, religious and corporate elite that determine the prevailing bounds of reality. People know their own experiences and what they have undergone does not fit with prevailing mechanistic world view. Large percentages of people seem to know there is an unseen world, or hidden dimensions of reality. The abduction phenomenon virtually forces us to consider profound questions about the nature of reality and how we, as a society decide what is real."

The awareness of Contact reality is changing and it is with thanks to so many courageous experiencers who speak up and to individuals such as Dr. John Mack, who are prepared to put their professional life on the line. This kind of commitment allows more information and research to be shared, promoting a tide of expanded consciousness, which will affect more questioning to the point whereby sheer weight of testimony and evidence must eventually gain some credibility for the subject.

"You have the sense that these people have actually experienced something of great meaning and depth and profundity and it is not simply a projection of their own unconscious," said Dr. John Mack.

There was a certain point in our history when overwhelming evidence allowed us to finally acknowledge what many had already known for years, being that 'the earth was round and not flat'. For the experiencer perhaps, Contact realisation may be closer, but as yet we will doubtless have to wait until the mass consciousness can no longer deny it. At present however, we can learn, as Dana Redfield says: *"When to speak out, when to remain silent, each weighing the risks and consequences."* So at this time you may only find understanding and acceptance through your own process.

What are the psychological explanations of Contact? Am I going crazy, or is this real?

It is normal and understandable, given the nature of this experience for individuals to question their psychological health. *"I must be crazy"* is a very real fear and I've included some information to help you with this so that you can find out whether this explanation is a valid one for you. Is Contact experience a form of mental instability, or is it a bizarre, but real one? To understand more about the explanations given for Contact experience, we need to explore the symptoms of mental illness and also look at how Contact experiences are explained using traditional psychology. Only then can we find out whether traditional explanations are valid for your experiences. Towards the end of this chapter there is a segment called: "Contact, the Chrysalis for Change", which gives you a step by step process, enabling you to honour your experiences through to gradual integration and full acceptance.

Elle and Karen are both experiencers:

Elle: It's just that my life feels so bizarre, like living as Batman or someone. It scares me to think that this is all real.

Karen: *Isn't it better to know that it's' real rather than to find out you're crazy?*

Elle: I don't know, at least I could be given medication and it would all go away.

Karen: *But it wouldn't you know, it would all keep going, they would still come to you.*

How do you distinguish Contact experiences from psychiatric illness?

Ask yourself the following. The questions are intended as a guide only, to help you to evaluate your own experience.

- Can you distinguish between inner and outer experiences? In other words, can you tell the difference between what's going on in your mind as opposed to what's happening in the outside world?
- Are you clear about which inner experiences do not fit with the prevailing world view of reality. In other words, do you know what other people consider to be 'normal'?
- Are you able to function in the three-dimensional reality?
- Can you cope with the everyday practicalities of life?
- Can you still make discerning judgements?
- Do you have control of your emotions?
- Do you generally react in an appropriate manner to outside stimuli, without excessive mood swings?

If you are at all unsure about these, then it is wise to seek the advice of a professional, but ideally it should be someone who is educated in Contact reality. We should also remember that some people, who have had very traumatic Contact experiences, can be affected by them so much that they can lead to some form of mental instability.

What are the traditional and psychological explanations for Contact experiences?

Are they fantasy or confabulation? Imaginary, not real and individual fantasies are as unique and diverse as the person. In Contact experience, there are millions of people around the world having very similar and classic Contact scenarios, which follow the same patterns of experiences. This means that if Contact were imaginary, multiple participants of this experience would all be fantasising the same thing. Interestingly, a school teacher in America asked 30 children to draw a picture of an alien and the pictures were as diverse as the kids' imagination (and not one of them resembled a 'Grey').

Biophysical disorders, such as sleep paralysis and *temporal lobe epilepsy*. This is the effect of the electromagnetic field of the brain. In Contact, this hypothesis fails to explain the depth and volume of details and the multiple witness matching imagery. People do draw what they say they have seen and there are numerous matches and similarities. This hypothesis also does not explain how two people can begin a period of simultaneous, total amnesia without injury or cause and then return to consciousness without any meaningful trigger.

Delusions. A distortion of our 'known' reality. These are usually the result of deteriorating relationships and ineffective coping. In Contact however, millions of people have 'identical delusions' or memories and some people with Contact can be very young. A client of mine told me that her daughter who was 18 months old at the time, picked up the book "Communion", by Whitley Strieber, pointed to the grey face on the cover and said: "Look mummy, this is the man who comes and gets me." Small children do not experience delusions and with Contact experiences, research suggests it could start very early, or even from birth.

Brain Tumour. A tumour or some abnormality would be evident to the practitioner. There would be physical evidence from a brain scan or similar procedures. However, (as an example) Whitley Strieber had a brain scan and no tumour was found. Several of my clients have also had brain scans that did not show any abnormalities.

Hallucinations. Perception without objective reality, delusion carried through injury, substance abuse, or a brain tumour. In Contact, none of these criteria are present.

Shared Hallucination, 'Folie a Deux'. Shared hallucinations only occur between two persons who have a close symbiotic connection. This is not the case with multiple Contact experiences.

Jungian Archetypes. The collective unconscious theory is that all human beings share basic primitive imagery. In Contact this does not explain the intricate and specific detail of experiences, which describe emotions and behaviour accurately. Jungian imagery cannot explain the conscious sightings that do not rely on unconscious memory recall.

Suggestibility. It is said that therapists can lead the client, or give them certain scenarios in a relaxed state, so they take 'on board' suggestions as if they are their own personal memories. In Contact experiences, a good therapist will take great care not to lead their clients. To check validity, some therapists will deliberately make a contrary suggestion only to find that the client will correct them and say something quite different, which demonstrates they are not being lead by the therapist. Further, there are examples of clinical hypnotherapists working many miles apart who have found that participants of the same event have had precise corresponding details.

Repressed Sexual Abuse. That human beings are creating 'space age imagery' as a symbolic representation of repressed sexual abuse. In Contact, research has shown that hardly one in a thousand who have had this experience have revealed such an underlying connection. But the reverse has been shown to be true; a memory of human sexual abuse can be a 'cover' for alien intrusion.

Influence of the Media. It is suggested that the media encourages individuals to believe they are having Contact experiences. In Contact, this does not explain the emotional accounts of children who do not watch or understand television, adult programmes or talk shows. It doesn't explain how people with Contact can know specific details that are not published or known to the general public through the media.

Hoaxes. Fabricated tale or practical Joke? In Contact experience the individuals relay similar 'markers' and accounts with little evidence that would suggest another experience or fabrication.

Attention Seeking. It is suggested that some individuals seek attention by saying that they are having Contact. Research shows this is a rare occurrence because in reality it sets people up for ridicule, or the prospect of being perceived as mentally ill. I have not had any client do this and in fact I would say that the contrary is true. Individuals would prefer not to own their Contact experience and would happily accept some other medical label which would better explain it.

Is there any psychological testing being done with those having Contact?

Yes there are, these tests include:

- Minnesota Multiphasic Personality Inventory
- Wechsler Adult Intelligence Scale
- Thematic Apperception Test
- Lie Detector Test
- Brain Scan

In terms of psychological health, individuals were found to be well within the accepted norms.

There are several books available that cover the subject of psychological explanations for Contact experience. These hypotheses have been thoroughly discussed and satisfactorily answered. For example, books written by the eminent psychiatrist, Professor John Mack and researcher Budd Hopkins. For more information, see page **.

Apart from these tests, what evidence qualifies Contact as being a real experience?

- Marks and scars on the body, sometimes bruises and rashes (some of these glow fluorescent under black ultra-violet light), with no knowledge of how they got there.
- More than one person in the household having the same experience. The 'missing time' episodes happen to more than one person in a household, or when travelling in a car.
- Implants and anomalies in the body. Objects have been seen on X-rays and some have been surgically removed and documented on film (see Dr. Roger Leir, "*Aliens and the Scalpel*").
- It affects all age groups. Children as young as two or three years old are having this experience, without prior knowledge of the phenomena.

- Marks on cars after some experiences. For example, in "The Oz Files", author Bill Chalker documents the story of the Knowles family. In 1988 they were crossing the Nullarbor Plain in Australia and claimed to have seen an 'egg shaped object'. They believed the object had landed on top of their car and that the car was being lifted off the road. Later Mrs Knowles put her hand on the roof of the car and found it was covered in black/grey dust and had a foul smell to it. All the four family members witnessed this.
- Unusual animal behaviour at the time of these occurrences. Animals can react strangely when Contact occurs.
- The emotional impact of the memories and dreams.
- Millions of people from all cultures and belief systems around the world are having this experience.
- There can be emotional trauma such as Post Traumatic Stress Disorder (PTSD).This does not occur without real trauma.
- Many individuals can be physically missing from their beds.
- Many individuals have been psychologically tested and there has been no physical, psychological abnormality found.
- Individuals have had unexplained and documented healings from their Contact experiences.
- Transformation of the individual on all levels, physically, emotionally, psychologically and spiritually.
- High Sense Perceptions (HSP) are noted from those having this Contact experience, e.g. clairvoyance, telepathic skills, healing abilities, awareness of a multidimensional reality.

It is reasonable for most people to look to conventional psychiatry for more understanding of this. For many it is a necessary part of their process, even if it ultimately only shows them that their answers are not to be found there. However, mental illness does not lead to a positive transformation of the individual on many levels, as it does following Contact experience, nor would mental illness activate High Sense Abilities, healing and clairvoyance.

"The psychiatrist was clear, Jason is not mentally ill", said Ann Andrews, Jason's mother (and author of the book "Abduction"). In November 1995, Jason's GP also said that in her opinion Jason was not psychotic and her unambiguous statement of his sanity echoed what the psychiatrist had already told Ann, that Jason was not hallucinating. However, anti-depressants and further medication were still prescribed to help him sleep. Jason and his parents believed that continuing to see the psychiatrist was fruitless: "He would emerge from his talks with her in tears, insisting that he wasn't making it up," said Ann. As any mother would be, she was happy for Jason to see someone who could try and help him, but she maintained that he got the best support from those that knew and believed in Contact phenomena.

What's more, Ann also said that Jason had shown the psychiatrist the marks on his body but this was not explored or explained. This is a common occurrence and many clients have mentioned unusual marks, scars and lumps to their doctors and these have been dismissed or negated as being unimportant.

Many of the clients I have seen, who have gone to mental health professionals have found the response to be varied. It is quite common however, for a psychiatrist who cannot make a proper diagnosis as no mental abnormality can be found, (e.g. when the unexplained cannot be conventionally explained), to offer medication to assist with poor sleep patterns, or depression.

The information we supply here is intended to help guide you and help you evaluate your experiences. With it, you can decide for yourself if your experiences fit more with Contact reality or psychological illness. If you decide on the former interpretation and feel your experiences have some validity then this information will act as a catalyst for a new process or 'paradigm'. It is a broader one, a multi-dimensional one and it will inevitably change many, if not all of your previous beliefs.

This process of awakening to your new paradigm I call 'Contact, the Chrysalis for Change'. It is a paradigm shift you will need to make to integrate new information and beliefs about your multidimensional reality. If this challenge is 'real' then what does it say about your world and what you believe in? The shift starts with your acknowledgment of the reality and triggers the process of change in you.

Contact, the Chrysalis for Change, The Shift in Paradigms

Acknowledging Contact is a huge leap into the unknown. For many it is very frightening to accept that this experience has reality, has basis. When you finally realise that traditional thinking has no valid explanation for this you may feel 'out on a limb', fragile and disconcerted. Acceptance does require a huge paradigm shift, but becomes the chrysalis for change.

From Confusion to Living with Close Encounters

The Contact process explores the various stages individuals go through until they reach a place of acceptance and healing. In Chapter 1, David demonstrated his ongoing Contact process and he experienced several of these stages simultaneously, vacillating between them. This is a normal part of this Contact process.

So let's look in detail at this process and try and explain what some experiencers say it feels like. The common, initial responses to Contact experience, is usually fear and confusion. But there is also provoked curiosity and questioning, which encourages people to study resources in an endeavour to understand. The question undoubtedly is: *how real is this?* Often, a trigger event will finally give confirmation of the reality, which I call the Realisation Event. But there is an ongoing struggle to acknowledge this greater reality and to let go of the previous 'limited' one.

But slowly, through more information and more openness, a contactee will find that they are able to reach a place of acceptance and begin a 'conversion', a change in worldview. Fears calm, through gradual integration, until they feel ready to embrace more fully their new reality. Personal transformation will follow as it leads to the unfolding and awakening of higher perceptions, the 'normalising' of these abilities and living and growing with Contact.

What is the Value of Identifying this Process?

For most of us, when we have any difficult life experiences, it often helps to have reference points. Despite initial feelings of confusion and fear, many individuals do come through their Contact experiences and manage to reach a place of integration and healing.

The Ten Step Process from Fear to Transformation:

1. *Confusion.* Being 'in the fear place', feeling isolated and fearful.
2. *Curiosity.* Questioning, wanting to know what is going on!
3. *Controversy.* Seeking out more information.
4. *Crazy or bizarre.* Wanting to know whether you are crazy or having a multi-dimensional experience?
5. *Confirmation.* The Realisation Event, e.g. this *IS* real!
6. *Conflict.* Denial versus acceptance, e.g. what do you want to believe?
7. *Change.* The new paradigm, a change in your worldview.
8. *Conversion.* The acceptance of your multi-dimensional reality.
9. *Calm.* Integration and opening up to transformation.
10. *Contact.* Living and growing with awareness and Contact.

As with any process, the individual will vacillate between these markers for some time. This is quite normal, but as they slowly integrate their experiences over time, they become more stable.

Let's look at the ten-step process for change in a little more detail.

1. Confusion. Elle best describes this:
Q: So what is it that you fear?
"I fear that 'they' and my experiences are real. I fear that my world as I know it is becoming redundant. So many things are losing their relevance and meaning. I fear the experiences and interactions my daughter will have with 'them' in the future. I fear I will not be strong enough to cope with the people around me who may discount my experiences and intense emotions and they'll think I'm crazy.

"I fear the uncertainty of whether I am doing the best thing for my family by revealing all of this."

2. Curiosity, what is going on?
Many with Contact experiences are fearful of something but are unsure about what it is. They have lived with unusual paranormal phenomena, strange dreams and experiences that arouse feelings of apprehension and anxiety without quite knowing why.

They may believe that they are just different, or 'weird'. One individual said: "I've always felt as if I was just messed up in the head." The fear of being perceived as being crazy can mean that these thoughts are not shared or expressed; they are buried until it becomes a private nightmare. At some point there will be a catalyst. It may be a life crisis, even a sighting of a UFO, or a book about Contact experiences, a picture of an ET face, or a TV programme. This can propel a person to explore this phenomenon when previously they had shown little interest. The trigger can even sometimes make them feel obsessed for a short while, with a need to seek out more information in an effort to understand, even though a part of them may feel bewildered or very uncomfortable about this obsessive need.

3. Controversy, seeking out information
This is an important time for the experiencer as the more information they can collect from different sources, the more opportunity they have to acknowledge this reality, as it can be very validating and healing to hear your experiences being described by someone else. It is also very important to

find out if there are professionals nearby that work in this area as most of us are programmed to more readily accept information from those with certified credentials.

4. Crazy and bizarre, or is this a real experience?

We are exploring this issue within this chapter to help to give guidance as to the reality of your experiences. If you find that information in the previous chapters fits or 'resonates' better with you, then this offers you more clarity about the reality of your situation. When you are in the psychological shock of this discovery, you may feel as if you are going crazy, so it is very important to seek appropriate help and support from those you trust, or someone who has some understanding of these phenomena. It can be a time to actively seek support and resources and there is more help for you further on in this book.

5. Confirmation, the Realisation Event. Is this real?

HELP! This is real! What happens when you finally realise you are having Contact? This is the moment when you finally receive absolute confirmation and you find that you have to acknowledge that your experience has reality.

6. Conflict, denial verses acceptance. What do I believe?

I am not sure I really want to know! For many experiencers this is the dilemma. If you believe you are psychologically sound, in other words, a 'sane' individual and if you believe that the phenomena has 'physical' reality, then you inevitably have to conclude that at some time in your life you have had interaction with non-human beings. The initial response, in my experience, is usually: *I don't want to believe this.* Many people have actually said that it would have been easier to cope with the thought of being mentally ill as opposed to facing the truth of the experience.

7. Change, the new paradigm, a change in my world view

"Thread by thread, the fabric of my known reality was torn apart. I was confronted with more and more segments of the greater picture of life than I ever believe existed." (Elle)

Finally there is a change in worldview as you open up to the reality of Contact and the acceptance of these experiences begins. Gradually the myriad of confusion or unusual events starts to fit into a pattern, confirming your experiences. Many discover during this process of acknowledgement new triggers for more information, which confirm this 'new' reality all the more. It takes time and courage to adjust to this as the previous familiar and secure boundaries of reality dissolve. As you are going through this process it can be very destabilising and you will still constantly question the reality of it. But when you can finally embrace it and take it on board, you should feel a huge sense of relief. However, support and understanding are crucial at these times and if possible it is important that you are able to connect with other experiencers to help reaffirm your reality.

8. Conversion, the acceptance of your multi-dimensional reality.

"The first publisher who read my book said: *Do you really want to do this to your life?* Well, I went public and have lived with the consequences - some think I'm insane, others think I'm brilliant. For sure I have no more secrets, which means no more fears."

Excerpt from a letter from James Walden,
Author of *The Ultimate Alien Agenda*

When you come to terms with this reality, you are able to create a new base to work from as you are starting to integrate and learn more. Unfortunately, you will still have to cope with a closed and sceptical public mind, the uninformed or 'misinformed' and those who are locked in fear. You will realise that your 'secret life' is not something you can share with everyone, although there is a growing number of people who become more confident as they begin to talk openly about their experiences. This is not because they want to confront people, or gain notoriety, but in an effort to gain acceptance and help to raise public awareness. Many also want to give information and support to those isolated and frightened, those who are still too afraid to acknowledge their own Contact experiences.

9. Calm, acceptance and opening to transformation

James Walden best describes this, he says: "I've learned experientially that my human life is much more comfortable when I accept without fear or judgement other beings and other worlds, with the love that my human spirit can manifest and express. Yet as I sit and listen to all those others who walk the same path, who describe this very same understanding, who in their sessions with me recount lives on other planets, in other dimensions and who are normal, everyday people - from university students to secretaries, to lawyers or psychologists, these people generally possess the more advanced capacities of healing and psychic ability. They are evolving in a very different way, understanding why they are here and what the greater picture of life is all about."

10. Integration, healing, living and growing with Contact

"When I healed my victim consciousness, my world shifted to a positive pole. I am now a full-time physical, emotional and spiritual healing practitioner, hypnotherapist and holistic educator. My primary goals are to help people take responsibility for their own health, attitudes and awareness. This is what my 'abductors' (teachers) were trying to help (force) me to accomplish." (James Walden)

Contact is the catalyst for transformation on every level, physically, emotionally, psychologically and spiritually and this experience changes the whole person. The acceptance and integration of these experiences allows the individual to balance these two realities healthily, with this comes the desire to seek greater understanding as awareness grows. Experiencers notice that their Contact interaction changes as they become a more conscious participant. Many lose their fear as they begin to actively explore their Contact and gain greater understanding of themselves and their personal reality.

CHAPTER FOUR
Now I Know I'm Not Crazy

"Jason does not need as much day-to-day counselling as he did at first, because he now understands what is happening and because he has supportive parents. I am sad for him that he has been forced to jump through other hoops, like seeing a psychiatrist. So many young 'abductees' are sent to see psychiatrists, behavioural psychologists and other 'so called' experts. They are given tests for epilepsy and many adolescents are diagnosed as psychotic - either schizophrenic or manic-depressive. It is depressing for them, because in the end, if nobody believes them they really do question their sanity."

Excerpt from *Abducted* by Ann Andrews & J. Ritchie

Contact and the psychiatric paradigm

I feature in this chapter Sandra's case study. It is a story of a young woman's Contact and it demonstrates the potential consequences when Contact experiences are interpreted purely from traditional, psychological models. The conventional interpretation of Sandra's experiences drastically changed her life and the trauma of its effects left her not only heavily medicated, but even more confused, very depressed and at times suicidal. Sandra was unable to accept the psychological interpretation given and despite the overwhelming odds against her, she determined to find out what it was she was experiencing. By researching herself, she gradually found out that her experiences were not unique to her, many others had been having them and they had been categorised under the label "Abduction/Contact". This understanding brought Sandra into the realms of the incredible and bizarre, but through it she gained new understanding of herself and her world. For me, Sandra's story also demonstrates the resilience and courage of human spirit. With no-one to turn to, she embarked on her personal question to find out what was really happening to her.

At the age of fourteen, when she shared some information with her doctor she told him that she saw aliens. The consequences of this disclosure resulted in a sure diagnosis of mental illness. This was devastating for her and part of her was unable to accept this explanation so it became her personal mission to try and understand what these experiences were. The psychiatric treatment compounded and exacerbated her difficulties, leaving her even more confused. Not only was she living with this ongoing and frightening Contact, but she was also experiencing the uncomfortable side effects of powerful anti-psychotic drugs. All this, not surprisingly, took a massive toll on her health and wellbeing. Psychologically, Sandra was bewildered and fearful and there were times in her life when these feelings brought her to the brink of suicide. But despite what she had been told to believe about her experiences, Sandra continued to question and gradually she came to the conclusion that her experiences were valid. She bravely sought the help that she felt was more appropriate and applicable to her and through that support she gained the courage to honour her 'reality', which ultimately transformed her life. Sandra's story is by no means unique, although her personal management of her experience is. For that reason alone, I feel her story needs to be told and it also demonstrates perfectly how the process from confusion and fear evolves through to living and growing with Contact.

Sandra believed her Contact experiences began as early as three or four years old when she said she was too young to vocalise what was happening to her. She struggled with the impact of them, thus creating fear and confusion, which affected her both emotionally and psychologically. Her parents were totally unaware of what she was experiencing, but were concerned about her behaviour. At eight years old she was taken to see various mental health professionals, when at fourteen she finally disclosed to a psychiatrist that she saw aliens. She was flatly told that there was no such thing and was diagnosed as schizophrenic. Medication did not stop her experiences however and the psychiatric 'label' was devastating for her. The powerful medication she was taking made her feel like a zombie most of the time she said. Her self-esteem plummeted as she lost motivation, feeling worthless and stupid, life lost all meaning for her and several times she attempted suicide.

Sandra takes us through this Contact process from the moment it began (as a young child), explaining her confusion and fear. Feelings of isolation developed because she didn't know how to explain these experiences, or who to tell. Finally, feeling so trapped in her fear and isolation, she felt she had no choice other than to trust her doctor by being honest and open, so she told him about what she thought had been happening to her. Sandra recalls how betrayed she felt by his denial of her reality, the invalidation and the subsequent psychiatric label that was placed on her. Intuitively she sought understanding, until eventually she gained enough personal evidence to convince herself that her experiences were real and this gave her the courage to get the appropriate and necessary support she needed. But paradoxically, the Contact 'reality' also challenged her at the same time. Once she acknowledged her experiences, as being real to her, her fragile world rocked, as she realised that to accept this fully she would need to make huge changes to her worldview perception. This was as terrifying and confrontational as believing she was mentally ill. But with support, she gradually came to terms with her experiences and started to integrate and accept them. This has since lead to further exploration of her reality and a focus of personal growth and new awareness.

The impact of all this on Sandra's parents was huge. It is important to remember to acknowledge the difficulties that close relatives and loved ones experience in these kinds of situations and how much they are challenged, as they too struggle to decide whether Contact is possible, real, or if this could be mental illness. Ultimately, they will experience a certain amount of fear, or even terror. After all, if Contact is a reality then it's been happening under their roof! What's more, as any father or mother knows, we have a built-in need to protect our young. If this is happening to their son or daughter, how powerless must they feel, helpless! In a crisis it would be much easier for the parents to 'hand over' the problem. Find a vicar, priest or psychiatrist, any kind of professional to take this problem over and sort it out . . . please! Dealing with mental health issues is difficult, but probably easier than facing the prospect that aliens have been visiting your house, interfering with (or 'abducting') your young, from babies upwards. Absolutely terrifying!

Sandra's Story – A Case Study of Contact

"I didn't have the language as a child, to explain why I was so reluctant to go to bed at night; I didn't know how to say that strange monsters came for me at night. I lived most of my young life in terror and isolation. I didn't understand what was happening and didn't know how to talk about my experiences at all. My family were unaware of all this until I told them finally, but by then I was already in my teens. We are a religious, Christian family, what I experienced did not fit within our beliefs, except as the possibility of evil spirit presences, so I was taken to see both psychologists and psychiatrists and over several years was given a multitude of diagnoses and a variety of medications. There were times during this period when I became so desperate and despairing. I contemplated ending my life and at one time I almost succeeded.

"I was eighteen when I saw a television programme, which terrified me. The documentary was about the exploration of archaeological evidence that supports the possibility of extraterrestrial Contact throughout human evolution. It was more concrete evidence for me - that my experiences could be real and it really did disturb me, but I just knew I had to do something. So I contacted a local UFO organisation in Perth, "The Australasian Society for Psychical Research (ASPR/ UFORUM)" and they gave me Mary Rodwell's phone number."

I can remember Sandra's initial call to me quite vividly. She said: "No one knows I'm ringing you, but I just have to talk to someone, I just feel as if I'm falling apart." I asked how I could help and she said: "I just want to understand my experiences. I feel so isolated and alone."

Sandra then told me about the programme she had seen and how it had evoked such terror in her. "I just don't know what to do, if the documentary is right, then I know my experiences are real. I need help to sort this out. It's like a private nightmare! I feel I am frightened to go to sleep at night. I try to keep awake as long as I can, but the night terrors are so bad I often go and sleep in my parent's bedroom. I just feel like it's out of control."

I asked if there was any particular experience that she remembered: "I remember this vividly, I was just eight years old and I never knew why this experience was so clear to me, because many others were just like vague dreams with a sense of dread and unease with them. But it was as if this experience had some special significance. I remember my mum tucking me into bed; it was about eight thirty at night. I don't remember actually falling asleep. The next thing I remember, I suddenly woke up, I was not in bed, but in the lounge room, I couldn't understand what I was doing there. There were flashing lights in the room and I felt absolutely terrified, it just didn't feel right, I felt really traumatised and I ran straight to my parent's bedroom. I have never sleepwalked in my life, so that didn't fit. It's strange whenever the subject of ETs comes up, my mind instantly goes back to that memory."

Throughout my childhood and adolescence I have seen lights in my room and at the window and sensed 'presences', which I knew were not human. I often felt paralysed, as if these beings were watching me. I was terrified and found I couldn't bear to sleep near my bedroom window as it felt too unsafe.

"In my early childhood, I believe I was a happy little girl, with a loving and supportive family. But from my earliest memories I can recall fear coming into my life. At the age of four I just changed. It was as if some 'reality' hit me. I found it was not such a good world. I don't know what made this change within me, but I believe this was when my Contact experiences began, it would certainly account for it. One time I remember lights in my room and being taken away by a group of beings, which I have always known was a part of my reality and not something in my imagination. This continued throughout all of my childhood. The strange and frightening memories always seemed to haunt me, but the only time the fear seemed to be reinforced on my young mind was when I saw pictures of the 'Greys', or television programmes, or anything on UFOs and ETs, anything at all on that subject, impacted on me profoundly and would trigger something in me.

"Even as a little girl I was continually asking questions about the world and the universe. At six years old I saw a documentary on UFOs, this was when my fear really began. I soon found that anything I saw on UFOs or ETs absolutely terrified me. One time, I saw the author Whitley Strieber on television and he was talking about his abduction experiences and his book 'Communion'. It was the face on the book cover that really scared me; a face I recognised, the face of an ET (a Grey)! I became too frightened to watch television just in case I might accidentally see a program on UFOs or aliens. It was strange really; I was not in the least bit frightened by horror stories, or weird crime shows, just programs on ETs or UFOs.

"There was a spate of sightings of UFOs near where I lived, one report mentioned that people had been lifted up by a UFO; this was shown on a TV programme.

It was at this same time that a neighbour, a young boy, told me that he had seen lights outside my bedroom window and I felt awful. I would wake up several times at night and turn on the bedroom lights just to check there were no Greys in the room. I desperately wanted to find other, rational explanations for my experiences. My religious beliefs gave me even more terrifying explanations, such as being visited by some 'evil' spirits or other. This made me even more frightened and confused. The 'night terrors' made my childhood so difficult and unhappy, not just at home but also at school. I became very lonely, it was hard to make friends and I felt like I didn't fit in. The academic pressures of school life made me feel continually anxious, I often felt like I couldn't cope. I remember being mostly tired and frightened. Even from the age of eight, I started to distance myself from my peers and spent my time alone in the playground. It was my choice not to make friends at school, I just felt different and separate from them. I felt no connection or common feeling. Some of my teachers embarrassed me, they told me I was not very bright, I felt I lost my will and just became a dummy. I always felt I was an 'outsider' and I just couldn't wait to get out of there. My fear consumed me and I never felt free of anxiety. I was taking in more and more information about ETs from the media. I lived this solitary fear and I never spoke to my parents about my 'secret life' until I was about fifteen. In my teens, I would often wake up so tired and lethargic I would take days off from school and caused problems. I fell behind in my studies and I became more anxious and depressed. I was very lonely, I still found it hard to make friends and I think I was more mature than other girls of my age, anyway they would all laugh at me because I wasn't cool.

"By the time I reached the third year of high school I was almost fifteen. I just didn't want to be at school anymore and I didn't feel as if I belonged. I had no friends, I didn't like my world. I felt all the pressures on me and I tried to cut my wrists, but my mother caught me. She took me out of school, but later they tried to get me to go back, but I would do anything to get out of it. Finally, I was allowed to stay at home. I left school full of confusion and isolation.

"When I left school the strangeness of this reality began to impact on me to the point that I became completely consumed with fear and the dread of waiting, feeling watched and ready for them any minute of the day. This was very frightening and bewildering. I had temporarily moved in with my grandmother, but I found that 'they' followed, they went wherever I did! So it began all over again, the lack of control and sleep deprivation took me to the point of terror. After eight months I moved back home with my parents and they took me to see a psychiatrist. I had decided to talk to him about my experiences and felt that I had to tell him I was afraid of aliens. But he had no belief or understanding of the abduction experience I talked about. I was told not to be ridiculous, there was no such thing, and they didn't exist.

"By Christmas 1994 my mother told me that the doctors thought I had schizophrenia. Apparently, the psychiatrist had taken my case to a panel of doctors and they had concluded that I was schizophrenic. It was pretty horrific and this information was very disturbing for me because from the moment I was told this, I knew it wasn't the truth. Despite the fear, I was also fascinated and drawn to the UFO/ET phenomena. I began to read many books and magazines and as I became more informed I learned about the reality, the physical evidence, such as marks and scars on the body and I recalled my own bruises, scratches and marks. I also woke up feeling tired, with throbbing and uncomfortable headaches, I knew this meant something, but whom could I talk to? I felt no-one would ever understand and the only support I could ever get was if I went to the United States and somehow find one of the psychiatrists that I had heard about who specialised in this kind of thing. But this was not possible, I had no money and nobody believed me anyway.

"When I turned seventeen I had been in hospital three times and the abductions were not stopping. The medication was only sedating me to the point of exhaustion and I felt my life was *hell*. No-one would believe me, I had revealed my experiences to my parents and doctors and they kept telling me I was mentally ill.

"When I left school I stayed at home, I was alone too much of the time because both my parents were working. I was so shy and nervous and I was frightened of going out alone. I had no confidence to get a job and it would have been very hard for me anyway because I was exhausted and sleepy all the time. I spent most of my nights trying to stay away so 'the beings' wouldn't take me. Then I would wake up so tired I would need to sleep for much of the day. It was a lonely and isolated life and I felt continually depressed and unhappy, I felt worthless.

"When I was seventeen, I had an experience when I was fully awake, I felt paralysed and I saw an ET. I felt as if my soul was being sucked out of my body and through the window. I tried to call out but I couldn't speak. I tried really hard to call my mum and in the end I managed it, but she got very frightened. They took me to hospital and 'the experts' called it a psychotic episode.

"I continued to visit various mental health professionals throughout my teenage years. Different doctors and psychiatrists gave me a variety of diagnoses, they ranged from delusional episodes to severe depression and I received a cocktail of medications as treatment. I hated taking the medication, the drugs did not change my experiences or lessen my fear, they just made me 'fuzzy headed' and lethargic. I felt robbed of energy and robbed of the motivation I so desperately needed to change things. I believe now that my medication contributed to my depression instead of alleviating it. "

I spent so much time on my own, I had plenty of time to think and to try and analyse what was happening to me. I knew I had some definite experiences, because I was wide awake when some of them happened and I also had strange bruises and marks on my body. I often wondered why I had bizarre feelings and marks on my body. I often wondered why I had bizarre feelings of terror over anything to do with UFOs and ETs. I was desperately trying to understand what was really going on and I became increasingly dissatisfied with my medical diagnoses. I was eighteen when I watched a programme about ETs, so I decided to contact the local UFO organisation and they gave me someone to ring. The television documentary had finally given me the information I needed for me to gain the courage to find help. It felt as if the jigsaw pieces were beginning to fit together, I became desperate to find someone to help me make sense of it all."

When Sandra phoned me, I was able to give her the information she needed and I invited her to come in for counselling. Sandra hadn't told her mother that she had been in touch with me; she said this would be hard as she knew it would be difficult for her mother to acknowledge that these experiences had any reality whatsoever. I suggested to Sandra that she should tell her mother anyway and that I would be very happy to speak to her and offer her some support and reassurance, if I could. Sandra's mother phoned and asked me lots of questions about these kinds of experiences, my professional background and my research work. She looked into my references and career history and only when she was fully satisfied would she bring Sandra in to see me.

Sandra came to me over a period of several months and when she felt ready she joined the support group. She was still feeling very vulnerable, shy and self-conscious, but through counselling she became more confident and stronger. Sandra felt that it would help her to meet other experiencers and talk to them, even though meeting strangers was very difficult for her. It had taken huge effort and courage on her part to come in and meet the group. It was also very confronting for her parents having to bring her, as they were still feeling very uncomfortable with the possibility and likelihood of what was happening to their daughter and in their world.

When Sandra joined the group it was a momentous event for her, by acknowledging her experiences she took a huge step forward. Her anxiety was very apparent, she moved restlessly in her chair, hiding her eyes from the others. As she was greeted with acceptance and warmth, Sandra slowly lost some of her self-consciousness as she listened with rapt attention to the experiences from other members of the group. When it was Sandra's turn, I saw the effort it took for her to share her own experiences, slowly and haltingly she began to tell her story. But she had the respect and courtesy of the group and with this support she became increasingly confident. She bravely told everyone what had happened to her and divulged information regarding her psychiatric history. She was angry because her experiences had been so brutally misunderstood and misinterpreted in the past. The stories from the other members of the group finally convinced her of the reality of her own and she said: "At last, now I know I am really sane!"

The consequences of Sandra's Realisation Event came very soon afterwards. The next morning I received a call from her. She was distraught, she said: "I was awake all night; I want you to stop it happening."

A short time later she rang me again. She said that she thought it wasn't Contact after all, that she was just experiencing fear and that she might be crazy. Neither of these calls came as a huge surprise for me. As we discussed in the previous chapter, with confirmation and realisation there soon follows denial and an unwillingness to accept the experiences as they challenge our worldview perceptions. The support group experience had been very important for Sandra. It confirmed and validated her experiences, but she needed time to readjust to what this could mean. All her fears resurfaced because she knew that if she accepted her experiences as being real, it meant that she must face the fact that the 'beings' came into her bedroom at night on a regular basis. To really know this, was terrifying. We talked it through and finally she said: "Acceptance changes everything. I don't want to live in fear."

So Sandra experienced her 'conversion', she finally came to accept the prospect of a multi-dimensional reality.

Sandra's challenge she felt, was to accept that these beings were visiting her. She said: "I didn't believe that intelligent beings would come into my life without my permission and acceptance. This changes everything, it takes away my fear and makes me realise it's my life and I can accept them. They are not really monsters. The more knowledge I gain, the more I realise they are not evil. I learned from the others in the support group that they are not bad. Now I have to learn to accept that they are
a part of the Universe, and so am I."

Ultimately she was calm. She had moved from fear to transformation.

Integration - living and growing with Contact

Some months later I asked Sandra how she was coping with her Contact, "They come just before I go to sleep and I may be a little fearful just before, then I fall asleep and then the next thing I know is I'm just awake and it's the next morning. Nowadays, I don't bother to tell my parents. Most nights they come, it's just as common to me now as dreaming. What made it hell for me was the fear. These beings were not 'physical' as I recall it, most of the time they are simply around me, like guardian angels.

"I know they are there, I can feel them touching me. They are not trying to be mean or difficult, they are curious, really positive, loving energies and they have come to me because I have invited them in. These are not Greys, I can't even picture them. They are almost angelic, not earth based, but really cool! It's not abuse, or torture, but curiosity. They are interested in my body, prodding my toes, hair, face and nose, this is what I feel. I really believe they have a genuine interest in me, my soul energy, sometimes I feel I am sharing my body with them. Really cool! I am prepared to let them come in. I am in total control all the time. When I think of them (not the Greys), I feel different, different energy, pure spirit energy, like beings of light. Due to the drugs (medication) I wasn't open at all spiritually, it was like my whole potential was blocked, and the real me wasn't there. It was pure physicality, cigarettes and food was all I enjoyed before. My spiritual consciousness was not there, the drugs stopped it. It was as if things resonated but I couldn't understand why I was unable to take things in.

"It was really the world's view conditioning of ETs telling me from a young age that they were bad, evil, alien, not part of us and most of all to be feared, because most people don't even know they exist! The church didn't even talk about them and they say the world is what we have here . . . us and God . . . Animals don't have feelings or souls, plants the same, it's really pathetic. When the psychiatrist first asked me if I heard voices I wanted him to believe I must be mentally ill because I felt so different. But now I feel very differently about this. Having my experiences has changed my whole life; I believe the purpose of Contact is to change you for the better".

Sandra's gradual acceptance of her experiences had created some confusion and discomfort for her family. They too were challenged to explore their worldview. I had a phone call from Sandra's mother who said: *"if this is real and they come for my daughter, would the aliens come for me too?"*

So a family dilemma unfolds. Sandra's parents had come to believe their daughter had a psychiatric disorder. To acknowledge Contact reality was very difficult for them and acceptance of this experience meant a radical change in their personal world view as well as the anxiety created by the realisation that their home was not secure from extraterrestrial visitors. This was very frightening, understandably and opened up issues for them similar to their daughter's. But gradually her family were prepared to honour her experiences and do all they could to help her, even though this meant it would drastically change their own beliefs. This did much to help Sandra adjust and she was able to move forward with the new awareness and insight she had gained.

Sandra Today...

Sandra's process amply demonstrates the Contact experience taking her from fear, dread and confusion to the point of acceptance, thus integrating her experiences. The final acceptance of her Contact experiences meant that she could move forward and see how she has developed as a person through this. Her attitude has changed from someone who perceived herself to be a victim through to someone who now makes choices for herself and has taken control of her life. For Sandra, one of her challenges was to transcend her fear of everyday life and become integrated with society again. Her fear of criticism and judgement from others had held her captive within her home. Now she is learning to accept herself and appreciate what she has to offer. She is motivated now to make the necessary changes, not only to alter the course of her life, but to also become physically and emotionally healthier and more balanced. Sandra's commitment and determination to understand herself and her world has been quite remarkable. She reads prodigiously, absorbing many philosophical and spiritual works that have assisted her throughout this process of change. She also has learned to meditate and trust in her intuitive self. Sandra has gained amazing insight and understanding, not only of her Contact experiences, but of the normal life issues that surround her personal family. No longer feeling a victim, she views her life experiences in a different and more positive way. Through her own growth and spiritual exploration she chooses to see her experiences as important learning curves and has become more open and accepting of herself and others. She now believes she has a future and that she can follow her dreams. She is taking steps to improve her health and lifestyle and is looking forward to becoming independent and responsible for herself.

Interestingly, sometime afterwards, Sandra read her own story and said: "I couldn't write it, my 'secret life', I can't explain it to people, but it was just 'life' to me. But since I've read my story, it's like Wow! My life has some validity, some worth. It makes me feel acknowledged and maybe it can help other people."

My Assessment, Delusion or Contact?

It is important, when any professional is involved in the emotional/psychological field, to be clear about their client's mental health, especially if the client acknowledges that they have been treated for psychiatric illness. Although Sandra had the typical patterns of Contact, it could be said that she may have 'unconsciously' integrated her experiences with the information from the books she had resourced. This of course is possible and a good reason why researchers dislike experiencers to read anything until they have investigated the case. But with Sandra, we are reminded that it was the experiences themselves and her 'obsessive' and seemingly irrational fear of ETs and UFOs (even at six years old), which lead her to read about the phenomena in the first place, as she sought some understanding. However, many people with Contact experience have no prior knowledge or particular interest in Ufology. They are more likely to believe that these experiences are delusional. Sandra couldn't 'live' with her psychiatric diagnosis, so she educated herself regarding her own experiences.

There are many elements to Sandra's story that convinced me of its validity. A professional, exploring the possibility of mental illness makes a verbal and nonverbal assessment. For example, we observe how a client may present themselves to us, from the way in which they dress themselves through to managing the minor challenges of daily life. We assess their behavioural responses, whether they are appropriate or not, their level of reasoning and body language, for example. Sandra gave out normal responses and she is intelligent and articulate. In fact I could not fault her reasoning powers and information. She was ready and able to explore the possibility of mental illness, although she was depressed, anxious and fearful. I felt this was understandable given her circumstances - let's face it, who wouldn't be?

In spite of the fact that Sandra's lifestyle was unusual in many respects, I felt that he had coped brilliantly, despite the circumstances. She said that she believed her depression stemmed from not having her experiences understood and from continuously taking medication over the years. It had robbed her of the energy and motivation she needed to take control of her life. Another reasonable and logical comment!

Fully aware of her outer and inner reality, she was continually questioning, she was very aware of how unusual her experiences must have sounded to others. She continually sought confirmation that her experience did indeed 'echo' the patterns of Contact and she had physical evidence in the form of marks on her body with the emotional trauma being present. This to me was a very classic form of Contact.

In conclusion, I believe that Sandra's case is not at all unusual, although she dealt with it in a unique way. My research indicates many individuals like Sandra are misdiagnosed and sadly, this will not stop until the public is properly informed, especially professionals in the mental health area. Fortunately there are many open-minded, informed psychologists and psychiatrists working to support those with this experience (although unfortunately many more who are not!) However, the ones who are are helping to raise awareness, many risking their professional careers in the process. Some of them are experiencers themselves, so they know that it's like to be educated into one reality whilst experiencing another. The story of 'The Emperor's New Clothes' springs to mind, (when nobody dares to tell the emperor that he isn't wearing any). We all need to feel free to experience our reality and not fear the outcome should it be different to someone else's.

CHAPTER FIVE
In The Fear Place

"I think the ETs are using our fear to wake us up".

Julia

"The fear is the most difficult, it's like you are screaming inside but you make no sound! And then there's the confusion . . . WHAT IS THIS?"

Mark

"I don't know if you ever get over the fear. For me, when you think you are past it, it seems to hit you from another direction. You know what it's about, you've been through it many times, you've been through a plateau of coping with it and then it seems to sneak up on you again, just out of the blue and it seems to keep you in the same hyper-vigilant state that you've battled with throughout life. It makes you tired on a physical level, along with lack of sleep and the mind never stops worrying, the insecurity, never feeling safe and all the books that you have read - that you wish you hadn't! And now that you know, it prompts you to think again. "I think we need to know something about how to look after our bodies and minds; maybe something to strengthen our auras, or brain gymnastics to strengthen our minds."

Julia

Fear, Our Personal Armageddon!

Fear: A painful emotion excited by danger, or apprehension or pain.

Chambers Dictionary

This chapter is about our fears, how those fears can control our lives and what we ultimately experience. By challenging them and changing our attitude towards the things we fear, by choosing to do this we can use our fear as a vehicle for self awareness and understanding. I have described some techniques and strategies to help you understand, explore and cope with fear. You can allow fear to immobilise you, or you can find different ways to challenge and understand it. There are strategies for this, from conventional therapy to the more unusual and creative, which have been found to be effective by those experiencing Contact. Many have discovered that if you change how you react to your fear, it can change the experience altogether. I have found that what we believe in, (irrespective of what that might be), can often be the most powerful strategy of all. Fear is our ultimate personal challenge, we can allow it to block us and prevent us from moving forward, or we can use it to our advantage, by facing it and moving on. This is empowering and liberating, it gives us even greater understanding of our reality and who we are. James Walden (author *of The Ultimate Alien Agenda*), wrote to me and said: "Recently I started a process of self-analysis to determine how I've changed during the past six years since my first conscious abduction. Two realisations surfaced immediately. First, I am fearless in comparison to my former self. There isn't much about physical, human reality that frightens me now and when I released my fears I no longer needed physical and emotional pains. I've recognised wonderful improvements in my spiritual, emotional and physical health. "There is a place where you can always find peace and protection, the light and love of your spiritual self. My emotional pain caused me to forget for a while that I am spirit, as well as emotional and physical energy. I have learned to enter the white light, to heal myself."

How do *you* feel when fear takes over?

- Powerless?
- Isolated?
- Fear of the unknown?
- Fear of anything supernatural or paranormal?
- Fear of Pain?
- Fear of extinction of the self?

How to understand and cope with your fear

Step 1   Find out what it is you are frightened of. Become in- formed
Step 2   Explore your choices, work out who can help you
Step 3   Ask questions. Whoever you choose to help you should have understanding of this experience
Step 4   Resources. Seek information and emotional support.

Working through your fears, look at your choices

You can choose to deal with your fear differently. Sandra's story is a good example of this *(Chapter 4)*. I asked Sandra about her fear and when things changed for her, she said: "It was the realisation that I have control over this. I'd had enough, my mind was clearing. I became more focused and I thought I might as well try this. I do have a choice - by believing in myself and realising that I'm a part of this. I don't have to be if I don't want to be. It's my own fear and I won't let my fear control me anymore."
YOU helping YOU!

So how can fear work well for you, instead of paralysing you?

The process . . .

F *Focus*

Focus on what is happening, no more denial! You have had enough so you have the determination to do something different.

E *Examine your choices*

Choose to do something about the fear. Make a choice regarding the different ways in which you can deal with it.

A *Attitude*

For example: Sandra chose to deal with her fear by changing her attitude towards it and her experiences. With this new commitment to herself she was able to turn it around and it ultimately transformed her.

R *Realisation*

By believing in yourself and having confidence you have the power to change things.

Which strategies work best?

There are several which you can experiment with. What works well for one, may not work so well for another, so find out which is the most effective for you. Remember, if one strategy does not work, this is not failure! Have a go at something else. Learn to be creative and try whatever comes to mind, no matter how unusual, because by doing something differently, no matter how small, you are changing the experience and taking control.

Will these strategies stop my Contact experiences?

These strategies cannot guarantee that your Contact experiences will stop. Some of them may, but by changing how you react to them *will change your experience*. But ultimately, these techniques offer you alternatives to assist you. They are intended to help you gain some control over how you cope with your fear.

- *You* are choosing to change the experience by treating the experience differently.
- *You* have choice in your attitude towards the experience; you can change how you feel about it.

Strategies for coping with fear

Relaxation and meditation techniques

In the therapeutic area some of the more useful ways involve relaxation and meditation techniques that can help with fear, stress, and anxiety and/or panic attacks. Some people have rated the usefulness of relaxation and meditation as high as 10, so they are worth trying!

"I think that all the strategies listed would appeal to a wide range of people. Before attending the support group I would have tried all those examples listed. I have however; found that meditation helped calm my fears".

Mark

There are many ways in which you can help yourself reach a relaxed state and there are many books and tapes that cover this subject should you wish to try something different. They range from the relatively simple, to the more complex. Just try them out and see what fits. I have included a very simple relaxation technique below, which uses colour to focus the mind.

Colours are believed to have special effects on the body, mind and spirit. Scientific research in the 1970s and 1980s has shown that coloured light does have an effect on the body. Blue for example, has been demonstrated to be one of the most beneficial colours, it lowers blood pressure, perspiration, respiration and brain wave activity. Green is soothing, healing and gentle to the eye, which is why is it used in hospitals.

Colour relaxation technique

To begin . . .

Find a quiet place in your home and take some simple measures so you are not disturbed, such as removing the phone off the hook. If you can, try and devise a particular place in your home for this and make it your relaxing space, as your body will remember this place as being a place of tranquillity when you repeat the exercise. Ask your inner self to give you a relaxing and peaceful colour. Your mind will automatically give you one. You may like to ask your mind to give you a colour for healing, or for energy, or for dealing with fear.

This simple colour meditation can be done in just a few minutes if your time is limited, but you can also take up to half an hour if you wish.

Relax with colour . . . How to do it!

- Find a quiet place, preferable where you will not be disturbed
- Take the phone off the hook if necessary, to ensure that you will not be disturbed
- Find a comfortable chair to sit in, or lie on the floor, whatever feels best for you
- You may like to loosen tight clothing, take your shoes off
- Put on some relaxing music if this helps
- Close your eyes
- Start to breathe gently and become aware of each breath, as you inhale and exhale
- Let your mind bring you a colour and see the colour as a beautiful cloud, or mist - breathe it into your body
- When you breathe out, breathe out any anxieties or fears that you have.
- As you breathe the colour in, see the colour bringing you calmness, peace and strength
- See the colour filling the chambers of your heart, going through each cell and molecule of your being
- Exhale, pushing out any negative or disturbing feelings you may have, such as fear, anxiety, pain, hurt or sadness
- See the colour filling the air-sacs of your lungs and rising to your shoulders . . . Spreading down your arms, to your elbows, wrists, hands and fingers
- Now see the colour spreading upwards to your neck, chin, cheekbones, ears, forehead and scalp
- Now see the coloured mist travelling downwards from your heart centre to the organs, such as the liver and stomach
- See the colour filling them, as it travels down to your colon and lower organs, such as the liver and stomach
- See the colour filling them, as it travels down your thighs to your knees, ankles, feet and toes
- Finally see yourself completely enfolded in a cloak of beautiful colour
- Feel the change in your body as you do so and allow yourself to enjoy the peace
- Now allow yourself to go to a safe and relaxing space in your mind. Perhaps you could imagine a special safe space and fill it with

images that give you a sense of peace. Stay there for as long as you like!

The colour you visualise may change from day to day. If you ask your inner self each day for the colour that you most need or what will work best for you at that moment, then you may find that different colours will echo different moods and you will get what your body feels you require the most. Take as long as you like over this relaxation technique, from five minutes onwards.

It is perhaps worth mentioning that some individuals have found that meditation has opened the door to memories of Contact experiences:

"Meditation was too frightening for me and one of the things that forced me to start identifying what was going on with me. Anything that enabled me to leave my body was out, other than sleeping or being unconscious.

But I wasn't aware of being clairvoyant, in a conscious state of mind — so that when I started to do meditations I'd come up with stuff that would rock my brain and I'd wonder how on earth I could see this stuff . . . stuff that I'd got no knowledge of, like strange microbes and life forms, scientific machinery, computers and the inside of space ships, then of course some very strange people - and it all gave me extreme worry as it was all so cold and clinical and way out of anything I'd experienced on earth. I was expecting to meet with 'power animals', spirit guides and angels. It was all too much of a shock to my system, but meditation in a group was okay."

Julia

Note: The author has a range of meditation/relaxation CDs see www.newmindrecords.com

Again, this method may not be for you, so try another! By using the colour relaxation exercise you can go straight into the visualisation exercises below, or find a relaxation technique that works better for you - anything to make your body and mind feel totally relaxed and at ease.

Visualisation

In your relaxed and peaceful state, bring to mind a symbol that gives you a sense of safety, protection or control. For some, they may find it is a picture of someone they revere and trust, or even an animal. In the American Indian tradition, this is called a 'power animal'. So you can, if you like, think of an animal that represents power and courage for you.

One of my clients was attracted to the tiger and made it her power animal and she would bring it to mind whenever she felt afraid. By taking on this image in such a way you can either see it as protecting you, or you can feel yourself become the tiger, allowing yourself to feel its strength, the fearlessness, its power and courage. You can practise doing this in less threatening situations to begin with and then you may find that when you are very fearful you will be prepared and will be able to bring your power animal to mind. It can be beneficial to have a picture of your power animal in your room, this will help you to visualise it better.

Another way is to ask your mind to create a place, or symbol that may help change the fear or panic for you.

- Find a quiet place and use a relaxation technique to relax your body and mind (such as the colour relaxation technique, previously mentioned)
- Then ask your inner self to create for you the best place or symbols that would help change the fear
- Give you mind a free reign and see what your imagination comes up with When you are happy with some or all the images, try them out be doing the following:
- Briefly recall 'the fear place' until you feel anxious or frightened. Then imagine the symbol or image instead - replace it. Does this change the feeling of fear when you do this? Do you find that you become less anxious and fearful when you replace the fear with your symbol or image?

If this doesn't work straight away for you, try and experiment with different images, symbols or places. Keep going, as this is a very effective way of combating fear and negativity. Also within this safe and sacred space, use it to meet a wise and loving person. Just imagine someone sitting there with you. You can ask that person what you can do to help you with the fear. Have a conversation with them and ask them some questions!

You may find that you can gain new insight and even discover other ways you can cope with difficult and challenging situations. Try to keep your mind open and try whatever comes up. Trust in yourself, if it feels right then go with it.

Be patient . . . 'Rome wasn't built in a day!'

Like all techniques it can take time to integrate any new coping strategy. Try the techniques first using less threatening experiences, until the techniques become 'mechanical', automatic responses.

Affirmations, what are they?

Affirmations are statements that you say to yourself that have a powerful and positive message, such as:

I am strong
I am protected
I can deal with this"

Words can be very powerful. If you can say something (or even sing something) and repeat it, it can distract you from the panic you feel. For the more spiritually inclined this can take the form of a prayer or mantra.

"It is your own fear; I know the fear comes from me."

Sandra

The Mantra

'Mantra' is a word derived from the Sanskrit, meaning *man* 'mind' and *tra* 'to deliver'. It is thought that mantras are charged with vibratory power and within certain cultures and religions around the world the names of God of Gods are used. Concentrating on the word or words, plus repetition, is said to have the most impact within the being.

- A formalised prayer is a powerful mantra, such as "The Lords Prayer"
- The most sacred Hindu mantra is 'Om', the 'supreme reality'.
- They believe it is the sound from which the universe was created. The Buddhists uses 'Om mani padme hum', meaning: 'Oh jewel of the lotus hum', or 'the supreme reality'.
- The most sacred mantra for Krishna devotees forms sixteen words: 'Hare Krishna, Hare Krishna, Krishna Krishna, Hare Hare, Hare Rama, Hare Rama, Rama Rama, Hare Hare'.

Mantras can be repeated out loud, spoken silently, or said over and over in the mind.

"Mantras . . . They're on a scale of eight (out of ten). I've found the Hebrew mantra, 'Kodosh, Kodish, Kidosh, Adonai Sebeyoth' (Holy, Holy, is the Lord of Hosts) to be the best and easiest for me. They seem to understand that one . . ."

Julia

Sacred Objects

Special symbolic objects in the house or bedroom can give comfort and a feeling of security.

- If you have a Christian religious belief, then holy water, a crucifix, statues of Christ or the Virgin Mary, or saints you respect can help you to feel protected
- If you are Buddhist, perhaps a statue of Buddha . . .
- If you are more meta-physically inclined, perhaps you can light a candle, or incense, or have pictures of those you venerate or trust
- You may have belief that a power animal will protect you
- Or, if you find Feng Shui makes sense and helps, then use this.

Use whatever makes a difference for you. The purpose is to make you feel safe and secure in your environment.

Write it out

One young woman called Jenny was aware of ETs outside her bedroom, so she bravely decided that she would write to them as a way of dealing with her fear. It worked for her, because even as she wrote she felt stronger, as if the writing of the words actually empowered her. She found it strange that in the prose she wrote: *"You are tall and grey and very thin, and I want to ask you if you want to come in"*

She said: "I really didn't want them to come in at all I was terrified, so why did I write that?" But it seemed that although she was terrified, by writing to the beings, it gave her the courage she needed.

These words continue to empower Jenny. Whenever she feels frightened, she thinks of them, they comfort her and help her deal with her fear.

Jenny's poem . . .

How can I come to terms with this?
And how can I accept this as being
A part of my life,
A part I am so terrified of.
When I am in a state of fear,
I'm hopeless,
Fear takes over and controls me,
I forget about love and God,
I forget all things good.
Fear is the spider, black and ugly,
Cold and frozen, silently crawling
In a deep, dark, damp cave.
The cave is pitch black,
The air is pitch black and suffocating me
When I try to breathe.

I cannot move,
I'm frozen, too afraid to take a step.
Too afraid to move a muscle,
And I know I cannot stay here,
I know I must move on,
But my fear consumes me.

Because it's dark, I cannot see,
And because I cannot see
I'm afraid of . . .
I've lost my senses, and
Trust has walked out of the door,
And now I'm alone, really alone,
Who can I trust that will ever understand me?

When I looked out the window
You showed yourself to me.
I saw your eyes, glowing at me.
You don't show yourself clearly
Disguised within the blinds,
Yet that's your way of telling me
That you're around.

You are tall and grey and very thin
And I want to ask you
If you want to come in . . .

Somehow I fear we are somewhat the same
And we are,
All of us
Part of the game!
Life after life
We play out the rules,
Knowing the final outcome
Of this universal school.
You are here to tell me
Not to be afraid,
And this is part of something
I'm learning to understand.

There is a crack in the cave,
On a higher level.
The sun beams a ray of light
Warming the damp ground,
And the spider looks up to see
What's going down.

The light is new and suddenly he sees
As his frozen cold body
Takes the light generously.
His body moves, then cracks
And he sheds his old body
And crawls quickly up the cave wall.
Climbing closer to the source of light
Overwhelmed by its beauty
And sense of freedom.
He's now aware of entering, once again,
The familiar kingdom."

Jenny

Writing out your thoughts and feelings regarding your fear and experiences
can be very healing and strengthening. Jenny discovered, that not only did

her poem help her at the time whenever she felt frightened and thought of her poem it helped her with her fear.

Whatever works for you . . .

One of the most amusing and interesting discoveries came from a lady who had experiences throughout her life. She said that one night she 'inadvertently' left the electric cleaner plugged into the wall and that night she was not disturbed by the visitors. This happened a few times, but was it coincidence? This effect was noticed by someone else when an ionizer was left on in the room.

It would appear that some electrical currents might make a difference. Dr. John Mack suggests that: "The Greys are terrified of video cameras and they act as a deterrent. Also they dislike ultraviolet light, as it alters the magnetic field around you."

Books as a resource

In many spiritual, metaphysical, channelled and holistic books there are numerous coping strategies that are there to assist you. It is useful to read as widely as you can and see what fits for you. Many suggest visualising yourself surrounded by colour, white light, blue light or gold, when having a fearful experience. Try it and see if it works for you. If you are religious, you could invoke the Christ light, or ask the Angels to be with you.

"I thought, I have control of this! My mind cleared and I became more focused and I though I might as well try this. Now I tell them to go away and I use white light to surround me."

Sandra

Mental struggle . . . 'will power'

Some people find this technique effective. When you are experiencing 'paralysis' (through fear), make a conscious effort to make some small movement, move a finger or toe for example. This can remove the feeling of helplessness and can break the feeling of being paralysed.

Appeal to spiritual personages

Belief in the protection and power of a particular religious figure can be very powerful and prayer to them for help and protection has been a valuable way of coping with this.

Focused anger or rage!

Focusing strong emotions (such as anger or rage) when having the experience can sometimes change what is happening and this has been known to work for some experiencers, it can be mental or vocal rage. Some individuals during the experience have become so angry at the beings that the beings actually left. Both children and adults have managed to do this.

Talk to them

Tell them mentally, talk to the ETs and tell them what you do and don't like and what frightens you. Say how you want this interaction to be different.

"I now have the confidence, and know that I have the right to say go away. They respect that, that's the amazing thing for me. I just say don't bother me while I'm awake. It's the deal I made with them, I just told them."

Sandra

"If you are going to take me, wait until I'm asleep . . . I just don't want to know . . ."

Margaret

"Mental communications with the visitors . . . In the beginning, I would give this a zero - now I'd give it seven. Now I do this before I go to bed and while I'm in bed, trying to get to sleep. Originally, I would have been too terrified to even consider it and I was in 'fight or flight' mode . . . Mostly flight of course. Now I'm into a few years of conscious recognition, I just get cheesed off and say things like: look, I know you're there - but as you know, I've worked like a dog today . . . don't you think my human body needs some rest? I'm exhausted and I need to sleep peacefully and there must be an easier way to go about this - so back off!"

Julia

Automatic writing

"I think you have to find a way to meet on common ground. I have found that automatic writing works fairly well for me, but it could be anything that you feel comfortable with, if that is at all possible in the beginning. I can sit down and mentally communicate a question, and then the answers come through as I write them down. You have to find some way of starting to communicate with them, other than when you are going to sleep. For me it seems to lessen the disruption and shock a bit, it shows them that you are aware of them and gives you your power back as you are choosing the moment to communicate instead of them. Many times, when I have been at the point of hysteria about something I've seen, I've sat down and either written out my question, or asked it and then with pen in hand

waited for the answer. I have been pleasantly surprised by some of the answers, I've often got something I wouldn't have known, or maybe even thought of, and it's made me feel a lot better. The Aha reaction! The other thing of course is that I don't seem to ask enough questions . . ."

Julia

Crystals

These can be used when people are traumatised by Contact and do not wish to engage or they may feel invaded. Crystals are said to promote inner strength, greater awareness and understanding. Some alternative practitioners say they can programme crystals to offer help for blocking and protection with ET experiences. If you have a belief in the power of crystals, then this is something you could try.

Talk to the 'wise you'

Sit somewhere quiet where you can be undisturbed and if you want, put on some relaxing music. Have a pen and paper ready and have a mental picture of your 'wise self' sitting with you. You may see yourself as older and calmer and dressed differently to yourself now. Ask your wiser self anything you need to know that will help you understand more about your experiences, or ask for different ways to enable you to cope with them.

Yoga

There are many things that you can try to help empower you. Anything that helps you feel more in control or stronger. One of those in the Contact support group had said that she found Yoga to be very helpful, mentally and physically.

Internal Sound

This is a yogic doctrine that states that each person has their own personal and powerful sound, which can be felt in the head and shoulders. If you focus on this sound during the experience then it can change the experience, as well as give you some control.

Metaphysics . . . try love!

"All that exists are one!" If you are spiritually and metaphysically inclined then you will subscribe to the philosophy that we are all part of the 'creative force or consciousness', some call God.

If you believe this, then you will understand that 'they' are also part of 'his' creation and so they are also a part of God. If you subscribe to this philosophy then try to send a feeling of love and acceptance to the beings.

In his book "Sixth Sense", metaphysician Stuart Wild talks of his interactions with the Grey beings. "I sent them love in my meditations and if they showed up in my room, I'd project love and mentally try to hug them." He said that this seemed to work and they went away.

"I have to accept that they are part of the universe and so am I. I just see them as intelligent beings, but different to us, with totally different morals or ethics."

Sandra

Acceptance - by trying to have a more positive view of your experiences and how you see the ETs

Why have I put acceptance as a coping strategy? Because ultimately, you may try all these strategies, but none of them will guarantee that your fear or experiences will stop. Techniques and strategies will certainly help you to change 'within' and as a result the nature of your experiences may change, either way you will feel more in control. If you decide on acceptance and make this a part of your personal life script (difficult as it may be), then despite how challenging you may find these encounters to be they may enable you to find new understanding so you can move on and heal.

"I don't believe intelligent beings would come into my life without permission. Acceptance changes everything . . . it took away the fear, it made me realise it's my life and I have to accept them - they are not really monsters! The more knowledge I had, the more I found they are not evil. One day, I will be okay enough to see them properly."

Sandra

In James Walden's letter to me, he said: "In the moments of my discoveries, my comprehension was clouded by fear and therefore I wasn't able to glean from them what I would not like to have clarity of thought about and integration of my human and inter -dimensional existences."

As he stated previously, his self-analysis made him look at how he'd changed over the period of Contact experiences. He faced his fears, met them head on, and then transcended them. The results speak for themselves. James says: "I have recognised wonderful improvements in my spiritual, emotional and physical health."

Facing your fear, your personal Armageddon!

Is this experience an opportunity for you to embrace and explore your multidimensional reality? Is it the *ET Shamanic initiation?* Many with Contact who have worked through their fear see it as the ultimate challenge by their ET visitors and believe that if you can face your fears then you are ready to explore the greater reality. Many see the similarity with the ancient tribal cultures, the spiritual practices of the Shaman. The initiate or neophyte (after visualising their protection as being a circle of light), bring forward all the things they fear the most and if they achieve this then they are deemed ready to be a Shaman. The path of the Shaman is a process of facing what you fear the most and then you are deemed ready to be opened to the greater reality, which includes 'spirits' and non-physical beings. Shamanism is one of the oldest religions. Whitley Strieber mentions that this is the same experience the visitors forced him to do. Ultimately, it may be that through facing and dealing with our fear we are being prepared to cope with the greater reality.

James Walden also said: "My last conscious encounter was when a Grey being entered my mind and then my office. This Contact was a major confirmation because the dog stood up and barked at the being. I recognised Fred the dog's fear of the intruder, but for the first time I did not see the being as an alien and react fearfully. The being spoke with me mentally and shared significant information. I felt that I was participating in a tutoring session with a teacher who wanted me to accept a greater awareness of another world.

"There is a place where you can always find peace and protection . . . the light and love of your spiritual self. My emotional pain caused me to forget for awhile that I am spirit as well as emotional and physical. I have learned to enter the white light and heal myself and give healing to others. You can do the same. In fact, this is, I believe what my 'abductors' were trying to help me learn."

Dana Redfield also wrote in a letter: "In my case I was already experienced in coping with the fear and the concept of 'shields'. I was practiced in using them and much practised in prayer and meditation, with an inborn faith and trust. But still I did not have the experiences that invoke the kind of terror people report. Or am I just a good blocker/denier? I was plenty spooked at times, very uncomfortable. The scary part was all the stuff happening to my body, though never paralysis. Experiments with resistance didn't work and there was a determination to get to the truth, so this was some kind of co-operation I guess, I was going with it all, although there was some physical 'animal' body reactions, fear of the unknown and no control over what was happening."

The important thing to be aware of if that fear comes from you! You have the choice to do something about it and you are not powerless when you know you have choices. Fear is an opportunity, it can be utilised, enabling us to grow beyond our limits. In a sense, our fear is our personal Armageddon. Do you allow your fear to control you, or do you seek to control and understand it, to challenge and transcend it and ultimately move forward towards freedom?

Authors Note: There are a number of visualizations and relaxation techniques mentioned in the above chapter. To assist you with these techniques, I have produced my own series of meditation/relaxation CDs. These are suitable for the novice and for those more advanced in these practices.

The Inner Alchemy series has several titles, which can help with understanding and personal empowerment.

Suggested titles:
Inner Healer, Connecting to the Wise you, Inner Peace, Inner Child, Transcend Fear, Rebirth, Detox and *Connecting to your Power Animal.*

Individuals who wish to connect with the 'unseen realms' and explore their intuitive abilities: *Exploring the Angelic Realms* and *Meet your Spirit Guides.* Visit the website to see the full range **www.newmindrecords.com**

For those of you with stress related issues and struggling with health or psychological issues the MIND medicine series may be suitable: *Overcoming Depression* and *Reducing Stress.*

For individuals who have limited time, or are new to the relaxation process, the ten minute relaxation CDs series, *Take Ten* may be suitable.

Suggested titles:
Calm, Nurture your Spirit, Detox and *Optimum Health.*

All CDs have guided meditations and trance inducing frequencies, which make the process of achieving an altered state a simple and easy process. The subliminal affirmations assist in changing old unhelpful mindsets while encouraging personal empowerment.

CHAPTER SIX
Who Can I Trust To Help Me?

How do you find emotional support you can trust?

If you are undergoing Contact experience it is vital to access appropriate support. Often the first challenge for the experiencer is the fear of taking the step of personal disclosure, which is a huge one! The risk of sharing this information with someone is often quite terrifying in itself. Experiencers are often fearful of how their experiences will be received; this fear is a big block to overcome for many. What we think other people think of us bothers most people on some level. The perception of how we think others may perceive us can be a real issue for many - whether they have undergone Contact experience or not. There is also a fear of disappointment should the person they resource be unreceptive, derisive or think they are mentally ill. It is important for the experiencer to access the most helpful and open support all round. This should be a priority.

Within this chapter we shall explore the options and look at the support which is available and who you should 'trust'. I have devised a guide whereby you can check for open-minded and accepting emotional support. It looks at the differences between a researcher and counsellor and shows what they can offer you, highlighting the alternative options in healing modalities.

"How do you tackle the 'fear of humans' aspect? Maybe it surfaces as the consciousness expands and we realise how dangerous humans can be. It's all 'arms-length' until you have reason to protect yourself from the dangerous human. This is not the threat with a gun, or terrorist kidnap, but ridicule, deceit and ostracism - which can be just as harmful if not seen and averted. This is alienation in the extreme, because who can we trust to talk to about it?"

Dana Redfield

Who can offer emotional support?

- Family and friends
- Researchers
- Professional therapists and counsellors
- Complementary/Alternative healing fields
- Support groups (see Chapter 7).

Family and friends, what can they offer you?

- Ongoing emotional support
- Acceptance

But who can you trust?

A young farmer in West Australia experienced a 'conscious' Contact when he sighted a spacecraft. He also said that he communicated with the ET beings whilst living on his farm.

Desperately, he needed someone to tell, so he finally told his brother all that had happened. Shortly afterwards a psychiatric emergency team came to his home and he was taken to the nearest psychiatric hospital. Therefore, not only was he traumatised by the Contact experience, it was compounded by the misinterpretation of it by his brother, his lack of understanding and the well meaning but unaware professionals. He felt total desolation and termed it as being a 'betrayal of his trust' by his brother. Understandably the relationship with his family (especially his brother) was severely affected. But from this, he quickly learned to be extremely careful with whom he confided in. This story illustrates how difficult it can be for many individuals who want to (and often do) confront their families with this information.

Generally speaking, family members love and care for us, therefore it is natural to turn to them first for support, understanding and love. Most of us have this inbuilt trust. However, it is prudent to 'check' with any person first. See how open they are before you share any of this delicate information with them.

Family and friends . . . the checklist for help!

Your first immediate resource maybe to turn to a family member or a friend. If you do not want to experience disappointment or rejection, take your time to explore their personal beliefs first, before you share. If during this process they appear to be open to this phenomenon, then you can share what feels comfortable for you. Another option in the beginning is to tell of the experience as if it had come from a friend of yours. This is a useful check, if they seem open then you can decide how much more you would like to disclose. If they prove to be supportive, (even though they may not really understand what you are experiencing), they will be able to sympathise with your feelings, such as the isolation, fear, anger and confusion.

What questions can I ask to check for openness? What are the positive indicators?

- Do they enjoy books or movies on science fiction themes?
- Do they believe in the possibility of life on other planets?
- Do they believe extraterrestrials could visit us?
- Have they heard about the abduction phenomena?

If you get mostly negatives with these questions it could mean that you need to look elsewhere for support.

Alternatively, you could suggest they read some books, or show them a video on the phenomena and observe how they respond. It is wise however, not to share your Contact experiences until you feel the person will listen to you with an open mind.

Patience . . . it takes time!

Even if members of your family (or friends) are open to this information it is one thing to talk about it hypothetically, but quite another to disclose the fact that this has actually happened to you. It is important to be aware that although they may be supportive, it maybe quite a shock for them to hear it and you will need to give them time to adjust. It can be a useful strategy to show them a video about this subject, one initially that covers all aspects of the phenomena and gives a broad overview of its reality, possibly leading to more specific Contact experience. Watching it together is another way of opening up discussions between you and can provide you with an opportunity to talk about your own experiences. Not only will it make them more informed about the phenomena, but it will assist them in coming to terms with the 'reality shift'. If they are willing to learn more about it then books will help (or a ufology magazine that explains the Contact experience). In time they will come to understand more fully how best to support you. If you have already found support professionally, you can also suggest that they contact your counsellor/therapist (if you have one). This gives them the opportunity to ask questions, helps them to adjust and understand how they can best support you.

Checklist for your professional support

If you have resourced such organisations - as MUFON, or those specifically set up to support those with close encounters such as ACERN or ACCET, you will be given names of professional therapists who are informed about this phenomena.

But if it is difficult for you to access the professional counsellors they recommend, then you may have to find your own professional support. Having a check list is one way you can assess whether you have a therapist/counsellor who is likely to be open to this experience and support you.

The following checklist is intended to help you look for openness, so that you feel comfortable in asking the therapist any questions that you feel are appropriate. Remember that until you are feeling confident in them, you do not need to disclose your name. If you have any doubts regarding their suitability, (e.g. if they sound uncomfortable with your questions), then ask them to recommend someone else. They may know of a therapist who is better for the job! In this instance, remember, you are the client. Never be afraid to ask!

Initially it can be useful to simply ask in an open way what they think to the possibility of extraterrestrial life, or UFOs? If they seem interested, or receptive to such possibilities then you can gradually start to explain about your own experiences.

Alternatively, the kinds of questions you can ask are:

- Do they recognise alternate realities?
- Do they recognise non-physical realities and psychic phenomena?
- Do they accept the possibility of extraterrestrial life?
- Do they have an interest in Ufology?
- Do they know about close encounter/Contact experiences?

If these questions seem too threatening for you and you feel unable to ask them you can ask them to send you their business card as their card could give you a clue as to the types of therapy they offer. For example, those that offer alternative and complementary therapies, or show that they are open to alternate realities are more likely to be supportive. The only real way to find out whether they will be supportive to your situation however is to phone them. Again, you do not need to give them your name and through a phone call you can get the information you need.

You should remember that very few counsellors openly advertise their acceptance of this kind of Contact experience, as it can create professional difficulties for them. So phone them, find out if they can support you, often using the telephone is easier than meeting them face to face and you can retain anonymity.

What can the researcher offer you?

- Documentation and research into your experience
- Objective confirmation of your experiences

Researchers are individuals interested in researching the UFO phenomena. Many belong to a Ufology research organisation, such as MUFON (Mutual UFO Network), although some are independent.

What do they do?

The researcher is someone who is interested in documenting your experience. They will want the facts, such as places, dates and time of Contact experiences as well as any other witnesses to it. They will try to record details as accurately as possible, because it is important data for them and after all they are there to research into all aspects of the Contact/Abduction phenomena.

What are they interested in?

Researchers are interested in any new sightings and any interactions with 'non-terrestrial' beings. The details of your experience can help confirm other cases, as well as your own. Cases with multiple witnesses are particularly valuable, as well as any physical evidence. This all gives the phenomenon more credibility in the scientific community.

What can they offer me?

They can record the details of your experience, objectively. They can help you to discover any of the more tangible physical aspects of your experience. They will look at all the physical evidence, such as marks, scars, implants and they will want to interview other witnesses if there are any. If you have sighted a UFO for example, they will look for ways in which they can confirm this, not only from other witnesses, but also from physical evidence, e.g. if a craft has landed they would look for marks on the ground, soil changes, or damaged plant life. They would want descriptions of the craft and any occupants should you have that information and they would want to interview any other witnesses to compare stories and check validity.

They can also offer:

- An accurate/objective recording of your experience.
- They may know of other individuals that have had a sighting, which would validate yours.
- They may inform you that others have also witnessed the event but not reveal their personal identity as they may want to keep the information about the event as 'authentic' and uncontaminated as possible.
- They can offer you information to help you find someone who is trained to give you emotional support, such as a counsellor/therapist or support group.

Remember that researchers are not counsellors and most do not have the skills or training to offer emotional support, although many will try to be supportive by offering you referrals for this service.

Why should they be interested in what I have read about Contact?

If you are hoping to have your experience investigated by an organisation such as MUFON, then the researcher will usually prefer it if you read nothing more about the phenomenon until they have investigated your case properly. They will also want to find out what you already know about UFOs and abductions before your experience. In other words, what have you read, heard or watched on TV? The less informed you are about the phenomenon, the more credible your experience is, purely from a 'research' perspective. It means you have gained little or no information other than from your own experiences. This naturally gives it stronger validity, because there is less of a possibility you could have confused what you have already read or seen with your own experiences.

Can anyone be a researcher?

Yes! Anyone can call him or herself a researcher/investigator and again, it is important for you to satisfy yourself as to the integrity of the person you trust before you consult them and share your experiences. For most, researchers are volunteers who have been interested in the phenomena. This means that many do not necessarily have professional qualifications or training in any field.

There are individuals out there who have felt that some researchers have exploited them. When a researcher belongs to a recognised Ufology organisation then you are able to check as to the sincerity and integrity of the researcher. Some of the better known Ufology organisations will only accept researchers who follow strict, scientific criteria. A researcher belonging to such an organisation has to show that he/she will follow these guidelines. Many are selected due to scientific backgrounds and often they are university graduates.

Researcher or counsellor, who will meet my needs best?

Many individuals with Contact are disappointed that their emotional needs are not met when they report a sighting or experience to a researcher. Again, although a researcher may be supportive, most are not trained counsellors or therapists and may not be qualified with the right skills to meet your needs.

The Counsellor/Therapist will offer . . .

- Information
- Emotional support
- Therapeutic strategies, coping skills

Some common questions potential, new clients ask me are:

- What is a counsellor?
- What do you do?
- How can you help me?
- Therapy, what's that?
- What are therapeutic techniques?
- If I choose therapy, what therapeutic techniques will be used and what will they achieve?
- How do I decide what I need?
- How does this help me?
- What is the aim of therapy?
- Regression, what is that?

To answer these questions briefly:

The counsellor is someone who is trained to offer emotional support. The counsellor will be not only interested in your experiences, but will focus on your emotional and psychological well being. They will want to know how you are coping with your experiences and how they can best help you.

The counsellor is trained to actively listen, which means they will reflect back to you what you are saying, to be sure they have understood you. They will honour your view of the world, non-judgementally, with understanding and acceptance of you as a person. This is called 'person centred counselling'.

A counsellor who works in a 'person' or 'client-centred' way means they will not only listen to you, but will honour your world and will assist you, helping you to connect with your own inner resources (rather than advise or influence you regarding the direction you should take).

How will this help you . . .?

- It will lessen isolation
- It will make you feel more accepted
- It will make you feel supported
- It will help you to find new coping skills
- It can help you to tap into your own inner resources as well as external ones
- With it you will gain more information about the experience
- It will give you assistance with the understanding of your feelings, such as fear, anger, sadness, confusion, helplessness
- It will help unlock hidden memories
- You will be able to integrate the experiences giving you - greater awareness
- You can move forward with acceptance of your 'dual' life.

Therapy is a term given to the way in which a counsellor helps you to work through your own issues.

A therapist will suggest coping strategies and will use skills to help you work better in your world. With different therapeutic techniques they can help you to gain a deeper understanding of your experiences, so that you can assimilate them and function more healthily all round.

If I choose to have therapy, what therapeutic techniques will be used and what will they achieve?

We will follow on with a brief description of the types of strategies and techniques that may be used by a therapist. You may like to ask the therapist how they work and what sorts of ways they can assist you. When in doubt, ask! This enables you to make more informed choices with regards to what therapy you feel comfortable with. The therapist is here for you, *the client* and it is important that you feel safe enough to ask pertinent question

Some therapeutic techniques

The therapist will use to help you gain a greater understanding and deeper awareness of your experiences may be:

- *Coping strategies* - these are relaxation techniques for stress management, which help with the panic attacks and the fear. They are strategies to help you feel more in control.
- *Anger management.*
- *Re-framing* the experiences, learning new ways to look at them, seeing them from a different perspective.
- *Regression work,* enabling you to explore your experiences from a deeper level of your awareness. The therapist takes you into a more relaxed state and you are assisted by them to explore your experiences safely (there is a more detailed explanation of this later on).
- *Creative visualisation/creative imaging* can help you to understand the deeper meaning of your experiences. You are encouraged by the therapist to use your 'creativity' or imagination to explore (through symbols, or spontaneous imagery) the messages from your subconscious mind. The subconscious is the part of the mind that we normally only access when relaxed, or through dreams.

Who decides?

The therapist can assist you, helping you to explore your experiences to a limited or greater extent, but it is *you, the client who decides.*

So how do I work out what it is that I need?

How far you want to go with your exploration is often determined by how much you want, or are ready to know about your experiences.

It could well be that all you need at this moment in time are helpful strategies to control your feelings of fear and vulnerability. But if your experiences are becoming disabling, such as sleep disturbances, panic attacks, or phobic behaviour, then you may need to explore them in greater detail so that you can work them through. It may be that you feel an overwhelming urge to understand what these experiences mean to you on a deeper level, or from a more spiritual perspective. It is at this stage you may want to consider regression and/or creative imagery to assist you.

From the moment you decide to get help and support, you are empowering yourself. By this, I mean that *you* are changing the situation you are in, from being a 'victim' to taking back control.

- **You** are choosing to change your situation by deciding not to be alone any more; you are choosing not to be isolated any longer.
- **You** are choosing how you want to deal with this.
- **You** are choosing what kind of support you want to have
- **You** are choosing how you will explore this experience, in whatever way it feels helpful to you.
- **You** are choosing to have some control over it.

What is regression?

Regression is when a therapist takes the client into a relaxed state of being (this is the same as being relaxed while watching television or listening to music), where you 'switch off' a little from everyday noise and distraction. It is a normal state of being, it is when you 'tune out' and do things automatically without giving it any conscious thought. In this state you will still have complete control over what is happening, but you will feel more relaxed and peaceful. When you are relaxed like this, memories or dreams can be accessed more readily. *You are not unconscious, or unaware of what is going on around you, or what is being said.* You are simply feeling relaxed enough for deeper or hidden memories to surface.

Regression is a process facilitated by the therapist who uses words, music and imagery to assist you in reaching a relaxed state and a deeper awareness of your subconscious mind. If there are any blocks preventing these memories from coming to the surface it is usually due to fear, part of the subconscious can sometimes put a block up as a protective mechanism to stop your consciousness from being more aware of some threatening or frightening information. It is thought that blocks can also be put there from an 'external' source. By this I mean that some researchers and therapists believe that blocks could be put in place during Contact experiences, with the intention of clouding, or preventing you from accessing memories of your encounters with them.

"The most valuable help for me, apart from talking to experiencers, has been the regression. After that one session it gave me new things to contemplate and I have been much more at ease as I think about past events".

Mark

- Regression techniques can assist you to explore your experience in depth.
- Regression brings new awareness of the experiences and insight into what this experience might mean for you on a deeper level.
- Regression is recommended for those who want more understanding and integration of their Contact experiences.

Remember, regression may highlight certain aspects of your encounters that might be difficult to take on board, however, the therapist is there to assist you with this. But, you may bring up information that could well challenge what you know of reality, or what you perceive to be real! Be prepared to accept that sometimes this technique can bring up more questions than answers.

The ultimate aim of therapy is empowerment and understanding. It is a process that can enable you to come to terms with your experiences. Through exploration of your experiences you can find new ways in which to cope, integrate and heal so that you can move forward with this new awareness and get on with your everyday life, despite the restructuring of your altered world view.

Alternative, complementary healing and therapeutic options, what can they offer me?

Physical, emotional, spiritual healing and support. Support for this experience can be found from the complementary/alternative fields of health and healing. Complementary modalities of therapy 'educate' the practitioner to become (in many cases) more open to this multi-level experience. Through their work they can be more accepting of the non-physical world as they work in a more holistic way. They are also more likely to have had exposure to this experience, possibly without realising it.

Contact is often a trigger for individuals to explore their healing skills and they often become healers and complementary therapists as a result.

There are many different therapies and healing modalities that can help you, such as: kinesiology, the Bowen Technique, various forms of bodywork, natural medicine and acupuncture. Many forms of energy work, including Reiki (hands-on healing, originated from Japan) and spiritual healing. These can assist in a variety of ways with the rebalancing of your energy field and healing on many levels.

Do remember to ask your therapist questions and use the checklist (see Chapter 6) to discover whether they have an openness to Contact, particularly if you choose to disclose information regarding your experiences. Do this either before you meet them, or when you have your first session. This will not only satisfy you that your experiences will be honoured, but you may also find that they will understand from a personal level. This can be very helpful for you, the more aware they are, the more support you can access. Whatever option you choose will help you glean more information about yourself and your experiences. It will all help diminish the feelings of isolation and fear and may remove them altogether. You have another option open to you, which is I believe, the most valuable option of all - that is the support of those who are also having Contact.

CHAPTER SEVEN
Support Groups – The Experiencer Supporting the Experiencer

"The support group has been incredibly helpful. Talking to others and hearing similarities in things you have experienced, is both strangely alarming and comforting. The only people I can comfortably speak to about my experiences are the people in the support group."

Mark

This is one of the most valuable ways in which you can access support and understanding. Support groups not only provide the validation needed to help you come to terms with your expanded reality, but give you ongoing support through shared experiences. There are two kinds of support groups: the professional support group (PSG), or the group that is run by the experiencers themselves (ESG). As you will see, both are different but valuable and if there isn't a group near you then there is help here, which will show you how you can start up your own.

"The support group has helped me to integrate and understand by meeting others who live with the experience. It gave me courage knowing that I'm not alone, knowing that there is always someone there that I can call, knowing that I can get questions answered, that I can get regressions, healing, the latest information and the best books to buy. And having someone that will listen to my most bizarre moments, who probably knows someone else who's had the same, (like my 'man in flames' and the 'computer in my eyes'). By meeting each month, I am doing something constructive instead of feeling dumbstruck."

Julia

What is a support group?

A support group is a number of individuals that have had similar kinds of experiences that come together and meet regularly to share what they know and be supportive of each other.

What kinds of support groups are there?

- The professionally run support group (PSG)
- The experiencer support group (ESG)

"It helps just knowing that there are thousands of others just like me and then to actually meet them! Safety in numbers I guess. It makes fiction into fact. You begin to realise that you are part of something bigger than you realised . . . you get a bigger picture and find a great deal of relief. I've found that you can read about it and know about it for yourself, but when you join a support group something within you expands. From attending the group, I realised that there are many different ones (ET beings). I saw David's marks on his arms, he had the same as me, I thought, this is real, not a psychic shift, this is a reality."

Julia

The Professional Support Group (PSG)

A PSG is run by professional facilitators, trained in group work, who follow a structured, ethical framework. PSGs provide strict confidentiality and a safe, therapeutic environment in which to meet and share experiences with others.

What can a PSG offer?

You will have an experienced facilitator who will provide continuous monitoring of each person within the group. Therapists are trained to observe body language and signs of discomfort and anxiety and they will assist promptly if they think that someone in the group is struggling at any time. They can offer everyone within the group therapeutic techniques and coping strategies, with one-to-one counselling as and when required.

Who can attend a PSG?

A support group may not be appropriate for everyone because some individuals may be too fearful and traumatised to venture out and meet others at that time. If this were the case then a place would be offered within the support group at a later date when the person felt they could cope with it. This happened with Sandra (see Chapter 4). Initially she didn't feel able to sit in the group, it was only as her confidence grew that she felt comfortable and appreciated and received the benefits of attending the group.

How is a PSG organised? A PSG will usually have:

- Regular meetings.
- Minutes, proper recording of information that can be useful to the group.

- Organisation of a 'buddy system' (e.g. telephone/email contacts for other experiencers).
- Sharing of experiences and an understanding of them.
- Sharing of coping skills.
- Group therapy (e.g. techniques for integration and empowerment.
- Reading material and information.
- Public awareness programme (e.g. arranging talks with the families and/or community).
- Advertising the support group so that other people, 'new' to the experience (or realisation of it) can find them.
- A programme to inform and share with interested professionals
- Public relations, media and talks.

Are all people who experience Contact traumatised?

No, there are many that feel the experience has been a very special and beautiful one. Some feel honoured and even blessed. Many say that the experiences have been very loving and enlightening, whereby they have gained tremendous understanding of themselves.

It is hard to establish the percentage of individuals who are traumatised to those that are not. Often the people who are more traumatised will get the (media) coverage. The PSG can offer those who are comfortable with their experiences have the opportunity to share with those of similar understanding and openness. It helps lessen the deep feelings of loneliness and isolation many feel.

How do I find a PSG?

We have included some resources for you at the back of this book (see page 305-311). Other good places to look are local UFO groups, who may have, or know of support networks in your area. Also there is a mass of information available on the internet, within Ufology magazines and books.

Positive outcomes that can be achieved from attending a support group are:

- A sense of community, whereby all members of the group ultimately feel less alone.
- Increased confidence, which empowers the individual, enabling them to speak not only to family and friends, but even more publicly later.

- The sharing of coping skills and strategies.
- A fuller understanding of these experiences, which leads to acceptance and integration.
- Choices, notably the choice in how we decide to deal with any life experience including this one.
- Coping with fear. It is very valuable for those in the 'fear place' to talk with those who have reached a point whereby they are comfortable enough with the knowledge of what's happened to them, to actively be able to communicate with the 'beings' during their encounters. It can be very empowering for those in fear to see and hear how others have dealt with their experiences and that there is a good chance they too can ultimately reach a similar place.

Within a period of six months, two of my clients, who had been so paralysed with fear they struggled to talk about their encounters, were able to talk openly and with a confidence that would have amazed them before. So there is proof and reassurance here - what many perceive to be impossible can be achieved within a few short months. One client said:

"The hardest thing for me is that you cannot talk to anyone about this. If you go to work looking and feeling awful because you were taken the night before, how can you say the reason you look so terrible is because you were abducted by aliens during the night! If someone else comes to work and feels awful because of a bad cold, they can talk about it and get support. With this you can't."

The Experiencer Support Group (ESG)

This is organised by the individuals who have had experiences themselves and it can offer you many of the advantages of a professional group, but may not have the same professional safeguards in place. Before joining an ESG, it is wise to check to see if the group has professional support available to you, should you need it and also check the group for confidentiality issues. There is a word of warning here; some support groups can seriously damage your psychological health!

There is a danger, which has been vocalised by many people who have attended ESG's that some of them were very 'cult like', extreme and obsessive. If at any time you feel uncomfortable about the material shared in the group, or feel pressured, or pushed into believing things that do not resonate well with you, then leave! Look for another support group, or even start one of your own.

How to set up your own support group

If there is no support group in your area, here are some suggestions to help you set up one:

- First check! Look at and research the support that's already available in your area by contacting your local UFO research agency and local support or Mutual UFO Network. They are quite likely to know what support is available in your area. They might also be able to recommend a therapist that could help you. Also check in local magazines, or holistic journals, the library and of course the telephone directory.

- If you need to get in touch with other experiencers in your area, then try placing a discreet advert in your local paper, or holistic magazine. If you are uncomfortable with the words 'Contact/Experiencer', you could all them 'anomalous' or 'encounter' experiences. You can also advertise on the internet. By putting your email address on the numerous ufology/experiencer web sites, you will find that many people are happy to help.

- If you decide to use your home telephone number, a word of caution. Be prepared - not all calls may be genuine. To have an answer phone is useful, this will help you monitor and screen calls. It is unwise to list your home address, for the same reason. A PO Box address is well worth investing in if you are serious about doing this.

- Venue - would you want to use your home as a group meeting place? Think carefully about this. If you have the space and your family is agreeable, then there is no reason why not. But it may prove intrusive and often a public venue (if it's not too expensive) is a better alternative. However, the group should look at paying a small fee to be able to sustain this.

- Make a decision regarding who is suitable for the support group. For example, should it be available to anyone who calls and wants to be a part of it? Define your criteria, e.g. are you going to include all anomalous experiences, or just those very specific to Contact?

Here are some basic guidelines that you should incorporate within the group:

- Respect confidentiality.

- Consent of the group should an individual wish to introduce a new member.
- Discuss the aims and objectives of the group, e.g. what does each person hope to get from meeting together regularly? (There are more notes further on to help define this.)
- Acceptance of 'alternative' views and personal understanding often vocalised by each individual. The range of information and understanding around the phenomena is vast. It is important that each member generally accepts that everyone else is entitled to their own perspective and view point and that you all try to avoid judging others and the views that are expressed.
- Try to obtain professional and therapeutic contacts for the group.
- Try to have information available regarding other groups or organisations that are outside your area. Individuals often move away and you may find that people who are too far away to attend your group will ask you for help.
- There are of course financial costs to bear. Decide between you an appropriate amount to spend that will cover phone calls, photocopies, books and resources. This should be discussed within the group, so that the group as a whole takes some responsibility. It is important that the practicalities are clear from the start otherwise confusion and resentment over this can arise further down the line.
- You could also visit the local library for more information about support groups and how they are set up.

The life and times of any support group should include from the start its aims and objectives, such as:

- What are the subjects for discussion?
- What are the expectations of the group?
- Who can attend?
- Who will be responsible for organising the venue, advertising, finances and general running?
- Who provides contact numbers and so on?

The main objective of any support group is to give those attending, the chance to talk about the aspects of their life they are having difficulties with, within a group of people who are prepared to listen and offer support in return. Because all members of the group are experiencing some of the same issues, there is both validation and empathy offered. Many people are not particularly looking for advice. It is a chance for them to be heard, to feel understood and to be accepted without judgement by the other members of the group.

The first meeting . . .

The first gathering of any group is difficult for most people. It takes a great deal of courage to go to meet a group of individuals (particularly if you haven't met any of them before). In fact, many feel that the actuality of sharing a very private part of their life is as scary as the experiences themselves! If this applies to you, then always remember that these feelings and this kind of nervousness is felt by most individuals, it is normal and many will surely feel it as you do.

Interestingly, some individuals who have attended support groups may get a feeling that they have met some of the experiencers before. This is a fairly common discovery; many believe that they have met individuals actually during a Contact experience on the ships!

For some, the fear of attending a group can also come from a feeling that there will be some kind of retribution from the ETs. They feel that the ETs will know what they are doing and will try to stop them, or punish them in some way.

It is very important to respect an individual's feeling about this. It is also helpful to know that in all cases this 'retribution' has not happened. Experiencers, who have expressed this initial fear to me, have told me later that it was unfounded and they did not suffer any consequences.

As your support group progresses, it will develop to a point whereby sharing becomes increasingly easier as everyone becomes more comfortable with one another. If you want to make the most of your meetings then do try to have an agenda, but make sure it is one that is flexible, because often, as the evening moves on a wider agenda will present itself. It is best to allow this to happen, this natural evolution will flow through the sharing.

Once individual stories are fully explored, the group will look at 'ongoing experiences', e.g. what is happening in their lives, how they are coping and the difficulties they encounter. Future, regular meetings are an important part of any support group, as the ongoing Contact drama can be hard for some. The many multidimensional aspects to it incite further questioning, which will constantly challenge the individual and introduce them to new awareness. The process of attending the group can very much act as a trigger for this. Ultimately, after the acceptance and paradigm shift, the questioning will continue and a process of personal unfoldment begins, where the existence of this reality is no longer in doubt, but it becomes more challenging, opening up to further, more deeper questions, such as: 'what does this all mean?' Slowly, they realise that they are on a personal journey, reaching a point whereby they are able to understand who they are.

Support groups and meetings are invaluable because they offer so much by way of validation and comparison of new perceptions and altered reality. For anyone who is experiencing Contact, the support of like-minded others will help them during the integration of this reality into their everyday life. The sharing of experiences helps them to realise that they are not alone, that there are other people out there who really can understand.

CHAPTER EIGHT
Tracey Taylor's Personal Story of Contact

Expressions of ET Contact, a visual blueprint!

This chapter contains the story of a young woman who has been consciously aware of having Contact with extraterrestrial beings throughout her life. You will see, as she writes about her experiences, how instrumental they were in her expressions of geometric and complex artwork. This artwork she believes, acts as a catalyst or trigger for the awakening of human awareness, not just about the nature of our origins and past, but of who and what we are.

I met Tracey when she was in her early twenties, when she desperately needed to understand her Contact experiences. She is an articulate and intelligent young woman and as she questioned her experiences, continually searching for some answers, she was fearful that she might be mentally ill. She was relieved to have an opportunity to talk to someone without the fear of rejection, because when Tracey had shared her experiences previously, she received unwelcomed responses. She had contacted a well known author and researcher on Ufology and showed him her drawings; he then pronounced them 'evil' and told her that she should stop doing them. This reaction understandably frightened Tracey and left her even more bewildered and confused. It was finally through reading a book (written by an experiencer) that Tracey was put in touch with ACERN and myself.

Tracey's biggest challenge, she says, was having to cope with the denial of her reality from her fellow humans. Confused, she looked for psychiatric evaluation; she needed proof that she was not ill as well as a way of understanding her expanded reality. Confirmation of her psychological good health was given to her, not only through visits to several psychologists and psychiatrists independently, but also through a panel of eight psychiatrists. When Tracey spoke openly to them, she showed them her drawings of the beings and her 'geometric' artwork and explained how she had developed healing abilities. She told them she expressed her Contact, not only through artwork and symbolism, but through unusual scripts and language, which she feels, are natural expressions of her ET/human origins. The doctors were unable to explain her experiences, but they were prepared to sign a written statement which said that they were satisfied she was not mentally ill. Tracey felt that by doing this she also helped to raise awareness of this experience.

Tracey has written an account of what she went through as a child and adult, (which is illustrated on a DVD, "Expressions of ET Contact, A Visual Blueprint?") She has created these incredible geometric drawings and found that she can speak in several strange languages, as well as writing in unusual scripts. Some of this is illustrated on the same video and also the scripts and symbols are being investigated independently at present, by Gary Anthony in the UK. Gary has several researchers, two linguistic experts, two cryptographers, one psycho-linguistic expert, a phonetics expert and a symbols expert all working with him on this.

Tracey is convinced that she knows what some of her drawings mean. I have also come across many, many people who have found that their Contact experiences have affected them so much that they have been inspired to produce unusual artwork, not only of the beings that they have seen, but strange, scripted languages that they are able to illustrate on paper and actually speak out loud.

Apart from feeling impelled to produce this astounding artwork, Tracey tells us why she feels that her greatest challenge in life is in trying to be human and why so much that happens on this planet feels 'alien' to her. This feeling is common to many people who are being born today that are referred to as 'Star Kids'. Tracey has shown enormous courage, not only in honouring her experiences, but by intelligently and actively seeking to understand them. She was prepared to explore the traditional, psychological route, including having a brain scan. She wanted answers, but found that traditional psychology couldn't help her. Finally her answers were found not so much from the 'outside', but more from within herself.

There is one tangible mystery about Tracey's story that simply cannot be explained. Tracey went to see her dentist to have her teeth checked and when the dentist said that they are all perfect, she was puzzled. She knew that she had four amalgam fillings; however, the dentist couldn't find them and was baffled. Tracey does not know what happened to her fillings, but suspects that for some reason unbeknown to her, her teeth were altered through her experiences. I have heard many stories similar to this, whereby individuals have been healed of physical illness, or cleaned of pollutants etc. It is indeed a mystery!

Tracey's story . . .

Even from a young age, strange events became almost routine in my life. I would wake up exhausted and dazed after wild dreams of being taken aboard spaceships where many bizarre things happened. I was unable to accept that these were anything more than crazy imaginings. Dreams of my overactive mind, (as those who were close to me would put it down to). At primary school I had an invisible giant friend that I would talk to and to this day I can vividly remember the warm, large hand that would guide me around the playground, telling me jokes.

At night, I would sometimes have another visitor. I named him 'Father Christmas', he made me feel uneasy and frightened as he entered the room, but if I hid myself deep under the blankets, too scared to breathe, a strong sensation of calmness and security would suddenly come over me. I would then find myself floating in the night sky, looking at the millions of stars shining around me. But I always felt uneasy and frightened when these beings were coming to get me, as this was a natural reaction from the human part of me that was not totally aware of what was going on. The human part of me related to these beings as 'Father Christmas' and this is what I called them. My fear was the natural reaction of my human side on the 'earthly' plane. So I would feel uneasy at first when these beings entered my bedroom, then a bit later I would have this feeling of calmness wash over me and then a greater awareness would come through and with this awareness I found that I could understand very complicated concepts.

The tall, grey beings never conducted operations or experiments on me, not like the short 'Zeta Greys'. These tall, greyish beings were very different, I felt they were like family, as if I was at home when I was with them. I was much more afraid when the short, Zeta Greys would come, because I knew that some of the things they could do to me would be painful. To begin with, during my earlier experiences with them, I was paralyzed in every way, physically, mentally and emotionally. I felt too afraid to communicate with them, but each

time I had an experience with them they communicated more and more. I think it was because I was growing less fearful and more receptive. The more I began to understand these beings as well as the 'preying mantis' beings, (which I often saw together with the Zetas), the less fearful I became. I then found out that I could freely communicate with them and that they would do their best to help me to understand their situation and why they were taking people and doing operations on them.

From the moment I could hold a pencil, I would begin to draw. It was my passion and my gift. I began painting still life and landscapes and by looking so intently at people when I drew, I developed the ability to see auras. But until I read a book on this subject a few years later, I initially believed this to be a fault of my eyes.

At the age of fifteen I experienced a rapid onset of psychic and intuitive abilities, feeling a strong urge to heal people with my hands. However, I had never heard of such a thing and people around me just thought I was being excessively imaginative. It was with deep sadness that I suppressed these abilities for many years, due to the opposition of those around me who believed that I just had an outrageous imagination.

Unable to express myself freely, or communicate properly with others, I fell into a deep crevasse of doubt and confusion. At the public school I attended, I was very shy and tried to fit in, but if I tried to express my 'unusual' points of view, I was ridiculed by other students and even some of the teachers.

My English teacher was mistakenly convinced that I was taking drugs because of the extraordinary short stories and poems I would write for assignments. They would often tell me in front of the whole class that I must be 'on something' to be able to come up with such crazy tales. It all became too much for me and I changed from being an 'A' student, to a rebellious 'D', who tried to fit in as best she could.

I denied my 'inner truth' so that I would be accepted by others and not have to put up with the cruel teasing I had endured most of my school years.

In 1996, I won a competition and was catapulted into the fashion world as a model. After experiencing the invalidation and ridicule for who I was on the inside, I now had acknowledgment of who I was on the outside! I felt accepted and loved by the way I looked, but underneath, the secrets were building and my insecurity was growing. I was living a lie and it seemed there was nothing I could do about it. A professional modelling career proved to be a constant struggle for me emotionally and physically. In the house where I was living, I began to see 'spirits' and other strange beings, with non-human faces. My dreams were intense and sometimes I could not sleep for fear and anticipation of what may come. If I did sleep, my dreams were bizarre, such as undergoing physical examinations, or being in strange classrooms.

Grey beings, with large, black eyes would sometimes telepathically teach me to draw and write symbols in the form of holograms. These would often extend from my hands, via static, like beams of electric-blue light. After such nights I would lack energy and sometimes it was practically impossible to get out of bed in the morning because I was so tired. The model agency became suspicious because I was constantly calling in sick. I just didn't know what to say to them. I could hardly tell them little grey men had been abducting me or performing operations on me through the night! I couldn't even tell my partner, let alone my employer. It became increasingly difficult for me to cope, I was devastated and feeling guilty about what was happening. I honestly thought I was going crazy.

I went to see the doctor and explained the effects these horrible 'dreams' had been having on me. In a consultation, which lasted less than five minutes, he said I was simply depressed, so he wrote out a prescription for me for antidepressants and sleeping tablets. Although I wasn't comfortable with taking drugs, it was a relief to be able to have a decent night's sleep without these overwhelming experiences.

At Christmas in 1996, I travelled home to see my family. I was staying with my Grandmother in Perth when, one night, I had this really intense feeling that I should write something before I went to sleep. This was unusual for me, but I decided to go with these sensations and I wrote a page of information. Through this process, it felt as if I had little control over what was happening, the writing just seemed to flow. The next day I couldn't figure it out because I had actually written something way beyond my conscious understanding - I literally couldn't comprehend it. To my astonishment, this information was also contrary to everything I had been taught regarding human evolution. It said that the human race had been created by extraterrestrials! The writing also contained information about the genetic manipulation of human and ET DNA, used to create other species.

I was shocked and confused. I had never read, seen or heard anything like this, nor did I know anything about ETs doing genetic experiments with human DNA. I couldn't understand how I was able to write about something that was totally against any beliefs I had. I had heard of channelling, but my knowledge of it was very limited. Even though I thought this writing episode was just a 'one off', I began to get more and more urges to do it. The information that flowed was incredible; alien-human interaction, implants, dimensions, spirituality, the creation of human species, the raising of consciousness and so on. Then sometimes, 'involuntarily', I would find myself speaking another 'strange' language.

In 1997, when I was modelling in Japan, my dreams were more vivid and frightening than ever before. Because I was living on my own, I decided to delve into them more deeply and gained the courage to ask the beings why this was happening to me. To my amazement, I received answers in the form of dreams, writings and from a voice 'within' my mind. I was told that I had chosen for myself, to be a part of the evolutionary cycle in the creation of a new, more spiritually advanced species, which eventually inhabit earth. I also received information about the raising of human consciousness and of a dimensional shift that is presently happening on earth. It is going to assist us and enable us to access 'other realms' more freely, as well as increase our spiritual understanding. At the time, this was the most bizarre information I had ever heard and I did not know what its significance was for me.

I kept a diary of my experiences and one morning I felt a sudden urge to draw a symbol, which I had seen in a dream, during which many spaceships were moving around the night sky. The stars then moved into the configuration of a bird. As I was drawing this, my hand seemed once again to take over and I ended up completing a geometric symbol. Over the next two years, I completed other similar drawings and symbols, with little input from my conscious mind. In fact, the less I concentrated on this, the easier the information and drawings flowed. It was quite bizarre and I still had no idea why I was doing it. After Japan, I returned home and I felt that modelling wasn't for me after all - it was far too superficial. I was now keen to look more deeply within myself, beyond my known reality, as by now I felt I had conquered many of my previous fears. The time in Japan had given me a new understanding of reality and I could no longer deny my experiences. I had a new awareness, plus physical evidence of this reality, such as marks on my body (without knowing how they got there). Lots of things happened, like my watch working fine until I put it on and wore it, it was very hard to understand it all. And, to cap it all, I still had these ongoing interactions with alien beings and had to overcome my fears about that, plus worrying about what people might think of me.

I finally decided to tell my boyfriend and family about what had been happening to me over the years. My honesty was greeted with disbelief, I was seen as an attention seeker and that it was my attempt to avoid living in the 'real' world. My explanations became more and more hopeless, so I began again to question my experiences and my mental health. The isolation and embarrassment became so hard to bear, I sometimes thought about ending my life. No one seemed to understand what I was going through and I honestly believed I was going mad. I went to see a psychologist who told me I was perfectly sane; I just had an overactive imagination. I felt depressed, confused and filled with doubts about myself.

Whilst in a bookshop I reached for a book about Contact that had been written by a social worker and was about her ET related Contact experiences. I felt a strong urge to buy it, even though I didn't have much money. During the next few days I was glued to this book and I was amazed at how many of these experiences echoed my own. A spark of hope flickered within me; it was a realisation that I wasn't alone anymore!

The amazing coincidence was that I met the author of this book at the shop and she put me in touch with Mary Rodwell, a meeting that was to change my life! With Mary, I learned how to open up and accept my experiences, as well as realising that I wasn't alone with this. I went to a support group (facilitated by Mary), it was wonderful for me to be able to see for myself how 'normal' all these people were.

Before the support meeting I had a dream. In it, I was told to copy the geometric symbols that I'd drawn onto transparency material (acetate) and that they would all fit together in different configurations. To my surprise they did. I took them along to the support meeting, many of the people there felt very drawn towards them. Then they showed *me* how they should slot together, *they* put them together for me in different ways.

My friends at the group said that they had seen them before, during their experiences. Another young man had drawn his own symbols; some of them were very similar to mine. Another lady who studies ancient symbols and sacred geometry looked at them, she was able to recognise and interpret some of the symbols for us. She said that some of them existed in ancient temples and pyramids around the world, many related to star systems, such as Sirius and I was reminded that the symbols illustrated the links between ancient cultures and extraterrestrial life.

One symbol was similar to a crop circle that had appeared a few years earlier. A researcher in France had said that some were like the designs found in the Aztec pyramids. All this information was groundbreaking news for me, as previously, I'd had no way of validating what I was drawing, I'd had to live with the reinforced belief that it was all in my imagination. Also, I'd never been to any sacred sites, so this was further proof for me.

I also met another lady who, like me, found that she could speak fluently in another, 'strange' language. What's more, she had also written in an unusual script that was very similar to mine.

I was 22 at the time and had endured events such as visiting outer space in alien craft and watching alien life forms perform surgical procedures on me, before I was able to realise my connection to the Contact experience. I found that I had to search beyond the confines of conventional thinking. I have had a lifelong interaction with non-human beings; this realisation has forced me on a journey of gigantic proportions, changing me forever.

Contact with these ET beings has been going on for as long as I can remember. Experiences that most people would consider 'strange' have been nothing other than routine for me. As a child I would wake up some mornings, feeling exhausted after a night of interaction with a tall Grey, an intelligent being that I felt such a unique closeness to, he felt like family. Once I was onboard their craft I felt completely comfortable, more comfortable than I was in any earth environment. The result of this was that I felt compelled to create many geometric drawings that literally connected together in many different ways.

These drawings and combinations depict the important connections between humanity and ET beings, as well as demonstrating the workings of many technologies of ET origin. The drawings depict several scripts that relate to ancient texts from various cultures. These have shown that humanity is now at the stage whereby we are becoming aware of a greater reality and our true origins. They have shown controversial, but compelling information about advanced technologies, such as interstellar travel and communication. They also reveal the truth about the Egyptian pyramids and contain knowledge about many suppressed technologies that I believe have been hidden from the public by unacknowledged, underground government organisations.

The artwork comes to me during the experiences, or through an overpowering urge to put pen to paper. Whenever this occurs, my hand is taken over by a powerful force, with absolutely no input from my conscious mind. I am never completely taken over, or in a trance, although I do need to be sidetracked. At times I have tried to influence what is being drawn, only to find that my hand will stop and I'm unable to finish the drawing until I surrender my conscious input and control. After finishing the symbol, I usually receive a paragraph of hieroglyphic-type writing, which some people have said resembles hieroglyphic text. This depicts the drawings, interpretations and meaning, which are then translated into English for easier understanding and later reference.

The information and drawings come, I believe, through various extraterrestrial entities, most commonly through beings I would call 'geometric' or 'crystalline', when in visible form.

They have extraordinary features, translucent, like crystal, often showing faces within faces, which move and change constantly. Unlike the more common beings seen by experiencers, they have no obvious appendages, although they exude intense light and have a powerful presence of infinite wisdom. Each being is connected to the other, existing with a combined energy body, spanning solar systems and galaxies in this unified form. I describe them as 'grandfather beings'. They work within an energy body or council, which includes various evolved, enlightened species. This energy body provides a stabilizing, governing force over unified regions of consciousness, or within a specific focus, or related to an area within this Universe. It resonates at high frequencies and when combined with all existence they make up what is known as the 'universal mind'. The 'mind' exists everywhere, within all life, containing infinite information and knowledge. As everything in this universe is made up of the same matter resonating at different harmonics, these ET beings are able to communicate through all of us, directing thought on subatomic levels.

By doing this, the beings in geometric/crystalline form, communicate on levels comprehensible to humanity and by activating direct subconscious interaction. This is interpreted by the conscious mind into a simplified form of communication, such as the symbology I have shown within the geometric drawings. These drawings reflect humanity's consciousness and they are meant to assist us in understanding our link with the cosmic family. Focusing on the drawings can show you subtle images of the crystalline geometric features and faces within them.

There are messages within the drawings that are meant to communicate the nature of the macrocosm. We are learning to remember what we already know, to view this life and this universe in a new way and within a non-linear spectrum. This enables us to connect to our inner wisdom and awareness, bypassing linear space-time, thus allowing us to experience ourselves, as we are deeply connected to all life.

I have seen and worked with many different types of beings, including several 'Zeta' types. These little fellows (sometimes called 'Greys') have received much hostility and negativity from human beings. Many people seem convinced that they are trying to cause harm and disruption to humanity and in the past I felt that way too. I now realise it was my limited perception and fear, which kept me from understanding a greater truth. There are many races of Zeta type beings and through our perception of our experiences just a few are doing things that we perceive as being hurtful or even cruel. But this does not mean they all behave like that. If Zetas were to look down at the earth right now, they would see wars and terrible destruction that many people are causing, the devastation within our environment and so on, it would be easy to assume that 'we' are all the same (i.e. destructive and violent). The Zetas are only, I believe, trying to survive (as we are) and they have done nothing to me against my will. It has always been my choice and from my understanding, this choice is also respected by other beings.

The Zeta beings have played a great role in the evolution of humanity, within the 'denser levels' of our existence, teaching us much about ourselves. They hold up the mirror and many of us refuse to look into it for fear of what we may see. Their energy and presence comes through within my drawings, to show some of the past influences of the planet and how their evolution is directly linked to our own. As humanity moves to higher vibratory levels, the Zetas will be seen as allies and not to be feared. We shall also begin to perceive the ET beings working with us on finer levels as we move into their range of existence. As this happens, the Zetas will be less prominent.

The tall, greyish beings that I used to see, from birth up to the age of nine, always felt like close family to me. Taking me onboard their spacecraft, I was able to wander around at will and communicate freely with them. I felt a unique affinity with them, I easily forgot our physical differences, as there were no barriers, we were all equal. They were incredibly gentle beings who would communicate telepathically, demonstrating advanced healing abilities and reminding me of their technological ability to travel through interstellar space. They would take me to other star systems where I was shown the spiritually advanced practices and customs of beings on various planets.

I remember having an important role on board the craft. I assisted beings that were travellers and used complex star maps, which seemed to be transformed from my thoughts into holographic form. Often I would find that I was using complicated thought processes unlike anything I could experience on earth and we would engage in telepathic communication about concepts that defy the laws of linear space and time. I would experience interstellar travel beyond the light barrier where craft could operate on a non-linear frequency, allowing us to travel thousands of light years in a matter of a few hours.

I was very baffled at how I could know this information when I was onboard the craft, with this knowledge flowing effortlessly as if it were second nature to me. Since then, I have understood that I had access to this information from a very young age. When I was onboard the craft I had a shift in consciousness that allowed me to access information from a quantum field of thought. While in this altered state, I was able to interface with regions of my mind, which on earth were usually hidden within the subconscious or unconscious. It was very difficult to leave and return to earth, as I always felt I was going back to an unfamiliar, restrictive world, as I was far more comfortable in this 'other' environment.

I felt a very close affinity with the beings some call the 'Preying Mantis Beings'. They are often extremely tall, two to five metres (six to fifteen feet) and they have huge insect eyes protruding from either side of their head. I have learned to accept their strange appearance and have been taught much about humanity from these grand beings. They are extremely ancient and possess incredible wisdom. People often witness these beings during experiences with the Grey Zetas, enabling them to understand and work more closely with us.

The Mantis beings are incredible healers and are known to assist earth in many ways when intervention is necessary. Their wisdom and understanding often comes through my artwork I feel, as they are a significant link to our evolution. They are evolved beings who work alongside the crystalline beings within the council I previously mentioned. I have often found myself working with the young and newborn Mantis, as they are as curious as I am and we seem to learn much from each other. They are born with the

knowledge of their elders, as it is passed genetically. Yet only by their interaction with humans can they gain the wisdom to understand the knowledge they have been given.

Thousands of years ago, the designers of the pyramids came from a section of space called the Orion system. These beings were the original 'lion beings', the ancestors of the 'cat-like' beings from Sirius. The cat-like beings live and communicate in the same time frame as the Orion lion beings and these lion beings often come through my drawings as cosmic warriors of wisdom. They are called 'lion beings' for the obvious reason they have facial features similar to a lion's. They have beautiful soft faces, with cat-like eyes and golden, orange manes. They hold the key to our ancestry and are easily contacted by thought. They originally came to our earth during ancient times from the Orion star system, to oversee the creation and activation of the pyramids of Egypt and those existing elsewhere on earth. But the cat-like beings from Sirius were the prominent builders of the pyramids. The cat-like beings are descendants of the lion people of Orion, but 'live' in a different sphere of existence. The Sirius cat-like beings are physical beings, capable of building complex, physical structures. The Orion lion beings are in a non-physical spectrum that transcends space-time and they are the designers of such great monuments as the pyramids.

This is the multi-dimensional aspect to the construction of the pyramids, e.g. the Sirius cat-like beings, which interact with humans, honour the lion beings. Most humans know these cat-like beings as they are more prominent in the physical reality. There were many other races of beings involved in the construction of the pyramids, but the most prominent were the cat-like ones because of their direct link with their Orion ancestors, who hold the non-physical 'blueprint' of the pyramids. During the time when the earth was relatively untouched, the lion-beings were able to focus the earth's energies. The result was that this fertile planet was able to share its potent energy to accommodate the needs of many species on other planets that are thousands of light years away. These beings have now spread to other planetary systems to assist with similar energy activation throughout the universe. With strong connections to the beginning of humanity, they are often here to impart messages and some of the messages are depicted through my drawings.

I have also been told that a significant ancient identity, known previously as Horus, perceived to be a god of ancient Egypt, is another important key to our past. I have always felt an important connection to this being and I first saw him during an experience when I was seventeen. In this experience, I was underground in a cavern or passageway when he appeared in front of me and telepathically introduced himself. He said that he was most commonly known on this planet as Horus and sometimes as the 'feathered serpent, Quetzalcoatl' (this is what the Aztec people called him). He was standing side-on to me, revealing only the left side of his face, very similar to the ancient Egyptian drawings. I vividly recall his large, powerful eye and felt it penetrate me on all levels. He was floating and moving side ways along an underground hallway looking at the walls, which were covered in different kinds of hieroglyphics. I was told the messages within the hieroglyphs would be revealed to me during my lifetime. We stopped moving and then his snake-like tongue slid from his open beak. With his tongue he carved a symbol on the rock wall. When it was completed, he drew me towards it and it became very large. I found myself above ground, looking at a triangle with two concentric circles within it. In the distance, I could see a flat plain; I could see rocky mountains with the sun rising behind. Three tubular metal bars came down from the sky, one by one, joining the inner circle with powerful sounds of metal hitting metal. Three bars then descended to join the outer circle in the same way. An intense wave of energy enveloped me as I woke up, shaking in my bed. This experience prompted my ability to channel through the geometric symbols and messages.

This extraterrestrial being has had powerful influences on earth throughout our history, in many cultures. He has been seen as a messenger, here to plant 'seeds' within our consciousness, as part of our evolution. Many times he has shown us the potential of our advanced capabilities; that is why I call him 'The Architect of Consciousness'. I have titled one of my coloured symbols this, as it depicts his role in our universe.

There are some extraterrestrial people that look very similar to humans, commonly known as 'humanoids'. Once again, there are many different kinds, with different levels of spiritual and technological evolution. Many races of humanoids are technologically superior to humans. There are several types of ET humanoids that walk among humans virtually unnoticed, as they are curious about us. The humanoids that I interact with are very concerned with the suppression of technologies and mass extinction of the planetary species. I am told that if these technologies and energy systems were not suppressed then we would have an end to poverty and the preservation of our ecosystems. Some of these technologies are shown within my drawings and can be interpreted by those who choose to understand the links to the non-polluting zero point field of energy, i.e. energy that can be obtained through sources that will not threaten the ecosystems of earth.

There are several other ET beings that I interact with on a regular basis, such as those known as the 'Arcturians', the 'Pleiadians' and those from Andromeda. They are often mistaken for angels because of their incredible light bodies. They are also, a sort of advanced future version of the human species, who exude a body of light when interacting with me. They constantly inspire messages that are carried through into my artwork and geometric symbols. They feel concern for the path the human race has chosen to take and are patiently observing us with compassion and a hope that we will wake up before we literally annihilate ourselves. But all the beings make it perfectly clear that they are not going to interfere. It is up to us to make a global decision for peace and equilibrium.

Over a four-year period, I completed six coloured drawings and eleven black and white ones. After finishing seven of the black and white drawings, I had an intense encounter with the ET beings. They communicated, using a series of visual materialisations similar to holographic images. It was made extremely clear to me that the drawings were of great significance. This is when they told me that I should copy them all onto transparency material and that they would all align with each other, showing an important universal connection. As mentioned previously, I did this, found out that the drawings did indeed fit together in many different ways. For example, the triangles would fit with the others at exactly the same angles, all with astonishing accuracy, even though each drawing had been completed freehand and on separate occasions.

After this happened, the major turning point for me was when I met Mary Rodwell. Mary enabled me to acknowledge and accept my experiences and she taught me that I am far from alone in this. At the support group, at around about the time when the other members helped me to fit the drawings and symbols together, I had another encounter with the Council of Beings who conveyed to me that I needed to convert the drawings into a 3D format, onto computer if I could, so that the information held within them would be accessible.

Triggered by the symbols, I have found myself speaking languages that are not, I believe, to be of earth origin. I am now in the process of learning more about them, I have the information I need to convert these languages into English. I have often been caught out finishing sentences and naming everyday items using these languages involuntarily. The ability to speak other languages without consciously learning them is a familiar trait, I believe, of those who interact with these beings. It is commonly known as 'star language'.

I believe that many of the symbols have been used throughout ancient civilisations and are related to star systems. There is a strong link with the enigmatic crop circle designs found throughout the world, which could be another way in which some extraterrestrials are communicating with us. Also, there are electrical symbols within my drawings that relate to energy and alternative power sources. One has co-ordinates relating to areas of importance on earth, as well as complicated mathematical formulae. Key words around some of the coloured drawings are there to explain part of their significance.

The drawings depict a grand, universal connection, in a form that can be recognised by all intelligent life as a 'universal language'. The geometry and symbology act as a powerful trigger, awakening ancestral memories that exist within our DNA and within our minds on many levels. There is much we need to remember before we can openly join with the 'universal community'. Humanity first needs to realise that there is a greater awareness that allows us to initiate Contact and interact with ET beings without unnecessary fear and hostility. The illusions of space and time have been realised by many, as we understand the true nature of the cosmos and ourselves.

I now have a more conscious connection with the energy; this allows me to complete the symbols and messages. I have been preparing to create images and geometric symbols that will act as a trigger to accelerate personal development. These include geometric encoding, compatible with an individual's genetic heritage. As individual beings, we are made up of infinite geometrical encoding and harmonic frequencies, which exist universally, ultimately linking all life and consciousness together. We all react differently to them, developing at our own pace and in accordance with the evolution of our species. To put it simply, I can now complete drawings specifically for an individual's use. I call them 'personal blueprints'. They are intended to enable an individual to connect with their extraterrestrial origins, to reawaken inner abilities and understanding, triggering a magnificent new awareness of reality.

Planet earth has always felt unfamiliar for me, although it has provided diversity and learning. At times, life has been extremely difficult for me, particularly when I realised that people around me didn't accept my experiences and my way of thinking. This has forced me to question my sanity and the reality of my experiences, sometimes rising to thoughts of ending my life. Over the years, I have made several visits to psychiatrists and psychologists. I have undergone numerous physical and psychological assessments as well as CAT and EEG scans. No brain abnormalities or psychological problems have ever been found. Nor have I had any conventional explanations as to why so many others, (as well as myself) have had Contact experiences. So I have needed to look 'within' for answers. This has provided me with the acknowledgement of my lifelong connection to ET beings as being part of my reality.

I am now moving forward with my artwork, I have a greater understanding of its significance. I feel a true sense of purpose, as I know that the drawings will shed some much-needed light about the great mysteries of our planet. The transformations that I have witnessed within some people who have seen the drawings is incredibly inspiring. There is, I feel, a real need for society today to acknowledge extraterrestrial existence and human-ET interaction. It needs to happen now and I urge those who are aware to come forward and help us educate those who are willing to listen.

Tracey also has an account of the 'Star Children' phenomenon. We shall cover this in greater detail in the next chapter; however this is her understanding of them:

"Many physical alterations have occurred in the children who have cosmic awareness. The bodies of these children are stronger in many ways to that of a human child. They are children with a higher percentage of extraterrestrial DNA; and their molecular structure is arranged differently, allowing the cells and all that makes up the body to vibrate much faster. Everything is accelerated, including immune system responses, as the DNA is encoded to recognize all types of 'foreign' organisms.

The immune response of the body creates an automatic chain reaction within every cell of the body, which makes it integrate with the attacking organisms. This would normally cause disease within an ordinary person, but because of the response and recognition by the body to external organisms, disease is totally overcome as the body adapts spontaneously to that which is foreign. It is said that the Star Children have bodies of light in the physical realm, so anything which is normally viewed not to be light, becomes light when integrated into their system and becomes part of their body.

The DNA of a Star Kid contains ten fold the amount of information as compared to that of an ordinary human body. Things such as telepathy, manipulation of time and space, non-verbal communication and so on, are all very much conscious abilities for these children, as they exist for them naturally. Everything about their physical makeup is quicker; it vibrates quicker and is more efficient. Information passing through the brain pathways happens faster, so their learning skills and abilities are more advanced, as they are known to have photographic memories and extremely fast motor-neuron responses.

The linear-time format that human beings understand is irrelevant to them and the ability for these Star Kids to access memory is enhanced. Memory is not enhanced in the sense of time span, but in the memory of experiences throughout the life they are leading. They have a direct connection to a higher awareness, which is represented by enhanced (DNA structured) bodily workings and functions.

They can eat whatever they choose purely for taste and not nutrient, as their bodies at a very young age are able to go without food totally. Their bodies have a capability that enables them to turn foreign organisms and energy into nutrients that give them excelled growth and enhanced bodily functions. They are mostly vegetarian when they do eat.

The Star Children are extremely sensitive to all things. The emotional body of these children is balanced when they are brought into this world (emotions play a different role for them, where many of them are from), with emotions being used to direct thought and intention. When they are born there is a tendency for these children to form a strong link to the awareness of their mother, which helps them to stabilise properly within their 'earth' reality. The sensitivity of these children means that they feel exactly what their mother is feeling. Not all humans have balanced or harnessed the energy of emotions, so the child learns emotional reactionary patterns, which can cause difficulties later if not addressed in early life.

It is important for the Star Children to learn to have confidence in themselves and what they know, so that they are not tempted to rely on other people's opinions, which are usually emotionally based. It is also important for them to distinguish between their own thoughts and other peoples' thoughts. This comes naturally when they are confident about who they are. The emotions of other people can cause havoc in the life of a sensitive Star Child, that is why it is so important for them to express themselves and to be aware of who they are and choose to be. Learning to detach from other people's erratic, emotional energy is very important.

Star Children also have superior mental and analytical capabilities. With the mental understanding of themselves and the universe, balanced with spiritual understanding, huge leaps in human evolution can occur for the planet. Instead of using the mental abilities of the conscious mind (as experienced by humans), Star Kids are able to bypass the inferior, unsubstantiated clutter of the mind, to link directly to the subconscious with greater clarity and awareness, to connect to what is known as 'the higher self' or 'super-conscious'. The mental capacity of a Star Kid means accelerated, logical understanding and when attuned with the spiritual it will allow for the manipulation of time and space as well as the utilisation of spiritual laws.

Star Children quite naturally are born with great, universal wisdom and awareness. They have the capacity of seeing this within all things, no matter how vulgar or wrong something may appear to be. They have the ability to exude light and compassion, which can be mistaken for aloofness. Star Children see more than they let on, which cannot be adequately expressed through the use of words. This is where the Star Kids are often gifted creatively, as it is their means of expressing what cannot be shown in other ways. Star Kids do not need to be directed to express themselves in any creative sense, as this is a natural gift, which comes with the honouring of themselves and all life. They have a great feeling of 'being connected' to the universe, through their understanding, their links to nature and all that exists within their reality. Star Children are able to touch each other deeply; they can recognise each other and make a connection. They can do this by recognising the other's 'inner light', something that all beings are made up of. They need to develop discernment and resonance to all forms of energy. This will allow them to trust their inner knowing and help them understand that they are beings of light, here to show us a new way. They are connected directly to all things and all is connected to them. They know this consciously."

Tracey concludes her story for us:

"As far as my own Contact experiences are concerned, I slowly became very compassionate towards the ET beings, as there is so much that humans can learn and benefit from interacting with them. I was far more fearful of my experiences when I thought that I was the only one having them, I didn't know what was going on and why. But there has always been an equal exchange between me and the Zetas. I helped them achieve their genetic goals and in return, my healing and psychic abilities, **plus my understanding of life on earth and so on, has been enhanced. They** also protect me when I ask them to. If I need the answer to a question, telepathically they will tell me. Basically at the start, I misunderstood the Greys. The 'knowing' ET part of me initially made a decision to assist them. However, the understanding of this was overshadowed by fear, which stems from limited human perceptions and typical, 'knee-jerk' reactions to these experiences."

I have been privileged to see Tracey grow from fear and confusion into a person full of confidence and self worth. She is living proof that it is possible to achieve a healthy integration of multi-reality if the support that is needed to enable understanding is there. This kind of support can help a person overcome their fear, so that they are able to fully explore for themselves their Contact experiences.

To demonstrate Tracey's new confidence, in 2001 in Melbourne, Australia, she calmly faced a panel of psychiatrists and openly talked to them about her experiences. She held nothing back. All eight doctors agreed, they could not explain it away as being any form of mental illness. They were intrigued and they even wished Tracey the best of luck.

For Tracey - for her to agree to that interplay and for her to put herself on the line like that, it shows us how far she has come and how much integrity and courage she has acquired along the way. Her reasons were simple; she felt that she had to demonstrate that this was a reality for her and a positive one. What's more, she felt it was vitally important for the conventional establishment to become aware of this phenomenon. For me, she is certainly an extraordinary and courageous Star Child!

In the next chapter, we will study the evidence and look at the reality of the Star Child Phenomenon. As we explore this reality with real stories, you will be able to ask yourself the question: *Is my child a Star Kid or am I one?*

These amazing children display not only accelerated development, but also awareness at an age that would have previously been considered impossible. Dr. Roger Leir, author of "The Aliens and the Scalpel" has already shown evidence of this in his latest research. More and more credible researchers are noticing these changes in our children and I am certain that Tracey is one of these 'new kids on the block', a Star Child! Therefore, her personal understanding of the phenomenon, I believe, has much to offer us.

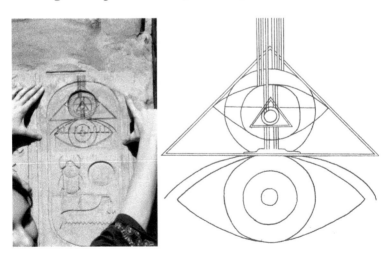

Above: Tracey with one of her black and white drawings. This drawing Tracey says was given to her in a dream by Horus, the Egyptian God, in 1999. In 2002 Tracey went to Egypt, and took this drawing with her. The image matched perfectly with a hieroglyph at Karnack Temple, Luxor. "Even from a distance I knew it would fit," she said.

CHAPTER 9
Star Children 'Homo Noeticus' – The New Humans

"Daddy I want to go to bed now, because I want to go home"

A 2 year old.

"Mummy strange lights came into my room last night and they took me and you and baby, and later they brought us back.'

A 3 year old.

"Mummy six little black aliens came to see me last night, they were very friendly and played with me, but I didn't like them touching me, they felt like dolphins."

A 4 year old.

"I believe that any mother that looks at her recently born child in comparison with children born twenty years ago will testify that there is a tremendous difference. Some look upon the differences in the 'new humans' and say the reasons have to do with better prenatal care etc. In my opinion this supposition is nonsense and in the light of my more recent studies and exposure to the abduction phenomenon, I have come to the conclusion that the rapid advancement of our human species is due to alien intervention in our bodies and minds."

Dr. Roger Leir, excerpt from *The Aliens and the Scalpel*

"Not long before Andrija Puharich's death, I was asked to write an article about him and rang his home in America. When I asked him what he was working on he told me he was working on the study of supernormal children. You wouldn't believe how many of these kids are out there. They seem to be on genius-level. I know dozens and there are probably thousands."

Colin Wilson, excerpt from *Alien Dawn*

"This would have been an area I would have never thought of in the beginning . . .but now, in the light of experience and knowledge, I would say it starts here. Parents need to understand that their children know what they are talking about and are not making it up. For me, I used to report all this to my parents and they used to say that I had an overactive imagination. That during the nights of being 'paralysed', it was quite normal and lots of people get that and that they often used to experience it themselves, (they said this probably out of concern and to make me feel at ease).

Now they are both 82 years old and as I've run all this by them, they now feel its okay to say: "Yes, we've probably been experiencers too!"

So what is the explanation? How do you honour a child's mental capacities, what do you say to your children and how do you handle it, should they start to report strange things? As a child, I knew what I saw and felt, but my parents would say that what I saw wasn't real. It's these kinds of responses that affect your life as an adult. It's like: I see it, but I don't believe it! Outside this experience your judgement becomes impaired".

Julia

This chapter is about *the new kids on the block*! These new children are given many names, but the name most commonly used is 'Star Children'. There is evidence which we shall look at, that supports the possibility of a 'new' kind of human. This takes the form of personal accounts and from parents who believe that their children are different, that they display many of the associated characteristics of a Star Child. We will also look at the different ways in which you can support your own child, should you believe they may be one! And as a parent, how do you cope with this information?

So what are these Star Kids, why are they being born and what is the Star Child phenomenon really about?

'Star Children' is a blanket term for these new children; I have personally named them 'the new kids on the block'. There are other terms, such as: Indigo Children, Children of the Blue Ray, Smart Kids, Children of Light, The Millennium Children or Golden Children. It remains to be seen whether they are all the same or different kinds of Star Kids, but certainly they portray many unique characteristics. This chapter looks at the evidence for the new human, or 'Homo Noeticus', a term coined by the noted author John White, a researcher of parapsychology and noetics, e.g. the study of consciousness.

There are many respected and credible researchers around the world who are realising that something incredible is happening. Mainly, there are some children being born now who are very different from those being born half a century ago. Some researchers suggest that there are many reasons for this, reasons over and above things like better parenting, improved nutrition and regular health care. These differences apparently, are far too profound and radical for that.

Dr. Roger Leir is one of many researchers looking into this phenomenon, this 'new humanity', or what many are naming the 'Star Child Phenomena'. Dr Leir is gathering data and evidence with regards to these children, he has spoken at conferences about the many differences these new kids are demonstrating, including accelerated physical development, higher intelligence and improved psychic abilities. With this research we have already seen:

- The ability of babies to read written print.
- Sign language used to communicate with toddlers not old enough to speak.
- Advancements in crawling, or age of speech.

Dr Leir says that he believes the answer to this involves the alien manipulation of human genetics. He is so convinced about it, he is presently conducting global research to confirm this hypotheses.

Psychologist and clinical hypnotherapist, Richard Boylan (secretary of ACCET in America) not only acknowledges the evidence for Homo Noeticus, but believes they exist in such large numbers that he is able to run workshops for them and their parents. He expands on these differences and has said that these special children, who have been 'touched by a heritage from the stars', will often seem like little adults in children's bodies. They have a gaze and a knowingness that belies their years, believed to be brought about by a telepathic downloading, often during the night, in what are made to seem like 'dreams', which increases the range and perspective through which these children operate. Boylan defines them as being 'children of both human and extraterrestrial origin', the ET contribution of the child's make-up coming from genetic engineering, or from biomedical technology and the linking of telepathic consciousness, or perhaps from directed 'incarnation' of an ET into a human body.

The child could be conceived from parents who are experiencers themselves, thus having genetic material that is part extraterrestrial. Or perhaps they have had their human genome altered by ET bio-engineering to bring out abilities beyond the average? Whatever the theory and beliefs, without doubt these children are much brighter, more cosmically minded, or more psychic, (or all three), than their human peers.

Recently, I have been conducting my own research into this fascinating aspect of Contact. I had been given some similar accounts from my clients after they discovered that their children demonstrated not only abnormally accelerated development, such as walking at eight months, or reading at two years old, but also show advanced psychic abilities. These reports mostly came in after I published an article on Star Kids and they came not just from Australia, but from overseas too, as far away as France, the United Kingdom and America.

Lori Codini, in America, wrote to me and said: "I remember as a child looking into the sky and wondering why the stars were in the wrong place. I felt my family from 'out there' had left me, and I felt so lonely." Lori said that when she was in her twenties: "I just knew I could have a special child". She said that her daughter, Jasmine, talked at four months, was reading before she was a year old and had intense conversations by the time she was two. Lori continues by saying: "Jasmine has an awareness of universal concepts and intergalactic citizenship that is way beyond her peers." Jasmine apparently struggled at school because she couldn't understand the 'silliness' of the other children. She found it hard to fit in and felt very isolated because of this. Lori added that she does have limited, telepathic communication with her daughter, but that they don't use it very often.

Boylan believes that these children are often confused by the primitiveness of earth and the bulkiness of their physical bodies. They can really unnerve their parents when they talk about where they came from and discuss their 'real ET parents'. I have also heard similar reports; one mother said to me that her five-year old child had told her: "You are not my real parents, they are in fairyland. You are just here to look after me." Then she said: "I don't really look like this; I am different on the inside." Her mother asked her what she felt she did look like and she replied: "I can't tell you, because you'd be frightened."

Ann Andrews, author of 'Abducted', writes of her struggle to support her teenage son Jason, who she believes is a Star Child. She says: "His maturity, wisdom and abilities are bewildering and I often feel out of my depth in trying to understand what he tells me. Jason regularly has conscious out of body experiences (OBEs) and says that he astral travels to do healing." This has been confirmed, because Ann has received correspondence from people around the world who have had 'visits' from Jason. Ann says that Jason expands on the subject of Star Children by saying: "The ETs choose the parents, not the children. The children are genetically altered before they are born, they are given ET DNA."

Ann believes the description of 'Star Child' certainly fits Jason as he often com plains of the 'bulkiness' of his body, saying how limited it is. "He talks way beyond my comprehension and gets angry with me when I don't understand. He is often very tight-lipped about his experiences and the reason for this is, he says, because it is hard to know whom to trust '*as you don't know who they are working for.*' I thought this was stretching things a bit far, but he was serious when he asked me if I didn't think it was strange that after so many hundreds of years of slow progress, we had suddenly come on in 'leaps and bounds' in the last fifty years. According to him, *they,* the ETs –

and he includes himself here, gave us the knowledge. They showed us how to split the atom and harness nuclear fuel so that we may finally meet them as equals. However, angrily he said that we turned all this knowledge into power over others less fortunate, for example with the atomic bomb." Ann says Jason is exasperated with how little 'we' know. He demonstrates this with the example that when she was learning a spiritual healing technique called 'Reiki', he said it was rather primitive and he could show her a much better way!

The understanding of energy and healing with the Star Children is further demonstrated by a story from one experiencer and their eleven-year-old son. She said he had been ill for several days, but when he was lying in bed she saw him staring intensely at the ceiling. She asked him what he was looking at, he replied: "My blue energy body, I can see where the blocks are, which ones are making me sick, but don't worry, in a few days I will be well again."

All these extraordinary children have Contact experiences. So how can you tell if your child is one of the new kids on the block? From various accounts I have received, I think that the clues can be present in the child even as a small baby. The parents usually notice unusual events or anomalies. For example, Anne Andrews says that Jason was only a few months old when she would put him in the cot and later find him lying under it, or at the end of it, despite him being far too young to do this for himself. But she never linked these bizarre events to Contact experiences, not until much later on when she understood more about it.

Another account I received was from a woman who said that her daughter (who was just 18 months old) went to the bookcase and, undaunted by the array of books, deliberately picked out the book 'Communion', by Whitley Strieber. She pointed to the grey being on the front cover and said: "Mummy, that's the man that comes and gets me."

The 'clues' as to these differences will usually continue as the child grows up. I received a letter from a lady called Louise, who was still struggling with her own Contact experiences, when she became very concerned because she felt that her son was having them too. She documented her son's experience and his *dreams* over several months because they were so unusual. What follows, I think, is very interesting. Her letter is a good illustration of how children can be affected by their experiences. It is also interesting to see how the 'aware' mother has coped with this situation.

Dear Mary,

My main concern in writing to you is not about me, but about my son Aiden. I am looking for someone that will listen and understand, but have only found this in psychics and they offer no real support, although in some ways they have helped. But with regards to explaining what they think my son may be seeing, it's like they think I'm crazy, or a 'few sandwiches short of a picnic', but I'm not. Please believe me when I say I am not filling his head with stuff, but rather, it's *him* telling *me* things. Because of what he says he sees, I bought a book about these phenomena to try and find some answers for myself. I won't go into details, but my little boy is four and a half years old, and yes, he does have a vivid imagination. But he does do and say things that, to me, he could not have picked up anywhere else. He knows what I am thinking, he finishes my sentences for me and he feels pain when I do. Lately he's talking about 'baddies' that steal him. He's worrying the hell out of me. I try to make light of it and support him at the same time, but he insists it's true. I believe him. I have a lot of things I need to ask you, and want to know, *are you sure it's really happening to me?*

It's important, because of my son. He is very blasé about it and also says that he will introduce *them* to me one day. Sometimes he acts like it never happens and I wonder if he's making it all up. As I told you before, I don't feed him information or hassle him and I wonder if I should pursue it any further, as I don't want his upbringing to be too unordinary and unsettling, (although as I say this, out of the two of us, he is the sanest at the moment)!

Please find enclosed my version of Aiden's *dreams* and the little things he says. Aiden is very 'matter of fact' about it all and I have had to tell him that not all his friends may see what he sees. This is unusual for him, but still he tends to talk to me about it instinctively. I'm a little alone and unsure about all this and not sure whether to talk to anyone else, or to just carry on as if nothing has been, is, or will happen. I realise I am one among many, but I would rather be educated than ignorant, for my child's sake. Otherwise I would probably just ignore the issue, out of fear."

Here are some of the instances Louise wrote about:

27/8/98

Aiden came into my bedroom this morning and told me he had seen two short ghosts in his bedroom with blonde hair, blue eyes, small ears, normal mouth and nice nose, *like yours Mummy*. At that time I was not in any mindset at all about ETs and I did not assume it was anything like that, nor do I quite believe it now!

16/11/98

Aiden sat next to me while I read a book and I asked him to "Shhh!" After a silence, out of the blue he said:

"I had a dream last night about a ghost."

I said: "Oh yes, what kind?" without looking up and trying to keep my response as normal as possible.

"Just a ghost," he said.

"What colour hair?" I asked nonchalantly.

"Red," he said. It also had a big smile, but he was unclear about the colour and shape of the eyes. He said it was happy.

"Was it a boy or a girl?" I asked, turning to listen to him because he obviously wanted to tell me about it and I knew that if it were his imagination he wouldn't have volunteered it in this open and honest way.

"Both," he said.

"You sure?"

"Yeah," he was definite.

"Both boy and a girl." I could tell it wasn't one of his *snecrets,* which is his word - he combines secrets with sneaky.

This description was similar to someone who came through to me during one of my meditations, who appeared androgynous. I saw them with red hair and deep green eyes, with no whites.

24/11/98

Today Aiden had his last DTP injection, (Diphtheria, Typhoid and Polio) and because he has bad reactions to them he was extremely groggy, as if he was drunk. He was also in some pain from localised swelling. He said to me, totally out of the blue: "You know ghosts? Can you see them? I don't see them, maybe just one, but I do feel them? See . . . here he comes now." He was looking through to his bedroom where he says he usually sees them. "Here comes the light . . . I feel them Mummy, not see them. They say: *don't hit them in the face, just the tail (bum). They don't like it."*

I laughed at this point as *that* was a big sign for me. One night, about a month before, when I had seen one of these beings, (after it had pulled me out of my body during sleep), I took a swing at it and my hand went straight through its head. I had dismissed this episode as a dream. I also sometimes tell 'spirit' to kick me in the arse if I need it!

Then Aiden said: "They are fantastic you know mum, really great, you should meet them. Maybe I show you them one day!"

I asked him what they looked like. The one I had taken a swing at looked like a *Teletubbie*, so I asked him if they looked like *Telletubbies*. He said: "Naw, aw *yes* . . . some are like *Telletubbies* yes. I show you them in the morning. I sink *(think)* they are hiding now . . . they hide." (as per children's series the Tellitubbies on Television).

I hadn't told Aiden about my dream. His description was totally independent of any knowledge I had of them. I had seen them before, just about the time I met his father, but I kept it to myself. Also, when Aiden is sick he doesn't go into detail like this and because I know him, if he was just dreaming, it wouldn't have made so much sense to me. He was definite in his attitude. He was groggy, but he knew what he was talking about.

Often when he wakes up he will tell me that he'd like to introduce them to me and that they wouldn't hurt me. These are strange things for a child of just turned four to say. To be able to associate the 'light' coming towards him and that he 'feels' them, this astounds me for a child of his age. That it would be something that coincided with my *dream,* something that he had no knowledge of, is quite remarkable.

9/2/99

Aiden was at pains to let me know, or to get me to help him stop seeing 'baddies'. There were two tall ones, he said, both with red eyes and they would get mad at him. But there were smaller ones, ones that came through the wall behind his bookcase, he said they were nice. He said that there are lots and lots of them and lately he says that these smaller, nice ones make the black ones go away.

12/2/99

Aiden woke up saying that he'd had a bad dream, that he'd had the 'aliens' dream. In it, they made him big and that his Daddy and I were there. We didn't stop them. He wanted to know why? He believed I knew, saw and heard everything, as I was in his dream. He said that he was bigger, not taller and that he liked going through walls. He said that later there was 'bad' music playing and that he was frightened by this song. He mentioned the tall, dark aliens grabbing him and hurting him. They hurt his shoulders where they grabbed him and then did something in his tummy, they also stuck their fingers in his ears. His third eye area hurts (the space between the eyes in the centre of the forehead, where we 'see' clairvoyantly).

21/4/99

Aiden says that the *Teletubbie* ones are the good ones who protect him from the baddies. He says he sees lots of these and they play with him and teach him things. There are only two of the tall black ones with red eyes, which I believe he thinks are baddies. He says he sees lots of angels and smaller ones, like *Tinkerbell*. They come to protect him and all he has to do is call for them. He sees them outside and in every room. Now he even sees them at both sets of grandparents' homes and lately they are even at school with him, but apparently they stay outside and look in through the window. He says that they hide and wait until dark, until he is asleep. But sometimes he says that they are even with me!

He seems honest and sincere and I can't see how anything could prompt such detail and the way he tells me all this, it's with knowledge, not imagination. It's like he has this look of trust, as if he is imparting some important information and that I will understand enough to know. A mother knows where it's coming from and his face shows honesty. He says it all with such confidence and 'off the cuff' eloquence. I'm sure if he was making all this up it wouldn't come out so quickly and it would sound more rehearsed, or with more pauses, or thinking spaces in between. Also, added to this is the fact that I know more about what I have seen before and he just fills in the blanks for me and it all seems to fit together perfectly, like a validation. I experienced the *Teletubbie* ones before, when I was single and not pregnant (I think) with Aiden. I did a drawing of what I saw and showed it to him to see how he would react. He said: "Yes Mummy, those are the ones I see. They are great you know . . . so funny."

12/5/99

Woke up at 5.45. Aiden was awake again too. Surprisingly, out of the blue, I though to myself *they have been*. I stretched and put my hands inside the tops of my leggings to keep them warm and felt a scab in the centre of my lower abdomen, just below my navel. It was a clean, round scab, not jagged, about the size of a mole. Just as I discovered it, Aiden said he'd had a nice dream. He said he and I were flying out of a castle, a small, grey castle. He was not sure how we flew and I was wearing my black clothes. This sounded like a dream I'd had not long before. It was about a castle and overhead I'd seen a 'mother ship' . It was the first time I'd had the feeling that *they* had been. I have dreamt of a castle twice again since then.

4/7/99

Aiden is sick with the flu and tonsillitis. He said to me, groggily: "I didn't want to go in the spaceship." I asked him when this had happened and he said: "Last night. I went with you Mummy. I didn't want to go." I asked him which 'ghosts' took us and he said it was the small ones. His third-eye chakra was hurting (energy centre in the forehead), maybe from the flu, I don't know.

28/8/99

Today, Aiden is sick and I kept him at home. He was chattering about his ghosts in the bedroom, the ones that were like the Teletubbies. He said they float, not walk, and that they talk to him all the time. Aiden has a knack of answering my questions before I ask them and this morning he told me what he wanted for his lunch, which was exactly what I was about to suggest. I find this happens so much it becomes the norm'. He is very empathic to other people's feelings and he seems to have a subtle understanding of things that are amazing for a five-year-old. The fact that he gives me details of the aliens in such a matter-of-fact way has actually made it easier for me to cope with the concept.

I still have my doubts about their intentions, but can see he is unharmed and somehow I can accept it now as being a part of our everyday life. He doesn't seem traumatised and if he talks about the scary ones, he doesn't appear to worry too much. He understands that they are only scary looking and not necessarily evil. He tells me that some follow him around and protect him from the bad ones. They come through walls and can become invisible when needs be.

When they visit him, he says that they teach him things, more than he learns at school. I have asked him a few leading questions, but the information he usually gives me and the way in which he describes it, can, in no way be just his imagination because some of his information coincides with similar things I have dreamt and seen and even read.

For example, I was reading "The Custodians" by Dolores Cannon, hoping it would shed some light on this particular being that I had seen. Aiden was apparently seeing the same one I was at the same time; he described to me similar characteristics that only an adult reading this book would comprehend. It all seemed really synchronistic. For a child to say that *they* only come out at night, that they can come through walls and float not walk, that they can become invisible, but are still around us – all this astounds me.

It is something that I, as an adult, am only just reading about, it depicts the characteristics of ETs and yet, Aiden seems to have first-hand knowledge of it.

29/8/99

I woke up to a buzzing fly and found that Aiden was awake with *that* look on his face, the look that tells me he has just experienced something. It was a look of stunned silence, like he has had a bad dream that was somehow real, but had left him too stunned to move, even to wake me up. He would wake me up if he'd been having a *normal* nightmare, but when this happens he seems to just lie there frozen, as if he is trying to fathom out what's just happened to him. On this occasion, he said that he'd had a bad dream. That in it, there was a bad space ship with people in jail and also a good space ship. There were children there of his age and some other kids there that were about year two (seven years old). He said: "There were millions of *Teletubbies*, and some were bigger and some were little. We had already learned how to fly, but were practising not to go over the edge."

He explained that to learn how to fly properly, as a test of skill you have to not go over the edge. "We had rockets on our backs," he said, "but some weren't working. Mine wasn't working. Some big kids got out of their seats really well too." I think he meant that they took off from their seats.

"They come in their space ship to earth from their home. They were teaching us to shoot other aliens with laser guns. The light went through their tummies and faces," he indicated the forehead. "Some aliens look like us. There are blue ones too, like the one I had seen in my mind's eye. We had to put our head down when flying so that the fire under the blast-off didn't burn us. We had glasses on."

I asked him if the rockets helped him to fly. In an indignant tone he said: "*No,* I already know how to fly!"

This was a very involved episode for him and he also mentioned a lady who was there with him. She had blonde hair and blue eyes, although he didn't seem so definite about her eyes. It turns out, according to Aiden, that it was the mother of one of his school friends and that his friend was there too.

This whole episode was said without hesitation. Aiden related it to me in great detail, uninterrupted, he was describing directly what was in his mind's eye.

12/9/99

Aiden woke up scared and sad. He said he'd had a dream about our dog. He dreamt she hadn't got out of the way quick enough and he had accidentally stood on her face. As he did this, she jumped back up and her face changed into a clown's, on top of her body - so it was half her face and half a clown's. It had long, red hair hanging down, with a fringe. He was puzzled and shaken and it seemed to be one of *those dreams*. He kept saying over and over that he wished he knew how this face changed because he couldn't figure it out. It was a happy face, but he was obviously freaked out at how it had happened.

I mention this as I'd had profound dream years ago regarding a clown. When I had stood up to it (because it scared me), it turned into a tall, ordinary man, with no hair. He was sitting in front of a warm ball of gold/white light and beckoned me to him. I flew up and around and landed under his outstretched left arm and I experienced the most unconditional love I have ever felt. I read that sometimes *they* show themselves as owls, clowns or maybe as dogs? So when Aiden said this, it rang true with me and it unwittingly verified yet again, that he was experiencing something similar to what I had experienced in the past and since forgotten about. My dreams and memories (and they all seem like dreams and not experiences), are very similar to Aiden's, but his are independent to mine; I have never divulged any of this to him.

20/9/99

Aiden was sick yet again, (with tonsillitis this time) and in his sleep he muttered something about *Teletubbies*. I thought no more about it until he woke up in the wee hours of the morning. He said he'd had a worrying dream. That he had shut our dog in the laundry cupboard and that she had jumped out before he'd closed the door. The scary part was that her face was half her's and half a male clown's, with long, red hair. Apparently it had a stunned look on its face and Aiden was scared because the clown's face mutated into the dog's body. He said he didn't know how it did it, but it just changed. He touched the red hair and it was scary too, but it had felt like cloth. He said it felt nice.

I reviewed many accounts from Louise, all written and documented like a diary. I think they portray good examples of how a young child with Contact experiences explains and copes with them. It is also interesting to note that Aiden, a bright, intuitive child, was extremely articulate and specific in his explanations and he seems reasonably comfortable with these experiences, far more than his mother. I have found that often, this can be the case and fortunately, in this instance, due to the honouring and intuitive understanding of his mother, Aiden seems to be very well balanced and able to cope with it.

It may be argued that some of his experiences happened around a time when he was unwell and that his physical condition could have influenced what he thought he was seeing. Louise responds to this, she says that even though he was ill sometimes, he was still quite lucid and very specific. "When he is very poorly, he doesn't go into detail," she says. "Furthermore, I do know the difference between his fantasies and his experiences."

The details in which he explores these experiences adds validity and I feel that I must mention, I only included some of this - there was quite a lot more that I could have put in. So, given the understanding that these encounters are related to us within the context of a four-to-five year old child, there is a lot of specific detail in his descriptions.

Elle also talks about how she coped with her daughter Jena when she was only eight years old. They were busy together; Elle was helping Jena with her homework one night, when they had, what appeared to be a Contact experience. Elle wrote the following account:

Suddenly, I felt an enormously commanding energy, a presence in the room. Feeling significantly dizzy, I looked at Jena. She had her head down and was busily writing out the spelling words I had given her to complete. Then I noticed that Jena had stopped her work again and raised her head, staring motionless ahead of her. *Mummy* she said, *I think the aliens are here.* I realised then that she was picking up the energy presence too.

Gently, I enquired: "How do you know?"

Jena said: "I just know." I knew on an intuitive level that she was confirming my feelings. The presence I was sensing was Et in feeling, there was no doubt. I couldn't dismiss this, I could do nothing but support her, and I couldn't deny this reality.

"Yes, I can feel something too," I said, in a very matter of fact voice. I smiled, then turned to the area in front of us and spoke out loud. I said: "Okay then, we know you are here and we're not afraid. Your energy is very strong to us and it would help us to cope better if you could move back and give us some room please."

I looked across at Jena and gave her a reassuring smile again and told her it was all okay. She looked down at her work and continued with her revision. I knew that because I had remained calm and because I had supported and honoured her feelings, I had been able to normalise this experience for her.

Elle said that after she had done this, Jena was fine all that evening and went to bed that night with no residual fear or anxiety.

Coping with Higher Sense Abilities (HSA)

It is recognised by researchers and therapists that children who have these kinds of experiences are often very intuitive and psychic. Whether this ability comes directly from ET Contact, or whether being psychic facilitates the Contact experiences in some way, is open to debate. Certainly many individuals have said that they feel their psychic abilities are enhanced by Contact and children with these experiences do seem to be more aware of non-physical reality. They can often perceive nonphysical beings (or 'spirits') and can feel quite comfortable about them being there, and are able to communicate with them. They may see them as being loving and protective and they often interpret them as being their guardian angel or 'spirit guide'.

Adults and children with Contact have told me that they can see and often feel ET energy, which they perceive to be different from spirit energy.

It is important to remember that even if you cannot personally perceive this nonphysical reality, it is very real to those that can. People who see, or feel the energy field of a person, or a spirit presence, are known as clairvoyant or clairaudient.

Teenage Contact

I met Chloe when she was attending my meditation classes. As Chloe was becoming more aware of her intuitive side, it was becoming increasingly obvious to her that she was having Contact experiences. But what concerned her the most was that she felt her daughter Miranda was having them too. Miranda was only 13 at the time and Chloe was naturally very confused and concerned for her. Chloe said that it all became evident to her, after Miranda had told her that she could 'see' clairvoyantly, was aware of spirit presences and had received information. Previously to this, Chloe had never suspected anything unusual in her daughter. She was experiencing strange things herself, which she was finding difficult to deal with, then to learn that Miranda was also seeing peculiar non-human beings was terrifying for her, as she had not had time to come to terms with her own Contact experiences. Surprisingly, Miranda had no fear, just extreme curiosity, as this account of her conscious experience graphically demonstrates. Miranda had told me that she always enjoyed writing in her diary and had written about her first Contact experience immediately after it had happened. Miranda was only 13 at the time, she wrote:

Lying in bed (just had an argument with Mum about talking to spirits), when what I thought was a human spirit popped up in front of me. Its energy was of a high level, so I decided to see if I could feel it on my foot. Mum looked at me weird, so I told her *it* was there. Who is it? Because I want to find out about these aliens and stuff. As soon as I closed my eyes I saw a really funny shape. I studied it for a short time and then it suddenly popped into my head that this was an alien, (I like to call them ETs). I froze for a second. I didn't get the shivers, but a funny feeling inside my stomach. I was more stunned than frightened, (I hadn't told mum yet), I told my Mum that it was not a human shape and drew an outline of what it looked like.

Then Mum realised what it was. I closed my eyes and it said it was more connected to Mum, but later I realised that it was for both of us. I then asked if it could show me pictures of what it really was, (I was doubting). I saw a table on a circular platform in a circular room, all white, with some sort of door. I then saw a close-up of the top half of the table and someone human, it looked like a live person's inner-self (energy body) was lying on it. *It* didn't seem to know where it was, but I knew it was in an ET ship. No ETs were anywhere to be seen. That image faded and I was seeing what looked like big doors, (metal, and steel, whatever), some were different. Mum asked: "Who are you, what do you want?"

I received answers straight away, the ET was communicating telepathically with me.

"We are your friends" it said, directing that to Mum, because it had already made me realise that it was a friend. "We are here for love and hope."

My mum asked me to call in Forever Life. I have a spirit guide I call Forever Life, who guides and protects me. *He* said it was alright to be in Contact with the beings, but he stood back because I had to experience and get through it myself (with the help of Mum, of course). The ET stated that it was from Sirius. It left after I opened my eyes. Oh! It also said that it just wanted to make itself noticed, as in *I'm here, and I'm real.* After it left, it told me I am in Contact with them and that I can communicate with them telepathically, whenever I need them.

Also when I finished I went very teary and quite red in the face. I was really blown away.

Although this may seem strange to some, Miranda was used to perceiving and communicating with beings from the spirit world, so she was not traumatised by this experience at all, only curious. She was able to feel energy and it was not unusual for her to see spirits. She knew this experience was different, but she felt it was not threatening. The being was communicative and it gave her some interesting information and for her, it was really an object of curiosity. Miranda had felt quite safe because she believed in the protective abilities of her spirit guide, Forever Life. Miranda is such a mature young lady, but despite her years, her confidence in dealing with the non-physical is astounding. She was also fortunate she had such an open minded and aware mother, who accepted and honoured her experiences.

Because of this, Miranda was happy to talk about her Contact and often enjoyed writing about some of her more unusual experiences. Wisely, she told me she had decided not to share her experiences with her friends, as she was unsure how they would react and did not want them to feel uncomfortable. Not only a balanced and mature young lady, but also a normal teenager that did not want to stand out from her peers. She enjoyed music, dancing and performed in concerts, in fact, she did all the things that most young people of her age enjoy. The only difference (and it was a big difference), was that she was aware of the non-physical, could pick up information about people intuitively and had dialogue with spirit presences. It would be easy for some to label this as being an overactive imagination, but apart from the very unusual nature of the experiences, fantasy would not have made such a profound emotional and physical impact on her, e.g. "I was very teary and red in the face, I was really blown away."

What are the indicators for a Star Child?

Statistically, if you are an experiencer then it is very probably that one or more of your children may be having Contact. Contact is inter-generational, which means it continues through the genetic line and occurs within families, with no discrimination over age.

Some indicators are:

- Children with memory gaps in their childhood. This can be a result of the trauma of Contact and Contact experiences are often blocked from a child's memory until they are ready and able to deal with them (if at all). However, memory gaps can also occur as a result of other traumatic life experiences.
- The basic pattern of Contact in children is similar to adults (see Chapter 2), such as night-time visitations or being taken during the day. The child may experience missing- time episodes, memory gaps or they may simply forget what happened altogether. They may have a vague recollection that something different or unusual has taken

place. They are often quite accepting of the experience however, as they have less 'programmed' conditioning from which judgement is influenced. The problem for a child comes when they try and vocalise their experiences, only to have them denied by members of their family.

- Unusual stories from your child. It is vital to be aware that children will often interpret experiences in their own way, through their own understanding. A child's imagination or fantasy will reflect what is seen in popular media programmes about spaceships and ETs, through television, cartoons, films or children's literature. And children do not generally watch talk shows until they are much older. So if you find that your child has similar experiences to you and they are quite unlike anything they may have seen, or read then this is another indicator of their Contact.

- In his book "The Uninvited" Nick Pope, author, researcher and ex-Ministry of Defence in the UK said: "Some children may interpret their Contact with beings as religious figures, such as Jesus, some even saw them as Father Christmas. This may be because this was the child's only frame of reference for their experiences." Children can also see ETs as clowns, cats, owls, horses, wolves, dogs and insects (such as spiders). They will often mention the fear of large eyes. One of my client's daughters called an ET Grey a *little grey mouse.*

- Children will also talk about their experiences with fluency and consistency. There is the appropriate puzzlement and curiosity that any unusual experience may evoke, but because, unlike the adult, the child is not hampered by what is 'okay' or 'not okay', they are able to say how it really is for them. This makes the Contact experience all the more valid and believable. A child's report of their encounter is more often than not likely to be true to their experiences, even though they have a limited range of vocabulary in which to relate it.

Elle told me of another conscious experience with her daughter Jena, who was seven years old at the time:

Jena said to me: "Mummy, the aliens are back."

"Are they?" I asked, in a light-hearted way,

"It's not funny" she replied.

"I know it isn't", I said, more seriously. "Which ones do you feel are here?"

Jena paused, staring ahead of her and then said: "The dragon ones."

"Why do you think they are here?"

"They're not hear for me. They took me to their planet once, in their spaceship. They can go, just go anywhere they want to go, you know. All they have to do is just go and they appear there."

Later, Jena described what they did with her. "They thought I was a frying pan", she said. "They were poking their forks and knives into me."

Elle said that when she heard this she immediately thought of surgical procedures as seen through a child's eyes.

- Strange comments by your child about their experiences, which do not fit with what your child, should know as being normal. For example, Elle mentions an incident where her daughter woke up to tell her about a dream she had about alien hospitals. Her daughter, an extremely bright, young lady said: "I had a dream about alien hospitals...it was so funny, because there were no toilets!" Interestingly, another child of seven, whose mother came to my support group made this same comment.

If you think that your child may be one of the new kids on the block, or undergoing some Contact, and then use the following for easy guidance and reference:

Their Feelings. .

- Very spiritual, often drawn to universal spirituality.
- Claim to feel different to parents and siblings.
- Feel that no one is the same as they are.
- Feel a sense of mission or purpose.
- Feel that their body is too heavy, bulky or dense.
- Feel very connected to all living things.
- Passionate about the planet and environment and will react very strongly to killing, even if it's a fly or ant, etc.
- Strong impulses to draw unusual pictures, symbols or scripts.
- Feel the impulse to draw beings they feel they have seen.
- Feel the impulse to speak in a strange language that feels very familiar to them on some level.
- Feel as if they are constantly being watched or observed.

- Feel that they have been touched when resting or sleeping by something that could be described as being non-human.
- Feel that they are sharing experiences, or sharing consciousness with another.
- Feel they are visiting other planets, planes, existences or realities.
- Feel that they are being given information telepathically, (e.g. in the mind, or by thought).
- Feel that they may have objects implanted within their body.
- Feel they can hear other peoples' thoughts.
- Feel drawn to travel to remote places.
- Feel that their body or mind has been altered in some way.

Physical . . .

- Unexplained marks on the body, scars that cannot be explained.
- Nosebleeds (a typical place for implants, see the chapter on implants later in the book).
- Unusual small lumps felt behind ears, legs, wrists and back of the neck.
- Sore eyes (some implants can cause irritation to the eyes).
- Bruises, scratches, rashes or soreness in various parts of the body.
- Very sensitive to pollutants, suffer from allergies.
- Refuse to eat meat products and are drawn to a vegetarian diet at a very early age.
- Bed wetting that goes on to a later age than is usual. High proportions of children with Contact experiences suffer from enuresis (bed-wetting) and this can be up to seven to nine years old. It is difficult to determine if this condition is due to Contact experiences, or some other cause.
- Wake up feeling tired and lethargic in the mornings.
- Do not like crowds of people.
- Irregular sleeping patterns.
- Experiencing 'extra' or missing-time episodes.
- Acute or very sensitive hearing.

Awareness, Psi Abilities . . .

- Perceive energy in their hands or around people.
- Aware of, or can see colours around people (the aura).
- Dreams where they feel they have been attending an unusual school.

- Out of body experiences, aware of having 'floating' dreams.
- Talk about going through solid objects whilst in a dream.
- Aware of past lives, either as a human, or extraterrestrial.
- Aware of a 'dual' reality or dual consciousness.
- Knowledge of spiritual, scientific, or other unusual information that they have not consciously learned.
- Awareness of events before they have actually happened.
- Can be aware that they can affect electronic equipment such as being able to turn lights on and off with thought. Many experiencers know they can do this with streetlights, for example.

Anomalous Phenomena . . .

- Drawing unusual symbols, or strange landscapes, or people.
- Talk about another 'eye' or an extra eye that gives them added information.
- Talk about energy surges within their body.
- Have unusual psychic activity, such as strange lights, or paranormal phenomena happening around them.
- They may go missing for a time, but do not remember where they have been. (Some kids have even gone missing from a school playground and have been chastised for it, but have no recollection of having gone anywhere. One child was even found outside the house at night, with all the doors locked from the inside).
- Clothing missing, or changed around, without the child having any recollection of moving it..
- The child says they see or feel energy and will talk about colours around people.
- They will often know, or sense what you are thinking.
- Imaginary friends that they say visit them, especially at night.
- The child may be unusually intuitive or psychic and have advanced development in that they may walk, speak, or learn to read earlier than average.
- They are very intelligent.
- Very sensitive.
- Extremely creative.
- Appear to have information that is unusual for their age and education.
- They can have difficulties fitting in at school.

- They are unable to wear a watch, (because the watch will break, stop, lose time, or they will lose them).
- Electronic equipment breaks down frequently around them.
- Your child may be diagnosed as ADD or ADHD (Attention Deficit Disorder, or Attention Deficit Hyperactive Disorder).
- See orbs and 'beings' around them, such as 'shadow beings.'

A proportion of experiencers have had their children diagnosed as being ADD or ADHD and this is relevant given how different the Star Kids are.

One young woman explained to me that some of the difficulties she experienced as a child was with her perception of reality. She said she was born without any understanding of what 'solid' was and initially she just perceived things as being energy. She struggled to understand when she was told an object was solid and had to learn what solid meant. Also, she did not understand the human concept of time being linear. She understood time, from a metaphysical perspective, how everything is all in the 'now'. She said: *"They* do get frustrated by how slow things are here, how long things take to do."* With her awareness of creativity being more instant, she said she just knew things, information was just there for her and it was all there without her having consciously learned it. So it was very hard for her to cope with the complicated and slow process of human learning.

If these different perceptions apply to Star Kids, then these children would indeed experience conflict between human reality and their own and it could explain perhaps, why many families with Contact have children who are diagnosed with ADD or ADHD. As my research began to lean towards this, I wrote to Richard Boylan and asked him if he had found any similar links. He replied:

"Some seem to think there is an ADD or ADHD disorder in Star Kids. What I think is the case, is that Star Kids are crushingly bored by regular school and other 'pedestrian' information presentations and they seem distracted. Their wandering attention is a result of their boredom."

I am inclined to concur given that these children are highly intelligent and many comment that they find our regular education does not stimulate them. And it seems that certainly some of the ADHD children perceive reality in a completely different way we have yet to understand and quantify.

Some fears that the child may have . . .

- Fear of the dark, this often continues into adulthood.
- Uncomfortable or fearful of sleeping near a window (they often say they see the ETs coming through them).

- Fear of clowns, cats, owls, spiders. The ETs try to appear as something more recognisable or normal to a person, this is called 'screen memory'.
- The child may follow you everywhere, feelings of insecurity because they feel they are being observed.
- Nightmares, then mention strange beings.
- Feeling paralysed at night.
- The need to search the house for 'monsters' they may think are hiding in the closet.
- The child is withdrawn and sensitive.
- Insomnia or unusual sleeping patterns.

How can I help my Star Child?

Listen to them! One of the most important ways you can help your child is by honouring their experiences and listening to them. Allow them to explore their experience in whatever way is useful and positive. It is only when you try to deny their experiences that the child will doubt themselves and their perceptions.

"As a child I knew what I saw and felt, but my parents would say what I saw wasn't real...which affects your life as an adult. It's like, I see it, but I don't' believe it, so your judgement is impaired."

Julia

Parents constantly ask me how can they best help their Star Child. Awareness and coming to terms with the fact that your child is having Contact is one of the most difficult issues a parent has to cope with. One of our most human needs as a parent is to be able to protect our children from any perceived threat or harm. This issue can leave the parents with feelings of anger as well as helplessness. Some parents say that it is far harder to live with the possibility of their child having Contact experiences than in dealing with their own. There is one account, where a mother was so afraid of the effects that regular Contact could be having on her young child, she actually communicated this to *them* telepathically and said that she wanted her child to be given a break. This request appeared to be respected and her child was left without Contact for quite some time afterwards.

What is most helpful for the parent, as well as the child, is to be as informed as possible. The more you understand about your own experiences, the more able you are to support your own child and yourself.

This is especially important if you are still very fearful about it, as your fear will be inevitably passed onto your child.

Remember to answer any questions they may have as simply and as positively as you can and try and explain things to them in a language that is appropriate for their age.

Tell them enough to satisfy their curiosity at the time, but say no more than you need to. In addition, if you have an older child having these experiences also, then it can be helpful sometimes if they talk to the younger one about it. We assume here that the older child is able to do this. Remember that at all times it is very unhelpful to communicate fear to any of your children. Instead, tell them that whatever happens, they are always brought back, remind them that they always wake up safe. Keep it simple and always answer directly and honestly and if you really don't know the answer, then say so. If your child does not appear to be distressed, then it is unhelpful to give them information that they would perceive as being confusing or frightening, just for the sake of giving them information. It would be far more useful to help them to find different coping strategies within themselves to help them rise above any fears. If however, you are unsure of what to say, discuss it first with your partner, or a friend who knows about this and preferably one who has children too.

If you remember having childhood experiences, then, (depending on the age of your child), it may help to talk to them about yours, reminding them that you are still in once piece! By doing this, you are normalising their experiences as much as possible for them. If you are fearful yourself, then you may communicate this to your child, so be careful. If they are okay with this experience, then you should try to be too, making them fearful will not help them. So if you find it difficult to explain anything, then I advise that you seek some professional support and as mentioned previously, try to access other experiencers. They may be parents who have a Star Child of their own and you can all arrange to meet up and talk.

Honesty is always the best policy. Also, remember that these children do seem to have access to knowledge and wisdom far beyond their years and may not have the same fears or conflicts that you may have. By honouring their awareness and understanding, you are helping them to cope in a healthy and positive way, allowing them to achieve their potential. Children have access to inner resources naturally. The more that you encourage them to have confidence in their inner wisdom and their reality, the better chance they have to cope with their Contact in a balanced and healthy way.

As Elle says so eloquently: "Jena is as much a teacher to me, as I am to her."

How much you say may depend on how much they remember of their experience. They may have very little recall and may only remember them as being vague dreams. If they don't seem upset, or traumatised in any way, then I recommend that you don't say anything to them until they raise it with you.

How can you help your child cope with fear?

Chapter 5 lists many strategies to help combat fear, which can be utilised also for your children. Fear is contagious and it's important to realise that if you are very fearful of this experience yourself, then your fear may well be transmitted (albeit unwittingly) to your child. We also know that fear can be generated by other sources, such as media, television and books.

A mother of a seven-year-old Star Child told me that her daughter had been fine with her Contact experiences until she saw the negative portrayals of ETs on television, then she became extremely fearful. Many individuals have become fearful of Contact, by watching television and being subjected to the media portrayal of this phenomenon. A child has no way of knowing, or of judging what is useful or harmful, so it is important to monitor this information as you would with extreme violence or pornography.

Fear is catching, and it is demonstrated graphically by the following account by Daniel, who was eleven at the time. He had been seeing the Grey ETs for a number of years. One of the beings in particular, he liked and he felt safe with it. He even had a nickname for him. But despite the familiarity, as time went on he became more and more terrified as night-time approached, which in turn impacted on his younger sister. She became equally frightened.

In desperation, the mother told me that it was becoming very difficult for her as both children wanted to leave every light on in the house, throughout the entire night. The mother had exhausted lots of different strategies, but it seemed that none of them worked anymore. I suggested a 'carrot' to encourage Daniel to face his fears, whereby he would receive a special star for every night he managed with fewer lights on. If he coped well, then as a reward at the end of the week he would get a special prize, or treat. Daniel's mother phoned the following week. The carrot tactic had worked well and Daniel had decided that he could manage with just one light on each night, to gain his star. Surprisingly, Daniel's sister managed this too, so it seems that with a little incentive, a fear can be faced head on and for some children, these kinds of strategies are vital.

"Often children have a strong, 'inner knowing' about how to cope, which can be encouraged", says Ms Truncale, in the book "Alien Discussions".

She also cites from her case studies that some children who expressed fear and reluctance to go with the beings, said that the beings left because of this and without taking them with them. It seems that some children find that they can say *no* to some of their Contact experiences.

Are all children traumatised by their Contact?

Many children are unaware of their Contact and research suggests that some children have little or no memory of their experiences until later on in life. In the 'classic' pattern, there are memory gaps in their childhood, which could be a protective mechanism there to prevent trauma. Some recall vague memories, they wonder about things and later comment they were surprised that they didn't investigate certain things further, at the time, because they were so bizarre. This is not a 'normal' response in itself, as most of us are curious and will explore the more unusual events in our life. But for those children who are aware of their Contact and are fearful, what else can you do to help them?

- Encourage them to talk about their experiences.
- Give them any strategy that will enable them to feel secure, (i.e. leaving some lights on, or having the room arranged in any way that will help them deal with this).
- If they trust in a religious figure, or object, then these can help them to feel more secure. Praying to some religious figure that they trust may help, or repeating some special words or mantras. Whatever the child believes in and is comfortable with.
- If you feel really concerned, then look for a professional, a counsellor or therapist who will honour these kinds of experience and who the child can trust.
- If the child does discuss the experience with you, how you respond will be very important. Remind your child that despite what happens, they are always brought home, in one piece! Although it is hard to understand what is happening at this time, they are loved and will always be loved and supported by you.
- If your child is receptive, then get them to write a letter to the ETs to say how they feel and what they like or don't like. If the child wants to, get them to draw what happens and how they see it.

Where do *you* go for support?

As this phenomenon is not understood or known about by most of society, you will need to resource all the information you can for yourself. Be prepared that it may not be something you can share, even with close members of your family. You may need to resource outside help. You may find also that you are criticised by family, or friends for supporting your child by listening to their 'wild imaginings', or nightmares. Daniel's family experienced this situation and his uncle blamed Daniel's mother for his fears. He believed that by accepting the experiences, she was encouraging Daniel's fantasy, (he ignored the evidence of the physical marks Daniel had on his body). She had tried to inform her brother about the phenomenon, but he remained unconvinced. Ultimately, Daniel's mother decided that there was no point in trying to convince him anymore and resolved that it was a subject that was best avoided between them.

To try and prevent this from happening, refer back to Chapter 6, which covers emotional support. Remember to talk to:

- Supportive family members and friends
- A therapist/counsellor who understands this experience
- Join a support group, or start one up
- Become more informed.

Star Kids, the new kids on the block

There are many books that mention these special children and one is by an American author, Dana Redfield, who has published two books about her experiences. Her latest book is called "ET-Human Link, We Are the Message". In it she asks the question: "Are we ET-humans, or humans awakening?" Dana writes about the Golden Children, Smart Kids and Wonder Children.

Another researcher and author, Kenneth Ring suggests in his book "The Omega Project" that NDE (near death experiences) and abductee experiences are the forerunners of a new breed of humanity. He feels that the visions and experiences are the 'growing pains' of this new human, the 'Omega' person. British researcher and author of numerous books on the UFO phenomena, Jenny Randles, also says: "Omega People and Star Children are one and the same." Dr. Roger Leir is now conducting a research project on 'The New Human' and asking parents to write to him regarding their exceptional children. The book, "The Millennium Children" by Caryl Dennis (with Parker Whitman) also documents many stories of special children that demonstrate amazing psychic abilities, high intelligence and an awareness of other dimensions.

In his book "Mysteries in Mainland China", author Paul Dong also talks about some extraordinary human faculties (EHF) found in Chinese children. Also the book "China's Super Psychics" focuses on these unusual children and their amazing psychic abilities. James Twyman, author of "Emissary of Love, The Psychic Children Speak to the World", tells of the children he has met in Bulgaria, who demonstrate the most startling psychic powers and wisdom. They are 'secretly' kept in a monastery where they are being trained. They call themselves the "Children of Oz" and though many others say they live in different parts of the world and have no way of communicating with one another, they claim to be linked. They have the power to move objects with their minds and can read thoughts.

Scientifically, there seems to be evidence to support the hypotheses of the emergence of the 'new human'. Dr. Berrenda Fox (DR of psychology and naturopathy and holistic practitioner) says that there is evidence through blood tests to show amazing DNA and cellular changes and that some people have actually developed new strands of DNA. This was discussed a few years ago at a convention of geneticists from around the world in Mexico City, the main topic of interest being these DNA changes. We are talking about major changes, according to geneticists, mutations that haven't occurred, since the time we supposedly came out of the water.

There are many different names given to these new kids, new humans. Are they one and the same though and are they all part of a new evolutionary phase in humanity? Certainly research suggests there could be several different types of Star Children and these types may vary depending on what their place, or role is within society. Furthermore, many seem to think there is a special task involved, or that they are aware of some kind of mission. They are the sensitive, shy and creative people, such as Tracey Taylor, who seem to be using creativity to awaken us through art and symbolism. There are the 'spiritual warriors', the more challenging Star Kids, such as the young girl, Jena. But whatever this phenomenon is here to demonstrate, it appears that it is global and that incredible numbers of children could be involved.

What about the Star Schools?

"Mummy, I learn more on the ships than I do at school".

Aiden (age 5)

There are many accounts that suggest that the ET visitors are helping us with educating our new kids on the block. Experiencer/Author, Whitley Strieber describes how he attended a 'secret school' where he and others were taught many things, from spiritual concepts, to understanding about our universe. Certainly, there are testimonies that suggest this, we find these children know things they have not consciously learned at school. They have an awareness of their origins and multidimensionality and demonstrate through their awareness that they understand energy and can use it for healing, art, the writing of unusual scripts and symbology. Some, like Tracey Taylor express it creatively through art; others may use music, or other artistic/creative forms of expression.

They seem to have a form of telepathic communication and are able to receive information, which helps them to understand more. But the largest obstacle, the biggest fear comes from the 'old model human', the person who desperately fights to hold onto their limited awareness of reality and attempts to contain the new human, to 'trap' them within it.

Dana said to me in a letter: "I don't know how to tackle the 'fear of humans' aspect. Maybe it surfaces more as consciousness is expanded, then we realise how dangerous humans can be. Can we always speak the truth and be safe among people?"

The difficulty for the Star Kids stems from the limited understanding of the phenomenon itself. Until more research is completed and there is some kind of professional acknowledgment of the Contact phenomenon that can help to bring it into 'mainstream' awareness, people in general will continue to categorise, medicate and hospitalise what they don't understand. By holding only old, limited (conditioned and 'pre-programmed') systems of what is believed to be the *norm,* the public at large will not embrace anything that these children are showing us, which may do untold damage to their psyche in the process.

It is very possible that many of these Star Kids choose to take drugs, or alcohol, because they can't cope with the restricted and 'conditioned' version of what 'we' are told to believe makes up our reality. The fear of something or thinking you are crazy may make drug taking an attractive option for some, because it shuts it all down! In fact, several young experiencers have told me that taking drugs became a means for them to escape reality, because they had been terrified of what was happening to them and scared of what others may think and do.

Therefore, unconditional support for the children who are displaying this awareness is vital!

But we do have limited data, so what this all means is hard to quantify at the moment. Certainly present research suggests a reprogramming, not only of our genetic make-up, but regarding a more deliberate and continuous non-human, educational program, facilitating a 'super awareness', which up until recently would only be visible within a select few. But in order to research it properly, there has to be an acknowledgement first of all - something that says there is *the need* to do it. Like Dr. Leir and many others, I feel we could be witnessing a rapid evolution of the species on many levels of awareness. If this is indeed the case, then it is vital not only to recognise it, but to instigate programmes to assist our new kids, to help them integrate and grow healthily with the correct support, the kind that is being pioneered by such people as Richard Boylan, the members of ACCET in America, and Dr. Roger Leir himself.

Authors note: Revised 2010
Since writing *Awakening* in 2002, my research suggests that ADHD children may be having Contact experiences and some Autistic children may also have experienced interactions with the angelic realm and extraterrestrials. This also may be the case with Aspergers Syndrome.

CHAPTER TEN
The Missing Pregnancy Syndrome

This chapter explores one of the most controversial and confronting aspects of Contact, the 'missing pregnancy syndrome'. We will begin by looking at the traditional medical explanations and personal accounts and ask the questions, can medical interpretations account for the emotive stories of women, who believe that this has happened to them? Can it explain the numerous physical anomalies these women experience and can it explain how siblings and other family members become aware of these 'missing' children?

We shall illustrate this phenomenon further by including a personal, emotive story from Ann Andrews, a woman who experienced a 'missing pregnancy', who eventually became certain that her baby son had been taken by extraterrestrial beings. It is, without doubt, one of the most difficult and painful issues she has had to face in her life. Ann was fearful, but determined to find some answers; she was resolute in her quest to understand what had really happened. Travelling half way across the world to explore and uncover her hidden memories, she asks the question: "Why did you take my son?"

Firstly, what is the missing pregnancy syndrome? It is a phenomenon that is connected to Contact experiences, which affects a high percentage of women who believe they have been pregnant, (experiencing all the physical signs of pregnancy, e.g. positive pregnancy tests, ultrasound, recorded foetal heart beat, etc), but then discover that their pregnancy has 'disappeared' after a few weeks or months. This does initially suggest a normal miscarriage, but many women who experience this phenomenon often feel this explanation doesn't fit into what they have experienced, or how they feel.

Following their miscarriage, they say they experience disturbing dreams and flashbacks, which indicate that something more out of the ordinary has happened. They feel very emotional and they cannot understand why and furthermore, some of these women believe that they have been pregnant numerous times with the same thing happening to them.

Some women also feel pregnant, even though they may not have been in an intimate relationship with anyone. There are also cases when doctors have queried scar tissue on reproduction organs, which can only be explained by pregnancy, when the female in question has never even had a child. In all of these pregnancies, the foetus is missing. The medical profession will explain this by saying that the foetus is reabsorbed. But some of these women have a very different feeling, or perspective and some definitely believe that their child has been taken from them during the first few months of their pregnancy. Many say that it was taken during a Contact experience.

What are the medical explanations for missing pregnancy syndrome?

The most common are:

- *Blighted ovum*. The embryo degenerates, or is absent from the start of the pregnancy. Placental tissue is present (often in a degenerated form) and secretes the hormone Beta-HCG that is assessed in a urine test. Thus a positive test does not in and of itself mean that a foetus is, or was ever present.
- *Spontaneous abortion*, or miscarriage, is the natural termination of pregnancy before the embryo, or foetus is capable of extra-uterine life (generally 20 weeks gestation).If no foetus is found, then it is a 'blighted ovum'.
- *Missed abortion,* when a pregnancy dies, but is not aborted for some time afterwards and may remain in the uterus for as long as five months. It is sometimes unclear why a non-viable pregnancy is not spontaneously aborted.
- *Hydatidiform mole* (1 in 500 pregnancies). For unknown reasons a fertilised egg degenerates into a rapidly growing mass of grapelike tissue that secretes Beta-HCG. Thus there could be a positive pregnancy test and enlarged uterus, but a 'missing' foetus.
- *Secondary amenorrhoea.* A cessation of the menses for six months or more, due to multiple reasons other than pregnancy, i.e. stress or anorexia.
- *Pseudocyesis* (false pregnancy, 1 in 500 cases). The signs of pregnancy are there, but the uterus is small and there is a negative pregnancy test. The woman in question will assume the role of being a pregnant mother and is often bitterly disappointed when there is no child.

Given the above traditional explanations, does this mean that all missing pregnancies can be explained and are all of these women just experiencing a natural obstetric event? Is it possible that the claim of these missing pregnancies and miscarriages due to Contact experiences have a 'conventional' and 'natural' explanation?

There has been much written in UFO circles about the missing pregnancy syndrome and most clinicians, without knowledge of any other possible reason will naturally subscribe to one of the medical explanations. Therefore, it is very hard to obtain more tangible evidence. But there is substantial, emotive and anecdotal evidence that should not be dismissed.

Let's examine the testimonies from some women who know that they have been pregnant and have had their pregnancy confirmed (with the foetal heartbeat recorded), but subsequently experience a miscarriage, with no foetus.

A mother's awareness!

Elle became increasingly aware that she might have experienced missing pregnancy syndrome. In an effort to find out more about her Contact experiences, she went to see an open-minded psychiatrist who agreed to hypnotise her. The psychiatrist regressed Elle through hypnosis and back to a pregnancy in 1991. I was present at this session, purely as an observer.

Elle said: "I feel very sad, it's hard for me to think about it."

"Why, what happened?"

"They took it. They have told me they are going to take it, they have come into my bedroom. They take my baby girl, they take me onto the craft and take her from me, they say that she is chosen to be a part of a very important race that is being created, to assist everybody, this is all meant to be and she will be cared for and looked after and that she will grow up here with my other children."

Elle then went on to describe another pregnancy. She talks about the procedure of taking the foetus:

"There's like a very large beaker with liquid in it. There's a long tube, a long, clear tube and there is something at the end of it."

She continues, very emotionally: "Little, *little* being . . . they are putting it in the water, the fluid. It was a boy. Oh God. (*upset),* my little boy . . .*oh, oh . . .*"

Women who have experienced this missing pregnancy syndrome have also described this type of procedure. Elle mentions great love for her child and says that she was shown him several times. She describes him as being gentle, vulnerable, very psychic, and telepathic and that he had some physical differences to humans, such as only a little hair and different shaped eyes. Many women have given detailed descriptions of their child, as well as showing very emotional responses to them.

In her book "Abducted", Ann Andrews recounts that Jason, her second son, was aware of her having a child on the ship and talked to his psychiatrist about *the baby that never was.* In a letter to me, Ann said:

"Some months ago, Jason asked me what I would have called his baby brother. I felt a chill go through me, but quickly answered 'Nathan'. Jason told me of an experience he'd had where he said, he knew an 'abduction/Contact' was imminent, but he wasn't afraid. Then, a blinding light had greeted him. In his next recollection he was being escorted into a large room that was dimly lit, but warm. There were babies sitting all around on the floor. He felt they were about a year old as they could all sit upright and on their own.

The ones that were close to him, he said, were blonde haired, with large blue eyes. He thinks that the babies further away were bald, but that may be because he couldn't see them properly. He said it was exceptionally quiet, but they turned to look at him as he walked amongst them. He then noticed a door open on the other side of the room and an older child walked in. He was about ten years old and had the same features as the babies. Jason said he recognised him instantly . . . it was *Nathan*."

There are reports similar to this account, where a human child seems to have had the awareness of their siblings on the spacecraft. Elle also recalls a conversation she had with her seven-year-old daughter, Jena, who said: "Mummy, I had a dream last night that you had a baby. They took us to the hospital, but it was the wrong one. They took us up to the alien hospital."
"Why was it the wrong hospital?" asked Elle.
"Well, they took us *up* to the alien hospital. I didn't like it, they were trying to trick us and we weren't allowed to take the baby home."
Jena then described the ETs, she said: "They had oval shaped heads, yes, they were aliens. The aliens had big heads and little bodies. They had stick fingers. The baby was a boy, called Julian."
Several of my clients have told me about their own missing pregnancies. These women were extremely sincere about it and often highly emotional. Many found it very difficult to discuss it properly. Pregnancies had been confirmed, with foetal heartbeats recorded and I have been told of anomalies being exhibited, such as scars appearing on reproductive organs that should not have been there. This substantiates their 'inner awareness', that their child/foetus was taken. From the accounts I have heard, I will list some of the anomalies that have been brought to me:

- Pregnancies experienced by women who have *not* had sexual activity but recorded positive pregnancy results, some with foetal heartbeat. But later, inexplicably, the pregnancy disappears, with little evidence of it ever being there and no evidence of the foetus.

- Women who have never had a pregnancy have been told by gynaecologists that they have scar tissue in their reproductive organs, suggesting they may have been pregnant many times.
- Positive pregnancies have been confirmed with foetal heartbeat recorded. Then after a Contact experience the women discover that they had a miscarriage with little or no evidence of conception (e.g. no foetus). One lady following this kind of event said that she experienced trauma afterwards in the form of disturbing and strange dreams, flashbacks and a memory of 'something' being removed from her.
- Many women experience strong emotions and feelings of having had a child on a spacecraft. They may even have a sense of it visually, with images of their child. These feelings are often confirmed by one of their human children, who seem to have an awareness of them, as well as other members of the extended family.
- Many women dream of being shown a baby they feel is their child and will experience deep love and a sense of being connected to them.
- Many women say that the visual images they have of their child do not look quite human to them; they seem frailer, with unusual characteristics, but nevertheless they felt a real bond with them.
- One women in her early twenties monitored her ovulation dates for several months, and found that she had Contact experiences just when she was due to ovulate. She told me that she was celibate, but had felt absolutely certain that she was pregnant. A few weeks later this feeling went, but as it did, she experienced a deep sense of loss and grief. I have heard many similar accounts to this.
- Many women have said that they experience 'dreams' of being secured to tables and having their foetus removed. Some women will consciously remember the method of extraction of the foetus and they show increased agitation and emotional response as they tell of this experience.
- Women have described seeing rows of containers with foetuses in them.
- I have seen unexplained emotional trauma, such as Post Traumatic Stress Disorder (PTSD). One young woman was told by a therapist that she exhibited signs of being extremely traumatised from having an abortion. This puzzled her as she has never had an abortion. However, through regression, she discovered that she had a foetus

taken by ETs and this had been extremely traumatic for her, "I saw my son" she said.

Elle, for example, recalls being pregnant and having the pregnancy verified by a doctor, only to lose it in a miscarriage. Her daughter Jena, was only a small child at the time and was unaware of her mother's lost pregnancy, but subsequently cried out in distress and said, through her tears: "The baby's in the dark!"

Elle says: "The pregnancy was confirmed at about five weeks, but after that, through the next several weeks, I retained this strong intuitive feeling that I may not be able to keep this one! At eight weeks, I found a spot of blood and over the next few days a few more."

Following an ultrasound, the radiologist said that there was no baby after all. Confused, Elle asked him to explain this more and he said that the sac grows but the baby doesn't. Elle was aware that she had only seen blood and nothing else. However, Jena, her young daughter, had not been aware of the pregnancy at all. When Elle arrived home from hospital Jena began to cry: "Mummy, Mummy, the baby's in the dark, the baby's in the dark!" Elle knew intuitively that Jena knew about this pregnancy. So to ease her daughter's distress she opened up the package with the bassinet in it. Once Jena saw the bassinet, she asked her to place it under a spotlight in the lounge room and then put a torch in it as well, so that the baby was no longer in the dark.

Again, Elle's description of her son was very specific, even with his age (seven years). She says: "I can feel his energy, he likes me coming, he's so gentle. He's very clever and telepathic, he's learning all sorts of things, he's very psychic and he's able to use his mind. His eyes ... *his eyes* are more like *their* eyes. He doesn't have much hair, it's blonde, light blonde. He doesn't react in the same way that earth children do, he doesn't quite have the same emotion, but he knows it's me. He's quieter and gentler, he seems more vulnerable."

There is no doubt that there is much regarding the missing pregnancy phenomenon that cannot be explained through conventional means. But ultimately, if you think this may have happened to you, only you can decide whether the traditional explanations fit.

I can give you some basic indicators that may suggest a Contact pregnancy, decide for yourself if you feel they may apply in your case:

- Positive pregnancy tests, some with ultra sound records, especially if you are celibate at the time.
- Contact experiences at the time of ovulation.
- Contact where you see a foetus taken and/or placed in a capsule of liquid.
- Visions of rows of containers showing foetuses.
- A terminated pregnancy after having Contact experience. Being shown unusual, rather frail-looking children, one you may feel a bond with.
- Being encouraged to hold, or cuddle a child during a Contact experience.
- Having emotional feelings about the child, as you would if it were your own.
- Being told it is your child, but that it would not survive in an earth environment

On an important note, many women who think they have experienced a missing pregnancy have no desire to be pregnant at the time, so this does not fit within 'wish fulfilment'.

How do you cope with the feelings of grief and loss?

- Name the baby, even if you are unsure of the sex. Giving the baby an identity can help you in coming to terms with this experience.
- Talk to someone close to you who will be accepting of your feelings and who will listen.
- Write or talk to the baby. Tell it of your love for it and feelings of grief.
- If you are religious, or spiritual, you may want to pray for it, or ask the 'angelic realms' to look after it for you. Whatever fits within your belief system.
- Plant a special rose bush, or shrub for them in a particular part of the garden.
- There are many books available regarding loss and grief, giving good coping strategies, which you may find helpful.
- If you feel there are some unanswered questions then you can try regression therapy. We have an example of this in Ann's story below, when Ann used regression to help her access information about her own missing pregnancy.

Why did you take my son?

Ann Andrews and her family live in England but they visited Western Australia in November 2000. Ann came over, not only to see a beautiful part of the world, but to also meet some of the people she had connected with, through her book "Abducted". I was one of those people, along with the other members of ACERN. How this all came to pass is a fascinating story in itself, but especially in relation to Ann's personal experiences, including her missing pregnancy.

Ann had two sons, Daniel and Jason, when her GP confirmed her third pregnancy. A few months later, Ann had a Contact experience. When she woke up, she found that she was no longer pregnant. Initially this appeared to be a normal miscarriage, but as time went on, Ann began to have these very disturbing flashbacks and nightmares that hinted something quite different could have happened.

What these experiences suggested was devastating for her, both emotionally and psychologically. Consequently, Ann's feelings about extraterrestrials and their involvement with us became dramatically coloured. Her experiences left her feeling angry, abused and extremely negative. But when Ann finally explored her emotions through regression, the information she gained and understanding of her experiences radically changed what she initially believed had happened to her, and as a result, her feelings about ETs changed for the better.

I was the facilitator for Ann's regression and helped her come to terms with what really happened, not only with the discovery of how she had lost her child, but the reasons why it had happened and the truth about why her 'boy-child', the child she now calls Nathan was taken from her.

Ann knew that she had to confront her 'demons'. I realised that she was propelled to learn the truth when I first contacted her, after I had read her book "Abducted". The book is set in rural England and it's a tale of human/ET Contact, the sort that has encapsulated for me, some of the classic Contact stories I have heard many times over. Ann's family had to face a series of terrifying and bewildering events, which escalated for them once their second son, Jason was born.

Throughout the book, Ann conveys sincerity, and a gentle warmth, which is practical and unassuming. She makes you feel she has her feet planted very firmly on the ground and is certainly not someone prone to fantasy. This is also true of Paul, her 'down to earth' no-nonsense husband. They did all the normal things that a caring, but confused family would do when faced with bizarre experiences that are a way beyond normal understanding.

They sought help from several professionals in the hope that they could explain for them, the unexplainable.

Anne wanted to know why her son Jason, from being a very young child, was terrified at night time. He was constantly disturbed by unusual and frightening dreams. Then there were the strange paranormal phenomena and poltergeist activity they had around the house, with inexplicable and continual harassment from what appeared to be 'covert' government forces.

Ann's main concern throughout her book is centred on her son Jason. Ann co-authored this book with a professional writer, Jean Ritchie and it tells of Daniel, the eldest and Jason the second, who both had Contact experiences. Daniel's experiences seemed to be less confronting than Jason's and Jason, Ann said, was lucky to be born alive because she was given a very poor prognosis for him. The doctors warned her that her baby was not expected to live and it is still a mystery to her that Jason was born alive and perfectly healthy. From the beginning though, there were many strange happenings around Jason. Ann's book highlights many of the more unusual, but it particularly mentions the trauma and fear that were part of Jason's everyday life, from being a small child.

Over the years, desperation eventually led the family to seek a psychiatrist for Jason, one that was prepared to listen to him. But Jason was very disappointed as the psychiatrist made it plain that she was unable to accept the strange world that was his reality. Fortunately for Jason, the psychiatrist found no evidence of mental illness. However, Jason was frustrated that his experiences were still negated and he responded to this by depicting extreme behaviour that became increasingly aggressive and disruptive. Ann and Paul still had no idea of the reality or true nature of their son's experiences. They had no understanding or knowledge about ET Contact and so they were at a loss as to know what to do next.

By chance, the family were watching a television programme on hypnosis and this was to be the catalyst that opened the Andrews family up to the understanding and possibility of what Jason had been trying to tell them all along. During this programme, a man who was being hypnotised spontaneously revealed that he had experienced extraterrestrial Contact. When Jason saw this, he erupted with anger and said that this was what he'd been trying to tell them all along. This was an instrumental moment as it gave Ann and her husband Paul a clue to the possible reality of his experiences. Before this happened, Ann readily admitted that the idea of alien Contact was such a bizarre concept to them, that they would dismiss it instantly. They understandably assumed that Jason's experiences were no more than the product of his imagination. Now finally, they both knew that they should explore this further, for all their sakes.

With determination, and some anxiety, their search leads them to a well-known ufologist in the UK, Tony Dodd. Tony was a policeman who had witnessed several UFO sightings himself. He provided invaluable support for Ann and her family during the many months of uncovering and integrating the bizarre and confrontational fact that her son, was not only speaking the truth about his ET Contact, but that Contact was indeed a very real experience for their family and many millions of people around the world.

Ann learned that this Contact did not just affect Jason, but that Daniel, Paul and she were also involved. The confusing jigsaw pieces of their experiences individually and as a family were finally beginning to make some sense. The deeper Ann delved, the more challenges emerged for her. But such was the courage of this family, they decided to 'come out' and tell their story to provide a way of helping others who may be having similar experiences.

Ann suffered greatly because she felt that she had let Jason down by initially dismissing his experiences, as they were so beyond anything she could understand at the time. This guilt still haunts her and the book was another way for her to demonstrate to Jason her sorrow for not believing in him.

I came across a copy of Ann's book and discovered that much of what she had written about was very relevant to my work. I had a client at the time, called Sandra, who had described similar experiences, including the many visits to traditional mental health professionals, (see Chapter 4). Sandra was also in her teens when her family took her to see a psychiatrist. When she told him she saw aliens, this admission unfortunately had a less than positive outcome for her. Subsequently, she was diagnosed as being mentally ill. Although Jason didn't feel that he was being believed, he at least had no psychiatric labelling to contend with.

It was the similarities between Jason and Sandra's experiences that gave me the impetus to contact Ann as I wanted to know if I could use her book as reference. Ann's response was both immediate and encouraging. We started corresponding and were quickly able to share many things, including our understanding of the implications of this experience. Ann's own paranormal experiences had frightened her and made her very wary and despite having two very intuitive sons, both who were extremely comfortable with their clairvoyant and psychic abilities, Ann still remained very frightened. She was however, far more intuitive than she wanted to acknowledge and as the months went by, I think she found it helpful to share some of her ongoing experiences with me. I appreciated and valued her trust.

Gradually, over the months, Ann disclosed to me a very difficult issue for her. This was the awareness of the belief that she had another son on a spacecraft! She mentions this very briefly in her book, as she found the whole issue too distressing to dwell on. To add to her pain, Jason was aware of her other son, his brother and he even knew the name she had secretly given the child, which was 'Nathan'.

Jason was quite angry with Ann because he felt that she struggled to acknowledge Nathan, who, Jason said, wanted to meet her and who loved her. Ann grappled with many conflicting feelings, which were clouded in deep pain and anger. She had always felt the aliens had used her and taken her baby, without her consent. How could she then meet this son, the one they had taken away from her like that, when she was feeling so much anger and pain? She felt she just couldn't bring herself to do this and Jason was angry with her, he couldn't understand why his mum would not want to meet her own son, his brother.

Ann wrote to me. In her letter, she said: "Just a couple of nights ago Jason came into my room and told me that things were being moved around his room and he had been woken up by a voice saying *Mummy, Mummy, where are you? Please, I have to see you!* Jason said that he could feel a very strong presence in his room and that I should at least speak to the child. At this point I felt a mixture of fear and anger and said that all they had to do was to arrange for me to be abducted like I had been before.

"Jason calmly replied that a meeting would only happen if I wanted it to. He explained that emotions such as love could not and must not be manipulated by *them*. The decision had to be mine.

"Mary, what am I so terrified of? Why can't I agree to see Nathan? I have always known that my son was out there somewhere, but, as always, I find it too hard to cope with. I put it out of my mind, but Jason won't let me do it any longer. I don't know if I'm refusing to see Nathan because it would be too heart-rendering for me to leave him again, or if it's because I'm angry that he has been taken away from us and isn't growing normally as my boys' little brother. I keep questioning myself, trying to understand my fear, but I can't and it's making me so miserable."

Ann had additional confirmation about Nathan, which came independently from her own brother:

"My brother said he had seen a very tall being, about seven to eight feet tall and very slim, standing in front of him and the tall being seemed to be holding the hand of a child about eight or nine, a human child. The being stated that the child and Jason are extremely close and Jason knows him as Nathan. I can't describe to you how I felt. I had told no one, absolutely no one about Nathan, apart from my husband Paul and obviously Jason knew. I suddenly knew that my brother was telling me the truth.

"After the initial shock, my feeling was one of anger and jealousy. Why would my son make himself known to my brother and not to me? So I have decided, I want to meet Nathan properly. "

I knew this was a huge issue for Ann as over the months she had confided in me her concerns over Nathan and she needed someone who could work with her, who had the therapeutic skills and experience in this area to help her explore this issue in more depth. This would give her a clearer picture, not only because she had been getting uncomfortable and painful flashbacks of the time when Nathan was taken, but because she needed to find out more about this limited jigsaw of events. She needed to understand, integrate and heal. There was no one else she could turn to as this kind of regression work in such a specialist area is only done in a very limited way in the UK, which I believe, is due to concerns with the process and its validity.

I knew that I might be able to help Ann explore this within deeper levels of her awareness and help her open up to the memories of particular experiences, to gain access to further understanding so that her healing could start. I knew that if we met, I could offer her this opportunity. We had built up such rapport and trust over a two and a half-year period and I was certain that she would allow me to help her should the opportunity arise. Finally, it did and the family came to Australia in November 2000.

Ann decided that she would bring the family over for a six week holiday, to meet the support group and the other friends she had made. I arranged for them to stay with a very open-minded, spiritual lady, who was a good friend of mine, so they could be themselves without any concerns. During the stay, Ann was happy to tell her story to the support group and other ufology groups. I was finally able to spend some personal time with her, not just to help her overcome her fear of the paranormal, but to offer her some intuitive tools she could incorporate to help manage her psi/clairvoyant abilities. We also wanted to explore Ann's wider understanding and unravel the truth about her third son, Nathan. It was one of the most moving and powerful sessions I have ever been a part of and Ann bravely recounts her experience in the sequel book to "Abducted".

I had known intuitively that a big part of the reason Ann had come to Australia was for her to finally work through her issues regarding Nathan. The hurt and anger she felt over what she perceived was the forcible removal of her child and without her consent was for her, unforgivable. Ann was terrified about exploring this issue, as the pain of it was so deep. To revisit it was unbelievably difficult for her. But I had Ann's trust and she knew that this might be the only opportunity for her to explore it properly and get it out in the open. So, bravely and with a certain amount of resignation and trepidation, she allowed me to begin.

Initially to relax her, we talked briefly about her conscious memories and the flashbacks before we went into the regression itself. The only positive thing that she could consciously remember was that she had a memory of one of the beings, a tall, gentle being she later recognised and called the 'soldier-man'. He stroked her forehead after taking her baby, saying that they would look after him. This was my only clue that there was more she needed to know about this harrowing experience. It was such a sensitive issue for her that to even broach it would bring her to tears.

I knew Ann had dreaded this session with me. Understandably she was terrified of the pain she would feel, revisiting snatches of memory she had slowly, over the years, become more and more aware of. I asked for all the assistance I could get from the loving, spirit helpers I truly believe assist me in my work. This for me is like a surgeon doing the most delicate of operations. We both had to trust that she was ready to see once and for all why her child had been taken.

Ann had told me that she had been almost three months pregnant. She had been told by her doctor that if she went ahead with this pregnancy, she would jeopardise her life and the baby's. Ann had already been in the process of trying to decide if she should go ahead with the pregnancy, as her GP had stressed earlier that another pregnancy was potentially dangerous for them both. It was a terrible dilemma for her. She had two small boys and a loving husband.

What would happen to them if she died?

Before she was able to make this decision, it was made for her. Ann woke up to find herself surrounded by blood and no longer pregnant. Strangely, there was no foetus. This was another mystery that for some time Ann couldn't explain and neither could her doctor. But slowly, through her dreams and frightening flashbacks, she had visual images and clues as to what had really happened.

What she felt she had experienced was far worse to her than any mystery and it was too bizarre to tell any doctor. Ann finally concluded that ETs had 'stolen' her baby and taken it from her. That he was alive, but with them, the Aliens! I did not know what this regression with Ann would reveal, or what we would uncover. I had thoughts in my own mind, a horrendous picture of ET abuse, or could it be something quite different? The last thing I wanted was for Ann to become more traumatised than before, I simply hoped that she would gain some understanding, healing and peace. So I carefully led Ann into her journey of discovery, when in my heart I hoped that whatever 'it' was, it would finally help her to understand and come to terms with why the ETs had taken her child.

The start was slow and painful; Ann was clearly struggling with her memory of that fateful night when her whole world was ripped apart. One day she was pregnant with a child, and then the next morning she had no baby, just pain and blood. A deep emptiness filled her soul, she was hurt and angry. Slowly, through her choking sobs, Ann recalled the night they came. She described how they took her to the ship and made her wait for the procedure. Ann was plainly struggling to revisit this experience; she needed a lot of gentle support and encouragement to be able to continue. The procedure was so painful for her that I changed her perspective so that she could view it 'detached' from her body. Rather than being 'in' the experience, she stood 'outside it', so she could look on and see what was happening, which lessened her experience of pain. Ann saw her baby being taken from her. She shook, her body racked with sobs as she described this procedure. She said they then moved the tiny baby to another room, where it was placed in a special receptacle. She knew that her child was alive.

As a facilitator, it was very hard to remain detached, as Ann's description of her experience was so heart-wrenching; another mother would relate to her pain. Ann's deep emotion surrounding this experience completely negated any suggestion for me that this was a confabulation of events, as is often suggested by some with regression work, (in other words, a 'construct of the client's imagination'). The experience and its impact were almost too difficult for her to verbalise to me. Emotionally and physically she shook. I was concerned for her and distanced her more from the emotional content and the impact it was having on her because I knew that if I could keep her on track, we might finally learn why all this had happened. To bring her back to a fully conscious awareness at this point, would only awaken and reinforce all that she had originally believed, (such as: ET races being cruel and heartless, with no concern for human rights, or feelings). It would have been unproductive to have done this. Ann needed understanding so that she could start her healing process.

At this point, I talked to the part of her that knew all. It is an 'inner awareness' that we all have, (some call The Higher Self) and if you connect with it, in this space, it will answer. So I asked this part of Ann why they (the ETs) had taken her baby?

In reply, Ann spoke firmly and clearly. She described a special room that she was taken into and that the 'soldier' being was there, he radiated love and concern. He then explained to her that the only way to save her and the baby's life was to take the baby and keep it safe with them. If she had gone ahead with her pregnancy, then she would have died and so would her child. Ann had known of the serious dangers with this pregnancy, she had been given this information by her doctor. But it had been stressed to her by 'them' that this decision had to be hers. Ann said that she had agonized over it, but knew that she couldn't risk a pregnancy that might kill her and her child, leaving husband Paul alone, to cope with raising two small boys. So, having made this heartbreaking decision, she had agreed to let them take the baby.

She had made them promise that they would take the best possible care of him and that they must love him, she said, most of all to really love him and to tell her son that she loved him very much and that was why she had made the choice. Only when he (the soldier being) promised to do this, did she agree. She said it was the only way to save Nathan's life and her own. She knew that although he would never be able to live with them as a family, he would at least live. The soldier being promised that he would do as she asked.

It was hard to hold back my own tears as I heard this. Ann had been crying openly and I knew that there was one last thing we needed to do, so I said to her: "Now would you like to see your son?"

Ann nodded and as she did that her face lit up through her tears and she beamed the most amazing smile. She said: "I see him, I see him. He's standing with the soldier man, holding out a red rose to me." Ann said she embraced him, "he's telling me he knows all about us, as Jason often talks to him."

I just listened in awe and relief, because Ann looked as if she could, at last, have some peace. I brought Ann back into a more conscious awareness and we hugged and both cried some more. It was a very emotional and moving moment. With relief, Ann had been shown what she needed to see, which enabled her to heal and move on. We talked it through for a short while until she became calmer, and when I felt she was ready I left her alone with her thoughts.

She needed to compose herself because Paul and Jason were outside. She needed a bit of space as she wasn't quite ready to face them with it; she needed time to integrate what she had learned.

I was relieved that Ann had finally received the information that would enable her to move forward, heal and integrate all her ET experiences in a way that would be beneficial to her. My job was done.

Ann continued to have more amazing experiences whilst in Australia and the family left with a vow to return. They said they had found true friends and an acceptance here, which they would miss, the most. We too, had learned so much from them, their courage and their honesty. My journey with Ann and the family continues today and we will stay good friends and lifelong companions through this incredible journey.

After Ann returned home, she wrote to me a few weeks later to share more of her story regarding her child Nathan. In her letter, she says:

"I have seen Nathan a few times since then, but strangely, I feel him more at first and then I can see him in my mind, very clearly. Usually when I am writing and getting stuck with words to express myself, that is the time he comes to me. The whole room changes, the atmosphere becomes warm and though it is hard to put into words, love and immense feelings of peace abound. It is a truly wonderful experience, every time.

"I used to ask if it was Nathan, and I would always get the image of him and the answer *Yes, Mum*. Now I don't ask anymore, as I know his energies and always there is the same love and inner peace. I know this will sound incredible Mary, but I feel he helps me with my writing. I always get over my word block, then thoughts and details enter my head and I can't get them down quick enough. I rush through the particular piece of writing and then, exhausted, sit in silence, just enjoying what we have together.

"He always says goodbye but I don't feel sad as I know he will always return and it's the greatest feeling in the whole world."

My thanks go out to Ann for allowing me to share with you such an intimate part of her life. We discovered that day, a part of the amazing enigma of our intimate relationship with our extraterrestrial visitors and we are still only scratching the surface of what our galactic neighbours are here to show us.

CHAPTER ELEVEN
Implants – What Are They and How Do I Know if I Have One?

"Signs of implants prevent against making it all some 'mystical change of consciousness' story, all in our minds…easily dismissed, millennium madness and other similar cop-outs. I say, in "ET/Human Link" that I don't know for sure if I was implanted, but I darn well found the triangle cuts in my hands and later a tri-scab on the chest and the ball beneath the skin. I showed them to a chiropractor, which helped with the credibility later. I saw that maybe the marks were a kind of language, or wake-up signal and this gives people another choice, if the idea of being implanted like lab animals is too frightening for them. Of course, the actual implants are of great interest to the 'nuts and bolts' crowd. They think they can prove something by extracting and analysing implants, but so far, the science community is unimpressed, or can't handle it."

Dana Redfield, letter to the author

In this chapter we will look at evidence for the physical and non-physical reality of implants. What are implants for, and why do so many people with Contact experiences believe they have them? Further, what do the researchers and experiencers themselves say about these implants? There is also the less tangible phenomenon, the 'metaphysical energy implant'. I can illustrate this more for you by sharing a regression session with you, where a woman had the opportunity to explore her own energy implants and review her incredible, but intriguing interpretation of them.

The implant phenomenon is part of the Contact enigma; it is understandably very emotive and is certainly a very controversial part of this experience. For a long time, the reality of implants has been dismissed by many as being mere fantasy, created in the imagination, by paranoid people making 'far out' claims. It wasn't until the pioneering work of Dr. Roger Leir, an American surgeon, who surgically removed some of these strange anomalies and had them scientifically analysed, that the subject gained any real credibility. However, some Ufologists and most of the general public, still treat this evidence with a certain amount of ambivalence, or disbelief. But for the individuals experiencing Contact, the reality of implants can have a huge impact throughout their own awareness, leaving many with the feeling of being watched, or monitored. They can be accompanied by a strange lump under the skin, with scars or bruising and there are cases where small, metallic objects of unknown origin have actually been sneezed out from the nasal cavity! All these individuals have said that they experience Contact.

I would like to look at what is known about implants through the eyes of the experiencer and also see what has been learned scientifically about the physical reality of implants. There is also however, another intriguing part of this phenomenon, which suggests a 'non-physical reality - that I call a metaphysical, or 'energy implant'. This is something much harder to scientifically quantify, but it does demonstrate how complex this issue really is.

The energy implant initially came to light for me when I undertook an intriguing therapy session with a mature lady some years ago. I recount her story at the end of this chapter and you will be able to read for yourself her explanation and understanding of these implants. For me, it takes the implant controversy to a new level, but real or not, that is for you to decide.

We know that even if we acknowledge that these implants have a 'reality', what lies behind the phenomena is still open to many interpretations. It is important to look at the many diverse beliefs and to explore their purpose in an attempt to find out why. As with much of the Contact phenomenon, it is difficult to offer anything more than personal viewpoints and understanding. The research as yet, is still unable to offer us any concrete answers and so it just adds to the myriad of complex pieces that make up the Contact jigsaw. We can however, look at how the experiencers think these implants affect them, both physically and intuitively and their feelings should not be discounted. There are many different interpretations on offer, such as a young man who sought his answers through anthropology and religion, a theory given credibility by several researchers. He discovered that the implant phenomenon has been known about for decades, by many indigenous cultures and that it has been viewed from a religious, spiritual perspective. There are also the science-based explanations given by the Ufologists who theorise about the purpose of implants. But whatever the interpretation, it is my belief that implants may well have a multi-functional nature.

But, despite the confusing information regarding their purpose, the implant phenomenon does provide a concrete reality for many experiencers, giving researchers and investigators additional evidence to back up its complex reality. This growing evidence, both within the physical and non-physical realm has made the acknowledgement of Contact far more real for the 'nuts and bolts' brigade and for all those still questioning the reality of their experiences.

So what do we know about these implants and what is their place in the Contact enigma?

Implants can be physical or non-physical and are believed to be placed in the body during a Contact experience. The physical implant is usually a small, solid object, whereas the non-physical implant is a 'block' of information, placed in the body in the same way, but undetectable by physical means. For the experiencer, the nonphysical implant can become a physical reality, as both physical and non-physical implants can show tangible evidence, such as scars, or lumps, or they can be in the form of an intuitive knowing of having 'something' planted within their body. Often, if the experiencer feels some emotion when asked about implants, which is a possible indicator to the presence of them, it can create a great deal of fear and some claim they would rather not know.

Understandably, it can be uncomfortable and alarming to be aware of something hidden in your body, which may have been put there by an unknown agent. I use the term 'unknown agent' because we should not automatically assume that because some individual is an experiencer, these implants are placed there as being part of, or through their ET related experiences. In fact, some researchers suggest that covert, government programmes exist that echo the ET Contact scenario and that some of these implants may well be human in origin!

But what is not in doubt is that many individuals, after a Contact experience, can find unexplained marks and scars of their body and see, or feel unusual lumps in various places. Many of these anomalies have been picked up on X-rays. Individuals have often intuitively sensed that they have had 'something' planted within their body, which then begs the question, if implants are real, either physically or metaphysically, then what is their purpose? Are they harmful, or beneficial and if they are beneficial, should they be tampered with, or removed? If we look at these questions, acknowledge what these experiencers intuitively feel, and take into account what some of the indigenous cultures know and understand about this phenomenon and combine all this with personal regression therapy, we may get close to uncovering the mystery of implants, whether they really do exist and if so, why?

The physical reality

Implants have been very hard to scientifically prove despite many individuals over many years having X-rays, which have shown very real anomalies, unexplained lumps, or objects in various parts of the body.

These anomalies or implants have often strangely disappeared, just as they were due to be removed, or they would dissolve or disappear just after removal from the body. Finally, a pioneering American surgeon, Dr. Roger Leir (author of "Aliens and the Scalpel") surgically removed some of these implants and had them scientifically analysed. This surgery was recorded in every detail and also formed the basis of a documentary called "Confirmation", which was first shown across the USA on television in 1999. Dr Leir discussed this groundbreaking surgery and the double-blind laboratory analysis of these implants, which show no apparent rejection from the body. They appeared to have their own nerve supply and contain unusual compounds and anomalies that cannot be explained through conventional science.

Therefore there is little doubt for those with an open mind that something very strange has been implanted into the physical bodies of some people. Dana Redfield wrote to me and said:

"I had a hypnotic regression, which showed me on a space ship receiving implants. I saw a long, thin rod with a triangle tip . . . I was being 'activated'. I see myself drugged-like! I don't know if what I saw in this trance state is actual, or the best my subconscious can do with the memory of how those triangle cuts came to be on my hands."

Often, the indicator of having an implant will come in the form of an unexplained mark or scar. These kinds of marks have been described by some as an 'alien tattoo'. American UFO researcher, Derrell Sims, discovered that following Contact, some individuals with these marks/tattoos, can glow fluorescent under black, ultraviolet light, displaying different colours, (such as orange, yellow-green, blue-white and lavender). So for some, there is a definite physical reality, whereas others may not display the obvious, physical clues. These others may still feel, however, that in some way their physical, emotional or mental bodies hold information in the form of energy implants and these they are part of their Contact experience. Commonly, these energy implants can be felt in the back of the head, behind the eye and earlobes, nasal cavities, sinuses, neck, hands, wrists, abdomen, legs, ankles and feet. Many say they can actually feel the lump and see the discolouration of them, some say they can feel them vibrate.

Those with implants behind the eye have said that it feels as if their eyes are being used to focus on specific things, as if they were a camera lens. It can make their eyes water when this happens. Those with implants in the ear have said that they can hear a high-pitched buzzing sound occasionally and they are very sensitive to loud noise. Also remember however, that there is a medical condition called 'tinnitus' that can account for this ringing, high-pitched sound too. So, if you are in any doubt, check with your GP before jumping to conclusions.

I have listed below some of the alleged reasons why we may have implants and their possible purpose:

- They could merely be a wake-up call to Contact reality, as Dana Redfield suggests: "Signs of implants in the body prevent a person from turning it into some kind of mystical change of consciousness story. If you know you have an implant, then your experiences cannot be so easily dismissed."
- The implant could be a conduit for receiving information. This experience is like having information 'down-loaded' into the brain (just as you would download information into a computer). Jena, (who was ten at the time) had a conscious experience when she became aware of a being in her room she said he was wearing a white robe, but had no eyes and communicated by using a sound, like 'Morse-Code'. "I can receive it as fast as saying 'hello'. Sometimes I get a headache, like my head's very small and can't take it all in so quickly. It's like having a 'knowledge bomb' dropped on my head."
- The implants could be monitoring a person's movements and also relaying instructions, (see Chapter 15, Ellis Taylor).
- The implants might be used to help us with certain tasks 'they' would like us to perform.
- They may be recording our responses to emotions, which could be used to help 'them' understand human feelings.
- Implants could be a device that creates increased awareness in a person and the psychic (psi) abilities used for healing and enhanced intuition.
- They could be there to increase our creativity. Tracey Taylor has a small lump in her arm, which she refuses to have removed as she feels this might be an implant which assists her with the amazing drawings and symbols she creates.
- Implants could be used to monitor the physical body, recording biochemical DNA changes, or measuring impurities and pollutants within the body. Perhaps they can also help with facilitating rapid healing.

- Implants could increase the healing ability of the physical body, speeding up the natural healing process, or enabling it to remain healthy. In the book "Confirmation", author Whitley Strieber mentions a gentleman who had an implant removed from his leg. After it was taken out, this guy said that for the very first time in his life he became sick.
- One woman has said that telepathically she was told that the implants were designed to help the whole psychological/mental process cope with the shock and integration of our alien bodies with our human bodies!
- They could be part of an 'ET shamanistic initiation', transcending the person into higher consciousness. The *indigenous* peoples' implants.

Simon Chrystal, an experiencer, independently explored the parallels between ancient shamanic techniques and Contact/abduction experiences and later learned that other researchers were also aware of these parallels. Simon believed he had implants of his own and that the procedure was identical to most of the 'initiation' and Shamanic ceremonies of the ancient and indigenous tribes. He believes he has several implants, one behind his eye and one in his neck and he has conducted research of his own, including anthropological and archaeological evidence, suggesting ET Contact throughout earth's history. His conclusion regarding this type of implant procedure is that they are put in through the nasal cavity and then into the brain, to activate the pineal gland (believed to be the main trigger for perceiving non-physical realities). Simon refers to an account in Professor John Mack's book, "Abduction", which he says is identical to his own, whereby 'Catherine' experiences a metal instrument being pushed into her nostril, inserted to about six inches and then feeling something break in her head. Simon said that this duplicated his experience exactly.

Simon also discovered through his research that Aborigines, as well as other indigenous tribes, have an ancient initiation ceremony in which they go into a cave and talk of being with their ancestors, then 'something' is put into their head. The outcome is a change in consciousness and access to greater psychic awareness. Many tribal people throughout the world have similar rituals, from the Mayans to American Indians. These rituals are ancient, the anticipated result being the increase in psychic awareness. He also maintains that the overall purpose is access, or to pierce and activate the pineal gland, triggering the pituitary gland, to release certain hormones, such as serotonin. These hormones help facilitate the ability to perceive the nonphysical and raise psi abilities. Often crystals are included in these rituals, as it is believed that they can store memory, again facilitating or magnifying these abilities.

Although Simon made his own deductions with regards to the shamanic parallels, several other researchers have independently agreed with his conclusions. Researcher and ufologist, Simon Harvey Wilson (MUFON representative for West Australia), developed a similar hypothesis in his thesis "Shamanism and Alien Abductions, A Comparative Study, 2000". So we have the hypotheses that implants, or at least some, may well be the modern day equivalent of the shamanic ritual of indigenous tribes. The outcomes are similar, an acceleration of higher consciousness, with appreciation of our multi-dimensional universe.

Whatever you believe regarding the theory of the implant, there is evidence to suggest that marks and scars on the body left from Contact indicate that there are procedures and possibly objects that are implanted during some of these experiences.

A few years ago, in Western Australia, I listed some of the physical signs that had been documented. Marks, indentations, scars, bruising, radiation burns, nosebleeds, scars round inside the sinus of the nose (where there has been no earlier surgery), lumps and bumps in places where they shouldn't have been - all with no explanation. I shall give you some brief examples:

- Male, aged 43, marks in the form of deep heavy imprints found on the body and face, a shaved area on leg. Scar behind earlobe with an unexplainable lump. Imprint of a 'being' etched into his chest.
- Male, aged 20, many small scars on the fingers of both hands.
- Male, aged 20, scars on the underside of the genitals.
- Female, aged 20, scars on her body and legs.
- Male, aged 20, severe bruising behind both ears after having an experience of being chased by a UFO.
- Female, aged 50 sneezed something 'metallic' from her nose. Regular bruises and marks on her body.
- Female, aged 30 scar on the chin and on the breast area.
- Male, aged 19, scar on the abdomen after a Contact experience where he said a round object was removed from his stomach.
- Male, aged 28, triangle marks on his hand which disappeared some days later.
- Female, aged 25, unexplained scars on ankle.

- Female, aged 45, unexplained scoop mark on her right leg.
- Female, aged 28, woke up with unexplained bruising under the nails of both big toes and later her sibling, living many miles away had identical bruising on the same toes.

So if implants appear to be quite common to the Contact scenario, why are not more of them found, or investigated?

- Ignorance or disbelief in the phenomenon.
- Many individuals are reluctant to go to conventional medical practitioners for fear of ridicule.
- Fear of the implant reality.
- Some individuals would rather not know and therefore will ignore them.
- Implants can actually disappear before they can be investigated.
- Many individuals say they have had their implants removed conventionally and they have been put down as anomalies with no investigation, or knowledge of what they might be. For example, one woman found a small lump on her son's neck, which was removed with surgery. The doctors said that they didn't know what the small lump was and surmised that it could have been a deformed hair, or hair follicle and it was never analysed. She thought that was strange, however, as the lump was in deep tissue, but no real explanation was ever given.
- A 40 year old male had a 5 mm piece of metal removed from his leg. He had felt this under his skin for many years, believing it to be a bit of chipped bone. When it began to bleed he had a doctor look at it and remove it. He then discovered it was metal with a little hook on it, this left him very puzzled, because there was no scar for the metal to have entered, but there was obviously a scar left by its removal.
- It may be that you simply have not noticed them.

Non-physical, metaphysical 'energy implants', what are they?

There do seem to be implants certainly, which are very real physical objects that have been seen on X-ray and felt by the individual. But there also seems to be a more subtle implant, which could be left by some ET involvement - perhaps to implant suggestions, or act as a 'block' to protect the psyche of the individual. Some people seem to suddenly have information, which could have been implanted as this knowledge has not been consciously learned. There are examples where such implants of information can be very uncomfortable for a short time afterwards, creating headaches and such.

Some say that this metaphysical implant programme, or the 'energy implant' makes them feel like they have been implanted with instructions, giving them an overwhelming urge to go to a particular place at a certain time, or behave in a certain way. Not withstanding, these implants, although they may not be tangible, or 'physical' as such, can be sensed by the experiencer, who knows that they are in his body and it does seem that there is a real physical effect derived from this type of procedure, irrespective of why they may be there in the first place.

In the case study that follows shortly, we look at this type of 'non-physical energy implant'. In this instance, the implant created a psychological block and as such, became a real challenge to the therapist. The client, on one level, desired help and needed to understand what was happening to them. On another level, they also felt terrified that if they 'tampered' with it (whatever it was), it would in some way trigger some form of retribution. From this, we can see that there is a real power to these implants.

This kind of experience is quite typical and can be very real for the individual. However, to my knowledge there have been no negative outcomes from working with these energy implants.

The metaphysical 'energy' implant, with a past life Connection

This story will certainly challenge some readers and I thought very carefully before including it. But, my philosophy has always been that no matter how bizarre the information may be, or the interpretation of it, *we don't know what we don't know!* So, unless we are open to different ideas and new possibilities, we cannot begin to find out what it is we don't know. I cannot properly quantify what was uncovered during this session, but from my own personal perspective, I felt I was there to honour the client's reality, allowing her inner wisdom to guide her to the understanding that made sense to her and fit within her beliefs. The outcome of this was healing and integration.

When one is prepared to explore certain issues with a client through regression, it opens up another realm of awareness. Whether the uncovered information is valid or not, is open to question for many, especially if this information does not fit into what they think is real. But the fact is, as with all past life theories and material, many credible practitioners, including psychiatrists and psychologist's have found that exploring past memories, ('past' in this life time, or a previous one) with some clients, can result in some remarkable healing. What's more, the client doesn't have to believe in their past lives in order for this to work well for them. Irrespective of what they believe to be true, they are still able to access these memories and be healed through this process. Many find through regression, an awareness of information (on some deep level) that suggests they have had previous existence. Belief is immaterial in this process of healing. The key here lies in re-experiencing the memory, even if this memory is perceived to be fantasy or a symbolic representation of something else.

The more you explore the possibilities of metaphysical implants, the more complex it becomes. I also discovered through my research that not all energy blocks of a metaphysical nature are implanted by extraterrestrials. Past life regression therapy demonstrates that many individuals have developed similar energy blocks in their body and that these have been set up when experiencing something traumatic, either in the present or carried forward from another past life. The past life blocks can still be there and if they are, they can affect an individual in this life, manifesting as trapped or unexpressed emotions held in the physical body. But in Julia's case example that follows, the energy implants thought to be there, appeared to be ET in origin and at the time did not suggest any past life connection, even though many experiencers talk of past life connections to extraterrestrials. In Julia's story, the information regarding her past life connection surfaced during the actual session itself. At the time, it came as a total surprise to both of us.

Julie is a mature, highly intuitive and spiritual lady, who told me she had been experiencing panic attacks on a regular basis. She would suddenly, for no apparent reason, feel very anxious and spooked and feel her heart racing. She felt this just before she consciously felt ET energy and knew she was going to have a Contact experience. This repetitious pattern left her feeling very anxious most of the time; she said she felt constantly afraid and unable to relax. She literally felt worn out with it, all the time.

Julia explained that, aside from this, she also experienced an array of paranormal phenomena, such as the television switching on and off on its own, unexplained banging noises, which were so loud they felt like an aeroplane shaking the house. All in all, she was extremely disturbed and felt very vulnerable and frightened.

Julia presented me with two main issues:

1. What was the origin of her panic attacks, why was she having them and where did they come from?
2. In meditation, Julia only saw ETs and space ships, which freaked her out. She wanted to know why she was having difficulty connecting to her spiritual guide. Julia believed that everyone has a spiritual guide, or a

spiritual being in their life and she felt this spiritual energy at certain points throughout her life. She was concerned that over the past few years she had been unable to connect to 'him' in the way she had before and so she wanted to know the reasons why.

To help Julia feel more secure with the process, we decided that we would access her spiritual guide first, so that she would feel safer as she explored her issues. This proved to be quite difficult and initially all she could feel were four entities with her, two of them were black, she said and she always felt their presence, but none of them were her spiritual guide.

In the beginning of her regression, she said that two of these beings showed her their world. It was very bleak and barren. Their voices sounded unusual, almost tinny, as if talking through a voice box and both had reptilian features. They would not answer her questions regarding their purpose.

Later she saw another presence; this changed shape and moved to show her an Indian reservation that was related to her past. Again, it refused to answer certain questions. With difficulty, we finally managed to connect to her spiritual guide, whom she recognised and he conveyed that these presences were not for her highest good. Apparently she had made some kind of an agreement with them in a past life connection. She felt that during that particular lifetime she had been desperate for help and had agreed to be of assistance to them. Then later, she decided that she no longer wanted to be connected to them and tried to break this hold they had over her. We explored the ways in which she could disconnect and remove the unwelcome attention she was receiving. Certain strategies were given, with the assistance of her inner wisdom and her life guide. We then looked at how she could bring healing to herself, then we identified the five implant blocks she saw in her body and cleared them away.

When Julia was in a focused but relaxed state, she did sense that some ET energy was blocking access to her spiritual guide. We used the metaphysical techniques of 'white light' protection before calling in her spiritual guide, as I always honour the client's beliefs and will incorporate them if requested, to create a safe environment for this kind of exploration.

For someone with more traditional beliefs, perhaps some form of prayer would have sufficed, or the calling for protection from a Guardian Angel or whatever fits within the client's belief system. Basically, I would use whatever is helpful to them.

The following notes are excerpts from the regression itself. At this point I am asking Julia's inner self, the part of her that intuitively knows what is happening, to look to the source of the difficulties:

Mary: *Do you feel your life guide now?*
Julia: Umm. . (nodding yes),
Mary: *Where do you feel him?*
Julia: On my right side,
Mary: *How does it feel to you?*
Julia: Solid.
Mary: *Does it feel okay?*
Julia: Umm, yes.

We established her guide was called Peter and that she was ready to cleanse her body of blocks. I did this by asking Julia to imagine that she could view her body as if looking at an X-ray, so she could readily see where the blocks were. She became very disturbed and said: "They *(the two entities)* can just switch themselves. I don't know if they are for good at all". At this point we brought in her spirit guide to offer her support and understanding as she was feeling quite confused.

Mary: *Have you agreed at some point to accept these presences?*
Julia: Yes.
Mary: *Ask your guide why you agreed to co-operate with them?*
Julia: I was desperate for help from anywhere.

Julia then said that she remembered being desperate (in a past life situation) and had called for help, these beings responded.

Mary: *So you called them in, but have they assisted you?*
Julia: Umm. . No.
Mary: *At a soul level, do you still want them to be a part of your life?*
Julia: (firmly), No.
Mary: *If they are not for your highest good, ask your guide what you need*
          to do to send them away?
Julia: To affirm my presence in the light.
Mary: *How does he wish you to do this?*

Julia: Affirm the words and say the mantras. Ask for protection and
           mentally let go, do not allow my thoughts to wander to them at all.

Mary: *So, to deny their existence?*

Julia: No, but if I see them, not to keep looking. To do the mantras to block it, yes. It's like when I'm looking around every corner, not to do that. It's not helping me. Actually, something's going on in my third eye, quite strongly, it feels like a cross there.

Mary: *It feels like a cross?*

Julia: Yes.

Mary: *Can you ask why this is happening?*

Julia: It's symbolic, seeing only the Christ light, that type of thing.

Mary: *Are there any blocks, or is there anything that we need to do to assist you with your protection right now?*

Julia: The connection seems to be in my heart area, it's like there's a line or a bar across there.

Mary: *Can you see it?*

Julia: No, I can just feel it.

I asked Julia to imagine becoming very small. To go with her guide and see what this connection looked like:

Julia: It looks like a brand new aluminium pipe.

Mary: *Has it been put there by these beings?*

Julia: Umm . . . yes.

Mary: *Why has it been put there?*

Julia: Something to do with not being for my highest good. So I can't reach higher.

Mary: *So you can't reach a higher vibration?*

Julia: Yes.

I then used Julia's own powerful imagery and with her spirit guide helped her remove the block:

Mary: *Has it gone now?*

Julia: Umm . . . Yes.

Mary: *What does your heart say to you?*

Julia: It's not there any more (the block).

Mary: *Is there anywhere else in your body where there is a block and can we remove them at this time?*

Julia: Across my hip bones, it's the same type of thing.

Mary: *Is it something to do with reproduction?*

It is often suggested, that the therapist can sometimes influence the client at this level. When I asked if it was to do with reproduction, it could have been interpreted as a leading question. But see how Julia dismisses my suggestion completely and gives her own interpretation. I have found that clients will always dismiss any possible suggestion that doesn't fit into what they perceive at the time.

Julia: I don't know, something to do with not wanting me to ... Um . . ..be concerned with the earth, not being 'earthed'.
Mary: *So it's preventing you from being stable, or earthed?*
Julia: Umm. . . Yes.

We removed this block in the same way, but this time Julia saw her spirit guide remove it. She then knew she had another block on the left side of her head.

Julia: I'm not sure if there is something in my head. It's on the left side of my skull and it's like, screw things have been staved in and not wires, but like knitting needles placed there.
Mary: *What is its purpose?*
Julia: Projection, thought transference, that type of thing.
Mary: *To help them influence you?*
Julia: Yes.

Once again, through imagery, we cleared the block and I asked her to scan her body again.

Julia: Well, I'm seeing the throat now.
Mary: *So, now go to the throat and tell me what you see.*
Julia: It's like feathers, similar to peacock feathers, they go down and irritate the throat . . . It's so I don't say any thing about this.
Mary: *So it inhibits what you talk about?*
Julia: Umm. . Yes.
Mary: *Scan your body. Is there anything else there?*
Julia: There is something around my ankle. The ankle, a pin stuck through, so I can't go anywhere.
Mary: *It's stopping you?*
Julie: Yes, from moving around the planet.

Once again I used the client's own imagery to remove both these blocks.

Julia: Yep! It's like a big nail between the joints, no . . . Making the joints stick together. It's incredible, but I can feel it coming out. I am to fill myself up with colour, a healing one.

Mary: *Can you see the colour?*

Julia: I can see a colour, hard to describe. Like pink and mauve mixed together, for healing and cleansing.

At this point I asked Julia if there was anything else she needed to understand from this:

Julia: Affirm what you are and what you stand for.

Mary: *Do you understand that?*

Julia: Yes.

Mary: *Is there anything else you need to know?*

Julia: I want to know if this is gone for good, this interference.

Mary: *Then ask.*

Julia: Yes, it's gone, as long as I choose it to be so.

Mary: *So it's your choice? You have control, you can say no?*

Julia: Yes.

This transpersonal way of working with the blocks was so real for Julia, that she said she actually felt lopsided for a time, due to the removal of the block from the left side of her head. Four months later, she was still free of the very distressing, sudden feelings of panic she'd had previously, which had preceded her ET Contact. She was also free from the paranormal disturbances that had been going on around her and she felt she was finally connected to her spiritual side. Julia had also regained her sense of control and was able to understand more fully and integrate her experiences.

A few years later, I talked to Julia about this session. I wanted to know how, with hindsight, she had interpreted it and what were her spiritual and metaphysical perspectives?

She said:

"Why did I see the blocks, or implants that had originated from a past life? In that life they were limitation blocks. In this life, I was able to find them and clear them. Actually, we can all put blocks on all future incarnations if we wanted to. Unknowingly, maybe we do! Maybe there are only certain potentials we can achieve in any given lifetime? My blocks were there even before that particular life though. I feel that I may have given myself these particular blocks, many, many lifetimes ago. This could have been possible if I had known how, through a connection to some religious or occult practice, such as the Egyptian priesthood, which is what I think it was. But, obviously, I didn't know what I was doing at the time.

"I have found one or two other things that I have unknowingly done and evidently they were secret practise used by the Egyptians. The priesthoods could put these bar/implants on all future incarnations or aspects of themselves, using ET non-physical technology. The priesthoods or ETs are the creator Gods for earth and they followed a particular path of knowledge. They created codes, (they created 'us' we were the hybrid) and they now create souls from these codes. They knew that they would be immortal, even if it meant only an aspect of them would continue to incarnate in the future. They aspired to work on themselves, undergoing initiations (e.g. barriers/obstacles to overcome), enhancing the desire to follow paths, and this path is contained within our etheric DNA codes, forever. However, it doesn't negate the ETs; it simply corroborates the issue and the Sirius/Orion data.

"These days, we search for enlightenment, a return to God, a going home within our religion and beliefs in God. We embark on paths of initiation, knowingly or unknowingly, it's part of the process, we are all initiates. It's inevitable, wherever you begin, however it starts, your thoughts eventually will encompass consciousness . . . the path".

Julia has moved on and has her own complex understanding of her implants. She no longer sees herself as being the victim of some manipulative extraterrestrial beings. In fact, she now believes that these implants, these blocks had been put there to enable her human-self to experience certain life challenges. It is certainly a complex interpretation, but one that for Julie at least makes sense. Of course, we have no way of evaluating the validity of her interpretation, not yet at least. Our 'reality blinkers' need to be taken off before we can begin to explore this in the depth that Julia has.

But, having said all of that, we can evaluate this regression therapy in the more tangible physical reality, by looking at Julie's obvious, positive outcome. Again, because *we don't know what we don't know*, if we seek to offer support for something that is not just physical, but non-physical, inter-dimensional and possibly nonlinear, then we have to be prepared to explore the experience properly and through our client's reality. It does not mean that we have to accept their interpretation, or agree with the way in which a person's psyche chooses to offer this understanding. If the aim is to help the individual find a way to understand their own experiences, then their interpretation of these experiences is all that's needed. To coin an old saying, "The proof is in the pudding". Julia was finally at peace, free from the harrowing panic attacks, able to integrate, heal and get on with her life. There will be many people who will believe that these metaphysical blocks are purely in the mind and that they are not 'real' implants. Well, in one sense, they are absolutely right, as there is nothing physical there. But, if they are affecting an individual in a very debilitating way then they are certainly 'real', whether they are made up of physical substance or pure energy.

Past life therapy is a controversial subject also, but it appears that having a belief in past lives, or Contact experience is not a necessity in order to regress, clear the issues and feel the benefits. Contrary to what many believe, this material will surface independently of conscious beliefs in either subject. The regression will offer information that may well be the opposite to what the client believes in and often past life experiences can offer important clues to the client's present-life difficulties.

Dr Brian Weiss, former Chairman of Psychiatry at 'Mount Sinai Medical Center' in Miami, now believes that up to 40% of present-day client issues are directly related to past-life trauma. It is true to say that under proper conditions, if past lives are explored, then very real and tangible results can be gained that can have definite, positive, therapeutic effects on the client. Dolores Cannon, a regressionist and author, has worked with many individuals with Contact experiences. She wrote to tell me about what she had learned about implants in relation to Contact.

Dolores, unlike some investigators who see all implants as being nothing other than possible 'controlling devices', said that in her work with experiencers, she learned that implants serve many useful purposes, such as monitoring the health of the body. Certainly she does not believe, as some do, that 'they' are using implants to turn the human race into 'controlled zombies', so that they can take over the world. She wrote: "That's preposterous; I want people to know that they have been taking care of us since the beginning of time and will continue to watch the development of their 'children' and their 'garden'. I think people are much better off looking at the phenomenon from this viewpoint rather than a viewpoint of fear, horror and trauma."

The nature of implants is still up for debate, with a myriad of hypotheses as to their purpose. But even though we have no scientific way of evaluating them yet, there is no doubt in my mind that there is sufficient evidence to support their reality, physical or non-physical. We still only have the individual testimonies from people describing how they feel the implants are affecting them; it is however, an important area to research. The fact is that physical implants, despite being 'foreign' to the body, show no tissue rejection. They could therefore offer medical science valuable information if they could discover how this was possible. But most importantly, what this aspect of the phenomenon shows us that there are many other tangible aspects to this phenomenon, which, despite the different hypotheses as to their purpose, adds to and provides further evidence with regards to the reality of Contact.

CHAPTER TWELVE
High Sense Abilities – The Fruits of ET Contact

"By their fruits you will know them."

The New Testament

This chapter discusses heightened intuitive perceptions, or high sense 'psi' abilities, which I call 'the fruits of ET Contact'. I'd like to explore with you what they are, how you can recognise them and why the experiencer demonstrates so many of them, compared to the average individual.

It is open to question what comes first. Do psi abilities within a person attract the ET Contact, as some believe, or are these abilities stimulated, or enhanced by these Contact experiences? Many experiencers feel these enhanced abilities have been deliberately engineered, some say by the genetic re-programming of their DNA. Others believe psi enhancement occurs through continuous Contact and they are taught how to use it, possibly through implants. It may well be that both hypotheses are correct.

Experiencers themselves have described how they are taught to use these abilities and there is no doubt that all those who have experienced Contact have some, if not all of these psi abilities. They can present themselves in many ways and as they are triggered, or awakened through Contact, it is understandable for a person to become very fearful of this awakened sensitivity, especially if they have no understanding of how these psi abilities manifest. This whole process can cause fear and confusion and many individuals can think that they are crazy at this point. Once the experience realises however, what these psi abilities are, they can then start to understand and work with them. Some of my work involved assisting these individuals consciously and confidently, so that they can work well with these 'new found' high sense abilities.

Let's look at what these high sense abilities are, what they may feel like, and find out whether you are experiencing heightened awareness.

The term 'high sense abilities' (HSA) is sometimes known as 'extrasensory perception' (ESP), or psi abilities. Whatever the label, it defines the human ability to acquire information from sources, which as yet, have no quantifiable, scientific explanation. The information comes from a 'sixth sense' and provides a knowing about people, events, universal concepts, or highlights an unconscious aspect of the individual. These abilities are heightened in those having Contact and they can change the individual on many levels. But the abilities themselves can be the cause of much confusion and bewilderment for the experiencer, especially if they have little understanding of what psi awareness is and especially if they have been taught to dismiss it, or told that it is unhealthy, or even evil! Contact can be confusing enough on its own, but adding it to new, expanded awareness and heightened sensitivity can often lead the individual to the point of thinking *I must be going mad!*

It would not be out of the ordinary for anybody in this situation to wonder if they are mentally ill, because in Western Society, this high sense ability is not taken that seriously and it is generally considered to be fairly rare, or unusual. But present research suggests that this heightened awareness is in fact 'normal' and a latent part of human nature. Many indigenous people are fully aware of these abilities and use them naturally. In turn they are encouraged, valued and respected. In contrast, in our so-called modern society, these kinds of practices are mostly scoffed at, considered strange or even bad. Most present-day beliefs suggest that unless we access information through an analytical or cognitive thought process, then it is unreliable and should be dismissed. Those with a fundamental, religious mindset have been known to suggest that these abilities are something to fear, that they are dangerous, demonic and evil. The traditional psychologists will mostly dismiss the paranormal in general as being imagination, or fantasy and particularly unhealthy for the individual if they are hearing voices in their minds, as this falls into the category of schizophrenia or paranoia.

Sadly, due to the limited psychological understanding that is generally the norm, it means that many individuals who develop heightened awareness will be understandably cautious of owning-up to having them. If anything, they may try to block them from their consciousness, in an attempt to ignore them altogether. The very last thing that some people want is to explore and understand it, it's much simpler to forget the whole thing and hope it goes away. But this lack of knowledge about psi senses means that if they do manifest, they become a bewildering unknown factor that simply generates fear and confusion. Although some individuals wake up, or access these abilities using spiritual practices, such as meditation, the Contact experience may not have had this spiritual education. So for most, these high sense abilities are perceived to be more of a curse than a blessing and rather than encourage them, they are discouraged. Limited personal understanding about this psychic, intuitive part of ourselves can make some individuals ambivalent to the point of denial. But blocking this ability makes them deny an aspect of themselves, which can offer them so much in understanding, not just about their true nature, but also about their Contact experiences.

Research shows that those with Contact experiences do have a very active, heightened intuitive sense and this awareness, added to their Contact can be a bewildering mixture. In my own research, (and through such organisations as ACCET in America), I have instigated special workshops, which explore these higher senses. They can help the individual enormously, as they learn to understand and work with their abilities. Having an understanding of this awareness empowers them; it reduces the fear and also enables them to work with this special part of themselves, consciously and with confidence. As they start to explore what their intuitive nature is showing them, working well with it, they can gain valuable insights that also help them to understand more of what their multilevel reality is showing them.

I would like to introduce you to your multilevel, intuitive abilities and help you to understand them. This chapter is only a brief overview, it is not meant to be a definitive guide, but it will hopefully explain how your abilities are presently defined and how they can manifest through your own experiences. For further specialist reading, see 'Useful Resources' page 285. Here is a list of some of the heightened perceptions, which for many, are considered to be paranormal, or supernormal. We may have them for one or many reasons, but whatever they may be, we can explore what they are and find out how to recognise them.

Heightened psi perceptions are:

- *Energy work* e.g. healing abilities, hands on healing, psychic surgery etc.
- *Energy Awareness* e.g. aura perception (seeing colours around people).
- *Astral Travelling* e.g. consciously leaving your physical body
- *Clairaudience or Channelling* e.g. the hearing of sounds, music or voices, not audible to normal hearing.
- *Clairvoyance* e.g. internal 'seeing' of symbolic images, pictures, or forms, spirit energies, etc.
- *Clairsentience* e.g. psychic sensing of smell, taste, touch or emotions, often known as 'gut' feelings.
- *Precognition* e.g. being able to predict, or see future events.
- *Telepathy* e.g. the ability to read another person's thoughts, or communicate in their minds in a non-verbal way.

- *Remote Viewing* e.g. seeing remote or hidden objects clairvoyantly with the 'inner' eye.
- *The Anomalous Phenomena,* such as, poltergeists e.g. paranormal activity when objects or other physical material are thrown or moved without obvious human intervention.
- *PK, Psychokinesis* e.g. objects moving with thought, or mind power.
- *Levitation* e.g. the physical body or other objects lift up into the air without any known physical means.
- *Telekinesis* e.g. being able to move objects through mind power.
- *Teleportation* e.g. being able to transport yourself energetically through space and time.

There is much evidence to suggest that we all possess intuitive and psychic abilities on some level, but most of us (in Western Society) distrust these sensitivities due to our conditioned emphasis on only valuing empirical, scientific data (and using our left brain, analytical and cognitive skills). We will often neglect our (right hemisphere) intuitive and creative side. As with anything, if it's not validated or used to its full capacity it can in effect 'disappear', or make us feel like it's not there at all. But if the ability is encouraged then most individuals can rediscover their psi talents – the ones they believed they never had! Those with Contact experiences exhibit many of these psi abilities and it does appear that they have them awakened, or re-awakened.

Energy Work/Healing

"I was able to receive visions and symbolic images from a particular area of the person's body. They provided me with insights and a deeper meaning as to the blocks or disease in that location. I was seeing more clearly into the body and as I connected with the body itself I could hear it *talk* to me, revealing the level of emotion restricted there."

Elle

Experiencers often discover they have healing abilities. By this, I meant they can 'feel' or see waves of energy coming from their hands, or see it around themselves and other people. This 'spiritual' or 'hands on' energy healing can happen quite spontaneously and many find they can be drawn or very attracted to healing - feeling almost compelled to touch an individual in pain. If they trust this urge, they may find to their amazement that this energy will manifest and flow from their hands to alleviate pain, or discomfort, or in some cases heal the condition totally. When some individuals use healing like this they can sense they are not alone and may feel other energies, or spirit presences around them. They can intuitively feel that these spirit energies assist and guide them to where the healing is most needed. Some individuals find they can 'mind scan' or clairvoyantly scan the body for illness, or disease. They discover that they intuitively know what to do to assist, or change the person's energy to achieve positive results. This healing energy also seems to affect and heal all living things, including animals and plants and some believe this energy can be focused and channelled to heal our damaged planet.

How does this ability relate to Contact experiences? Elle was exploring her extraterrestrial experiences through regression and said: "They put things in my head that trigger off abilities within me, so I am able to do more and see more, because they are interested in me doing medical work."

I have heard from numerous individuals who tell me that they have taken part in a process of healing other people on the 'ships', or have observed ET beings performing healing procedures as well as sometimes having healing performed on them. Elle discovered that her 'medical work' as she describes it, was in fact a form of 'psychic surgery'.

Psychic surgery or 'super-normal' surgery is a process of healing using the hands, whereby the physical body is opened up and closed again without the use of surgical instruments. Some psychic surgery has been known to be performed using simple objects such as kitchen knives; whereas other surgeons will simply go into the body using their fingers and hands! It is usually done to remove growths and tumours, whereby the healer penetrates the physical body of the patient. These operations can show blood and tissue, but these wounds close up quickly, almost instantly, without sutures, leaving very faint or no marks at all. Patients remain fully conscious throughout and say that they feel no pain. Some psychic surgery is less physically intrusive as it is performed on the energy body of the individual, sometimes called the 'etheric body' or 'peri-spirit body'. This kind of healer will not usually touch the physical body, but makes what looks like unusual hand motions, or sweeping motions in the air above and around the physical body. As the healer works on these subtle energy systems around the body, the changes will then manifest in the physical body as healing takes place. In the same way that a headache is caused by stress, the relief of the stress will manifest as the headache is healed, or relieved. Often the healer will channel the energy through benign, spiritual energy, or presences, and can be guided by their spirit helpers.

Elle says: "Slowly, I felt as if different doctors were taking turns working through me. I could sense a small, young female, then a vacating of that spirit being, then a pause or break, then an older taller male. I had no idea that so many different doctors were available, or willing to work through me in this way. Each time someone new would come through, I would feel them as they moved into my body, arms and hands, becoming used to the feeling of them working in my body, like trying on a new suit."

Elle discovered that she was assisted in her healing work by several spirit entities. She now works as a full time healer and has had success with many types of illnesses, including cancer.

Psychic Laser Surgery. There seems to be many variations of this type of healing and individuals who practise it have said that they had to learn to trust in it and work intuitively. Many can feel as if part of them is being guided and will therefore work with this overpowering desire to heal. Melanie told me how she unconsciously used her psi senses when she found herself doing healing on her husband. She had experienced many forms of Contact; one was particularly significant for her, when she was in a car with her brother. Not only did they see a UFO, but it also followed them home. They had both been terrified and afterwards, had significant missing time episodes and marks on their bodies. After this, Melanie discovered that she had healing abilities.

Then one day she received an urgent phone call saying that her husband had suffered what appeared to be a heart attack. Melanie said that the doctors didn't really know what was wrong with him, but that he had been unconscious for a long time. She said: "I just had an intuitive message that when I went to him I had to do some healing. So I went to the hospital, saw my husband who was still unconscious and looking so ill. I called on God and all the angels to help me and I heard something, someone saying *Do you have faith?* I answered desperately, *yes, yes.* Again, this voice said to me in a booming sound, *Do you have absolute faith?* I answered very loudly in my mind *YES!* Then, it was if someone took over my hands, it felt like a whole take over. It felt like I was working with laser beams, because laser beams were coming out from my finger tips, as if the fingers were synchronised, each one had a different colour and frequency, all doing different jobs, cutting and burning at a molecular level, changing the vibration of the cells. It worked three dimensionally, on each cell, all synchronously, as everything is mixed together with the different frequencies. It was like playing Brahms on a piano.

"Afterwards I was saying to myself, *How on earth did I do that?* I remember thinking, *please, stop me soon*, as it all felt too powerful, like it could destroy me, or take me over, because I didn't know when it should stop. It did stop, suddenly, and then I felt totally deflated, like I needed a strong whisky or something and I thought, *Oh my God, what is this?*"

Melanie said that there was a dramatic and positive change in her husband right at that point. "It was amazing; he just woke up and asked me what he was doing there!"

Nowadays, Melanie says that she can intuitively 'see' with some people, illnesses or disease and can spot where the problem is. Not only can she tell what it is, but also she can see any emotions related to it and the underlying reasons why the problem is there. She still feels very uncomfortable with her healing abilities, a part of her still questions and asks *is this for real?* Interestingly, she says that from being a small child she was always fascinated by crystals and by colour. This is something that I hear from many experiencers who seem to have an intuitive understanding regarding the correlation of healing with crystals and colour.

Psychic harmonics. A young woman, a Reiki Master (Reiki is an intuitive healing therapy that originates from Japan), had found herself doing a different type of healing to what she would normally practice. Intuitively, she began sensing the energy-body of a person through vibration and sound. Then she started to create sounds herself, saying that the sound she vocalised affected the other person's body vibration. She said it was as if she was moving blocks or tubes of energy that needed changing back to their original, healthy sate. It would take from one to three hours and she went into a light trance, having no sense of time whilst doing this. She also found that she was impelled to write in an unusual type of shorthand script. She was fully conscious as she did this and wrote with the speed of a secretary, at the same time vocalising this unusual, unknown type of language. Again, she feels that she is working on a molecular (quantum) level when she does her healing. These languages, as well as the strange scripts she writes, are I believe expressions of Contact. I have seen a percentage of people demonstrate similar abilities whilst experiencing this phenomenon.

Out of body healing and absent, or remote healing. Ann Andrews wrote to me describing how drawn she had become to energy healing and how her son Jason, then only sixteen, had explained his healing methods to her. He said his work is usually done when he is out of his body; although he can do this equally well in the physical dimension.

Ann said: "He tells me that many, many people come to him when he is present in this other dimension and they either tells him of their pain, or if their loved one is suffering. If it is the latter, then he says that it doesn't matter because the person asking for help can travel with him and guide him straight to the person who needs help. He tells me that in this out of body state, he will concentrate hard on the afflicted area and he sees the problem as a thick substance, rather like treacle. This is blocked and unable to go anywhere and as such, is disrupting the normal 'life force flow'. Then he sees in his mind a container, rather like a bucket, which has a small hole at the bottom of it. Into this he places the pain/problem and concentrates on persuading the pain/problem, making it slowly trickle out through the hole in the container so that it (a) is cleansed and (b) can then rejoin the life force flow around the body. He uses colours and other images to do this. On a physical level, he tells me he can locate where the problems are, just by looking at the aura of the person, as this will be distinctly discoloured (like a bruise almost). Where there is pain, he will use the same method, i.e. the container and the treacle, but he stresses that the aura has to be also healed."

This method can also be defined as 'absent healing' or 'remote healing', although not all healers will go out of their body and travel to the individual as Jason does. Many will just concentrate on sending healing energy to the individual in mind.

Some people who have been drawn to energy and energetic healing in this way, have found that they are not always able to define the healing process as clearly as say, Jason for instance. This does not give them or what they do any less validity, even if they find that they express their healing in different ways, such as: unusual hand movements, making sounds over the body, creating images or receiving information in their mind, which will assist them to know intuitively what part of the body they should concentrate on. Some people find this very difficult, because again, human nature is such whereby we would like to have it all explained properly, or scientifically, so that we can quantify these many different kinds of healing. But positive outcomes are the real tangibles, whether a person is helped by this as a result is what really counts, even if, as yet, we cannot understand the method properly. It would certainly be a pity to try and limit it until we do.

Jason asked me once about how I do my energy healing and I admitted that sometimes I am not that sure. Often I don't quite know why I am drawn to do something. He said that if I couldn't really understand it, then I was probably doing it correctly. I believe what he meant by this is that much of what we do intuitively, particularly if we trust this feeling or intuition, allows our inner knowing to work to its best capacity. Although he stressed to me that it is far better to show a person how to do their own healing than to become dependent on the healer.

Energy Awareness/Aura Perception

The aura is an envelope of energy that surrounds minerals, plants, animals and mankind. It is not seen easily with normal vision, but it can be seen as a ribbon of light by some people when the individual focuses less intently on something. The aura is also seen clairvoyantly, as a halo of light or as a multicoloured light or mist like steam. The aura can now be photographed, the pioneer and first to discover this was Semyon Davidovich Kirlian, from Russia. He invested a technique whereby it is possible to record some of the aura on film; this is now commonly known as Kirlian photography. The aura changes in depth, intensity and colour depending on the state of health of a person. Changes in the aura can alert a healer who is able to see this energy field clairvoyantly, to any part of the body that is sick or has disease.

Astral Travelling/Out of body experiences (OBEs)

OBEs are quite common for those having Contact experiences. An OBE is when a person feels separated from their physical body and their non-physical self seems to fly, travel to and perceive distant locations on earth, or elsewhere.

An OBE is sometimes called 'astral projection', or 'astral travel'. It is believed that at least twenty five percent of the population has this experience at some point. One lady told me that every night she used to look forward to going to bed because she loved to lie there and float. She was fully aware of this experience and it came as a shock to her when she learned that other people didn't do it. OBEs are a phenomena associated with altered states of consciousness, such as Yoga, meditation and hypnosis.

Lucid dreaming can also induce an OBE, although tests show that they do not correspond to a REM (rapid eye movement) dream state. The OBE state can be induced during waking consciousness, before, throughout or after sleep. The spirit, or consciousness, of the person is said to move instantly and freely, through the walls or objects, almost like a 'ghost' body. But it is said to be attached by an umbilical chord, often called 'The Silver Chord' and that the consciousness rises through the head, solar plexus, or simply floats above the body. In the book "Journeys Out of the Body",

Robert Monroe described meeting spirits on his astral travels, thought forms and sub-human energies (some pleasant and some unpleasant). Monroe believes that there are many levels to this experience and he suggests that it transcends time and space, parallel universes and multi-dimensional realities.

Robert Monroe (also the founder of 'The Monroe Institute for Applied Sciences') devised a program that can, if applied properly, take you to a different level of consciousness. Once in this state of being, OBEs have been known to happen. OBEs should not be confused with NDEs (Near Death Experiences). An NDE can happen when there is a physical trauma or crisis, where for a short time the individual is diagnosed as being clinically dead. During this time, the person will experience things like floating above their body, an absence of pain characterised by encountering a dark tunnel with a light at the end of it, where they meet deceased relatives, or angelic beings. Life reviews are also often experienced and many say that as these events are taking place they are reluctant to return to their physical body.

People have also commented that the experience has taken away the fear of death, as the process has been a beautiful one, which convinced them that the afterlife exists. These experiences appear to be quite transformative and individuals can change markedly, philosophically and spiritually, with parallels to the transformative effects of Contact.

Clairaudience

Hearing sounds, music and voices not audible through the ears is referred to as clairaudience. The term comes from the French for 'clear hearing'. It can happen in a dream-state, while you are fully awake or in other states of consciousness. It is common for someone with clairaudient tendencies to hear voices and sounds when in a hypnogogic and hypnopompic state, which borders sleep. It can also occur when undergoing past life recalls, spontaneously in meditation and through hypnotic regression.

Some say its like having a 'voice over' in the mind, or heard as an inner sound, when words are clearly distinguishable from one's own 'inner voice' or internal dialogue. Many people who have a sense of their spirit guides will identify these inner voices as belonging to them, as these voices will speak and convey information in a way that is quite different to how we would ordinarily think and say things. The information received may be about something that the person is consciously unaware of; it may be spiritual, or even scientific in content. A more highly developed clairaudient person can experience the sound as being 'external'.

Many oracles, prophets, mystics, saints and holy people in the past and present have been guided by clairaudient voices. It has occurred regularly throughout human history, as some of our great men and women were said to have experienced it, such as Joan of Arc. The Bible tells of numerous clairaudient experiences, where God has sent messages to both prophets and Kings (such as King Solomon, who described hearing the *voice of the Lord*). Many of these voices are perceived to be angels, spirit guides, spirits of the dead, The Divine Force, or extraterrestrial entities. Clairaudience can be cultivated if practised through meditation and altered states of consciousness.

It should be said that not all information gained in this way should be deemed to be accurate. If this applies to you, I suggest that you treat the information intuitively, as it is very important that it *resonates* well with you. By this I mean that if the information received in this way (or any way, for that matter), causes concern, or gives you a feeling of inner discomfort, particularly if it suggests a potentially dangerous activity, then it is imperative that you seek the help and advice from another experienced psychic. Remember, no loving, benign entity or energy will encourage you to do anything against your will, or instruct you in something that is potentially harmful or destructive to yourself or others.

Channelling

Channelling or mediumship is still clairaudience, as you are receiving information from paranormal sources, such as non-physical beings, angels, nature spirits, deities, spirits of the dead and extraterrestrials. Channelling can be spontaneous or induced. Spontaneously, it can put the individual into a sudden trance state or trigger a lapse in consciousness. Induced channelling can be brought about through practice, as you can achieve certain states of being through meditation, self-hypnosis, chanting and breathing techniques.

Channelled information can be received by:

- *Being in a Trance State,* where the individual consciousness leaves, allowing another spiritual energy to access their body and communicate through them using them as a vehicle. When this happens, the voice can change and the channeller will probably have no recollection of the content of the communication.

- *Overshadowing* is when the spirit energy is very close to the individual and they may or may not have voice changes, but will speak as the spirit, in the first person and will be aware of the process and to some extent what is being said. The channeller will often feel the emotions of the spirit energy and perhaps feel their own body vibrating with it. It can feel very energising, with feelings of euphoria and the channeller will have access to material they have no personal knowledge of.

- *Conscious Channelling* is the most common form of channelling. There is no loss of consciousness, the channeller remains in an 'alpha' state and will relay the information as they hear it in their 'inner psychic ear'. It requires the individual to concentrate and focus on the information, making every attempt to ignore the left brain analysis or input (until afterwards), so that they leave the material uncensored by the left, analytical thinking part of the brain. To begin with, some may find this extremely difficult as most individuals find it hard to give verbal material without thinking about it first and the information given would most likely be coloured by the individual's own thinking because of this. This is the main criticism of this method, and the reason why material derived from a trance state seems to be considered more valid is because there is less change, or opportunity for colouring, or misinterpretation of the material communicated. With practice however, this can be refined. This level of channelling is very simple and anyone who wishes to can learn how to do it. Channelling can also come in the form of 'automatic writing' where the channeller can first hear the information and then write it down, more or less as it is heard. This is not the same as automatic writing when another external energy will guide and direct the hand, with apparently no conscious involvement on the individual's part. Many experiencers, who have produced amazing scripts, symbols and drawings, say that this has been how they produced their work. They feel a real urge to draw something, which could be at any time of the day or night and they feel absolutely compelled to do it, with no conscious control. Throughout the process, if they try to redirect the flow of the movement then their hand can stop moving altogether. They have to completely relax with it, and allow the hand to be directed. This kind of automatic writing is often accompanied by a wonderful energy and many are disappointed when it stops, even to the point of feeling a sense of loss.

Again, if you are channelling information yourself, or with someone who practices this, then it is important to be discerning, make sure that the material resonates well with you. If you feel at all uncomfortable with any material you receive, then question it. Again, if the material in some way instructs, or orders you to do something that does not feel right for you, or if it puts you, or someone else in any perceivable danger, then you really should question the source of that material and never do anything that is in conflict with your inner awareness. When channelling, it is advisable that the individual is extremely well balanced, emotionally, physically and psychologically. It is also wise to avoid channelling if:

- You are physically, or emotionally unwell, or
- You are mentally ill, or feeling unbalanced in any way.

Clairvoyance

Clairvoyance means 'clear seeing' and it is the perception of events, people, or objects not discerned through the 'normal' five senses. Clairvoyance may manifest internally or externally, overlapping other psychic abilities such as clairsentience, clairaudience, telepathy, remove viewing, precognition and psychometry. It is a general ability among humans, as well as animals, being very highly developed in some individuals and some may indeed have a genetic predisposition for this ability. In its simplest form, it can manifest with the person perceiving symbolic images, which need to be translated by the person's own inner wisdom. In its highest form, clairvoyance is the viewing of the non-physical planes, known as the astral, etheric and spiritual worlds and communicating with beings or energies that inhabit them.

American psychologist Lawrence LeShan says that there are two kinds of reality:

- *Sensory reality* - normal everyday life, perceived by the physical five senses (e.g. sight, hearing, touch, smell, taste).
- *Clairvoyant reality* - no linear time reality, judgements are impossible, all things are seen as being interconnected.

The different states of clairvoyance are defined as:

- *X-ray clairvoyance,* the ability to see through opaque objects, such as envelopes, walls or containers.

- *Travelling clairvoyance* - the ability to see current events, people or objects that are far away.
- *Spatial clairvoyance* - seeing that transcends space and time, it also relates to precognitive clairvoyance (e.g. visions of the future).
- *Retro-cognitive clairvoyance* - visions of the past, this is used in psychic archaeology and psychic crime detection.
- *Dream clairvoyance* - dreaming of an event that is happening somewhere else simultaneously, this can be helpful within your personal life and can also be an early warning system.
- *Astral clairvoyance* - having a perception of the astral and etheric planes, perception of the aura, auric colours and certain thought forms.
- *Spiritual clairvoyance* - visions of higher planes, angelic beings and states of being, or knowing.

Clairsentience

Clairsentience literally means 'clear sensing' a 'super-physical sense perception'. It involves various senses including smell, taste and touch, with emotions and physical sensations that contribute to the overall intuitive or psychic impression. Depending on the individual, these can register internally or externally. Clairsentience is usually used in conjunction with clairvoyance and clairaudience. Many people experience clairsentience without being aware of it. They may have fleeting impressions and flashes, which they consider to be nothing other than imagination. But if they acknowledge them they may find that they can prove to be amazingly accurate. This can also be tied into a gut feeling or intuition, an instinctive knowing about something, without the usual ways in which one would gain such information.

Precognition

Precognition is having direct knowledge, or a perception of the future. It is the most commonly reported of the psi phenomena, with sixty or seventy percent of it occurring in dreams. It can happen spontaneously, as in a waking vision, or in thoughts that flash into the mind accompanied by a sense of knowing. Precognition can be induced from being in trance states and through mediumship. Mostly it will occur within 48 hours of the (predicted) future event. There can often be a feeling of severe emotional shock that accompanies this experience. Most predictions are traumatic events, catastrophes etc, such as earthquakes and natural disasters, or accidents and death. These experiences are particularly common with close family and relationship ties. Precognition and premonition should not be confused. Precognition is the knowledge of a particular event, whereas

premonition is more of a sense of feeling that some unknown event is about to happen. One third to one half of all information that is gained this way is considered useful.

Telepathy

Telepathy is the mind-to-mind communication of thoughts, ideas, feelings, mental images and sensations. It transcends time and space and in many tribal societies such as the Aborigines in Australia and other indigenous tribes, it is considered to be a normal faculty. Research shows that it can be spontaneous in crisis situation, when a person becomes aware of danger to another person, often someone emotionally close to them. Information comes this way through dreams, visions, or mental images. It can come as clairaudience or in words that pop into the mind. Emotions are an important factor of this experience, in both the sender and the receiver. In studies, the electroencephalogram monitors show the recipients brain waves to match those of the senders. Telepathic communication is one of the main features of the Contact experience. The majority of people say that the communication with the ET beings is non-verbal and that they could hear what was being said to them in their mind, (i.e. telepathically). Some say that this process is very easy, almost second nature and that the communication is usually very clear. Telepathic communication does not only happen during the Contact experience itself. Many people have said that they hear from the ETs who tell them to go to a particular location, or they find they are given messages and are acting as a channel for these messages or warnings.

Remote Viewing or Travelling Clairvoyance

This ability is one of the oldest and most common forms of psi. The ability to see remote or hidden objects clairvoyantly, with the 'inner eye'. The term 'remote viewing' was born by American physicists Russell Targ and Harold Puthoff, however Targ suggests that a more accurate term for it is 'remote sensing', as the process involves not only sight, but other psychic impression too, such as smell, sound and touch. This is distinct from SRV (scientific remote viewing), a method developed where there are certain fixed protocols and co-ordinates for the mind/consciousness to fix on. Remote viewing, experienced by those with Contact seems to happen spontaneously, whereby a person has the ability to see places, people, objects and so on, which appear to negate time and space. In her book "Remote Perceptions", Angela Thompson Smith talks about her remote viewing experiences and tells of her encounters with tall 'golden beings'. She says that she was not frightened and felt a sense of belonging, but she called her experiences 'interfaces' with the visitors and said that she was taught important things by them.

Anomalous phenomena such as poltergeist phenomena

The name 'poltergeist' comes from the German words 'poltern' *to knock* and 'geist' meaning *spirit*. Many experiencers talk of strange things going around them or in the household, such as unusual noises, banging on the roof of the house, the television switching channels or switching itself on and off, electrical failures, telephones and electronic equipment behaving erratically, loud noises, strange lights and sometimes vile smells! Researchers of parapsychology explain these as being 'mischievous' or sometimes malevolent spirits. But some believe that this energy could originate from the subconscious (PK energy) of an individual. Many of those with Contact know they have and can use this ability consciously, as well as unconsciously. There is no doubt that many Contactees do have unexplained, strange happenings around their homes, which can be very frightening. Where this originates from is hard to say except that it certainly is a feature of Contact for many people, but will require more exploration and research.

A client wrote to me and said she was having lots of strange, anomalous and paranormal experiences in her home. It had been happening to her partner also and she felt it was a form of 'out of body' psychokinesis, a physical materialisation, where he had the psychic capacity to influence matter in an out of body state. At this particular time, the city where they lived had experienced an electrical power-cut. While she was out her partner tried to switch the lights on, but due to this power failure they naturally didn't work. He was fed up and frustrated because he wanted to boil some water for coffee. He said he went to the bathroom thinking about how he could use the gas plate to boil up some water, instead of using the electric kettle. Then, when he went back through to the kitchen, on the draining board there was a hot, steaming cup of coffee. To his amazement, the spoon was in the mug and the kettle itself was hot. Apparently, he ran around the house calling her name, thinking that she had come home but she wasn't there, so he totally panicked and ran around, trying all the electric switches - but there was definitely no electricity.

She also said that apart from this strange event they often believed they had been broken into, or burgled, as things about the house went missing from time to time, but were then found months later. They even found one item in the airing cupboard.

These types of anomalous experiences are quite common when experiencing Contact. Certainly, many experiencers have told me that they know in some way they have affected some of their household equipment and have even found they have been able to turn street lights off as they have gone past them. Many have found that they cannot wear watches as they will stop or break as soon as they put them on. Some researchers believe that this is due to the unique electrical field that experiencers have, or perhaps it's just the enhanced psychokinetic energy they possess.

Psychokinesis

PK is when you are able to focus mental energy on an object and are able to create such an intense point of concentration that the metal bends, or the object moves. Some individuals with Contact experience find they can do this and it has been well documented and scientifically tested. One of the most well known people to demonstrate PK is Uri Geller, who also believes he has had Contact experiences. He has the ability to bend certain metals and is famous for bending spoons, knives and forks, seemingly at will.

Geller says that he has had many encounters with ETs, and that he has been in communication with them for years. In his book "Alien Dawn", author Colin Wilson asked Geller if he believed that his paranormal powers came from an ET source, or from his unconscious mind. Geller said that he didn't actually know, but that he felt it was external to him and that whatever lay behind his abilities, it appeared to be intelligent, even though it did seem to play tricks with him sometimes.

Ann Andrews wrote to me recently to tell me about her son Jason's ability to affect inanimate objects. Ann said that a well-known UFO researcher came to visit and wanted to take Jason's photograph. Jason said that he didn't want his photo to be taken and because of that he wouldn't allow the camera to work. It didn't! The researcher continued to ask if they could have just one picture, Jason finally relented and the camera worked perfectly, but as the researcher tried to sneak another picture, again the camera stopped working. Telekinesis and teleportation are also forms of psychokinesis.

Within this chapter we have only given you a brief overview with regards to the many enhanced psychic abilities that appear to run parallel with Contact experiences. It is certainly a valuable area to research and one that may help us to understand more of the Contact jigsaw. Certainly the new generation of Star Children appear to have these abilities in abundance, and do seem to be more comfortable with them, managing them well, if given the opportunity to have them accepted as being a normal aspect of who they are. Is it time to wonder perhaps, if this is part of an evolutionary change which is being encouraged, or facilitated by extraterrestrial Contact?

As a final note to this chapter, I have found that anyone who wishes to, can certainly enhance and develop their own psi abilities and indeed I have assisted many in this process. As a former nurse, I felt I was too practical and scientific for such intuitive work and believed I was about as psychic as a lump of stone! But I did discover, to my amazement that I was able to access my own abilities too. Having them has been extremely helpful because it has given me a greater understanding of what this awareness actually feels like from a personal level. This has helped in my work with experiencers enormously, because when an individual describes their psi experiences, I am able to relate to what they are saying using my own awareness, which intuitively guides me to find the best ways to assist them. Certainly I feel that those who would like to explore this part of them more seem to gain greater understanding of their Contact experiences in the process. So expanding psi abilities is a choice anyone can make for themselves and it is only a matter of desire and commitment.

CHAPTER THIRTEEN
From Isolation to Support

"You have read as much as you possibly can on the subject, which in the beginning is sheer torture, as the more you find out the worse it becomes for you on a personal level. Not only do you find out that people 'in the know' are describing everything that you have experienced, but that when you get to the more bizarre and intricate details, your mind is triggered into remembering things that you hadn't even considered being part of the process. What's even worse is you find that you seem to know a great deal about some of the stuff that's reported and yet, it doesn't make you feel any better. You start to wonder how on earth I could have known that. In the long run though, you start to get a light grip on it and you're able to remind yourself that there are thousands of others around the world that are just like you."

Julia

This chapter will give you guidelines to help you move from isolation to support, which is the first step to ending the isolation you may feel. The lack of knowledge and understanding about your experiences creates fear and the fear acts as a block, preventing you from resourcing help, so this in turn creates even more isolation. An example of this was demonstrated to me by a mature woman who told me that it wasn't until she was in her middle years she gained the information to help her to understand what her experiences were. I asked her why it had taken her so long to seek help and she explained that as a teenager she had told her mother that she's had these strange beings come into her bedroom at night. To her amazement, her mother said: "Yes, I know, I've seen them too, but we don't ever talk about it". Because of the fear and denial shown by her mother, she also remained fearful and isolated for many years. Once she became informed, she began to feel less isolated and gained the *confidence to face her fears and find the support she needed.*

"The isolation and embarrassment I felt became so hard to bear that I sometimes had thoughts of ending my life. No one could understand what I was going through and I honestly believed I was going mad."

Tracey Taylor

There are different ways in which you can access information. Remember that information is the first step in moving from isolation to support. You can inform yourself in many ways, the obvious being reference books, reference outlets, the Internet and the numerous organisations out there that have knowledge about the Contact phenomenon. Initially it may be difficult, as Julia said; it was like *sheer torture* for her. David also said (in his letter, Chapter 1) how difficult it was for him to read a book about this subject. But ultimately, they both found that by accessing the information (albeit eventually), the knowledge gained made them feel less isolated and through it, they found the support and reassurance they needed.

The steps to take that will move you from isolation to support are:

1. Information and resources . . . *Where are they?*
2. Check list . . . *Who can you trust? (see chapter 6)*
3. Emotional support . . . *Who will meet my needs best? (see Chapter 7).*

Information and resources. Where are they, where can I find them?

Once you take this initial step you will discover there is an enormous amount of information available to you. You will need to use personal discernment with regards to what information has any relevance to you and at all times be aware of the fact that however credible the source may seem, no information is totally objective or unbiased. You will need to trust your inner guidance and decide for yourself what information has integrity.

"It's like *us* against the whole world! People need to know that they are not alone and there is hope for them. In living and dealing with this mind-boggling and often terrifying experience, they can find the courage in themselves to overcome the fear and insecurities they have, concerning their own unique experiences. Most importantly for them, they must know that there is help out there".

Sandra

Reference books, magazines, TV, radio, the Internet, conferences and workshops

Books are the obvious resource and I have listed some of the better-known and most useful ones in the appendix at the back, (see page 285). I have categorised them regarding their focus and perspective and you must choose what is most relevant to you. You may find as you learn more about your experiences, that your focus will shift (i.e. the move from evidence of this reality, to the acquisition or realization of information and what it may mean from a wider perspective). This reference list is by no means comprehensive, but the books themselves contain pointers and further recommended reading to help guide you further. It is important to remember that not all the experiencer stories will fit yours exactly; we have to recognise that our own individual nature affects our personal perceptions and how we react and understand our experiences. If you are in a 'fear place', it may be wiser to avoid books that come from a fear focus, as they may give power to your fear, so allow yourself to be guided by your inner knowing.

Ufology is the second most resourced topic of interest on the Internet, which is a fascinating fact in itself and we may well wonder why that is? But is does mean that there is a vast amount of information out there for you to access. (For a list of resource information, see pages 307-313).

Apart from what is listed in the appendix, there are other resources available; you just have to look for them.

"In my desperation, I started flicking through the phone book and I looked under U for UFO, since that was the one thing on my mind. I finally found an organisation called UFORUM and spoke to a helpful man who gave me the number of a counsellor."

Sandra

Telephone for help

It may seem too easy, but in fact many Ufology organisations are listed in the white pages of your telephone directory. Mutual UFO Network (MUFON) is a well-known one. If you are unsure which ones are operating in your area then call directory enquiries!

In crisis it is useful to remember that there are many crisis telephone counselling services that deal with a range of issues such as: "Samaritan Befrienders (International)" and "Lifeline (Australia)". All counsellors are trained to honour individual experiences. But it may be wise, once again, to check their openness to this experience. Due to ignorance of the phenomenon they may find it difficult to give you the openness and acceptance you are looking for.

Professional help

How do you find a counsellor/therapist who will listen without judgement and who will honour your Contact experience?

The organisations listed on page 292 are made up of professionals from a variety of mental health fields, such as psychiatrists, psychologists, medical professionals, counsellors and practitioners of the healing arts. All are open to Contact phenomena, they are actively involved in sharing information and research and they can offer you consultation and referral options.

Obviously there are many organisations that can help you access information and support. Our list is not meant to be a comprehensive one, but it will enable you to resource professional help through the numerous options available to you.

Researching information is the first step in empowering yourself and by accumulating information, you can gain the confidence you need to acknowledge your super- reality. Reference material alone has the evidence to support your own experiences and understanding. Acknowledging this reality and *owning your own* is another crucial part of your Contact awakening, helping you to fully integrate. From isolation to support means you are able to access the emotional support available with confidence. The resources presented here are intended to help you to do this.

CHAPTER FOURTEEN
Expressions of ET Reality – Awakening to our Multidimensional Selves

"A human being is a part of the whole, called by us 'the universe', limited in time and space. He experiences himself, his thoughts and feelings as something separated from the rest, a kind of optical delusion of his consciousness. This delusion is a prison, restricting us to our personal desires and to affection for a few persons close to us."

Albert Einstein

"This is the new way. We are being taught to access the all-knowing aspect of ourselves, to realise the connection we have with each other on a cosmic scale. Once the entirety of existence and the personal connection we have to all is achieved, there is no need for tedious, verbal communication; we shall know instantly another thought, as there is no need for time as we know it, as all is all knowing, always. There is no always either, as the always is now."

Tracey Taylor

"It begs the question, not who are they, but who are we?"

Robert O. Dean

What are we becoming?

This chapter highlights the intriguing and transformative 'expressions' of ET reality, exploring the tangibility of these expressions, with fascinating outcomes, even for those who have had difficult and fear-based experiences. It is unfortunate that many of the fascinating expressions of Contact experiences have been negated or ignored by many UFO researchers and organisations, whose main focus in the past has been based on fear and trauma. This focus has obscured the fact that many of the traumatic outcomes are just the beginning of the human Contact journey. There are many experiencers who will admit that their initial difficulties stemmed from a lack of understanding and the denial of their experiences. It was only when they started to 'wake up' and understand that their negativity changed. Ultimately, with this natural process, many began to interpret their experiences not from a traumatic perspective, but through personal growth and transformation. Through this process Contact has therefore been acknowledged as being a catalyst for major lifestyle changes, triggering huge paradigm shifts within many individuals.

As the experiencer awakens to their multi-reality, many parts of their personal jigsaw will slot together, moving them through a transformative process whereby their experiences become a catalyst for many other intriguing 'expressions' of Contact. These expressions are not rare, nor are they exceptional. They have simply not been recognised before as being a valid or significant part of Contact phenomena. The reasons for this are two-fold: one is because these expressions have a less tangible nature and Ufologists and investigations have mostly focused primarily on scientifically quantifiable data. Secondly, the significance of these expressions has not been generally recognised. The intangible and often unusual nature of these expressions also means that many individuals have been reluctant to mention them, as they are unaware of their significance with regards to their Contact, they just don't make the connection.

I believe that these expressions are very significant, important parts of the whole Contact experience, because they show us in a very demonstrable way, that Contact affects many patterns of human behaviour. The person will experience unusual thoughts and feelings, changes in consciousness, they gain information, which is not consciously learned, or as Jena would say, a *knowledge bomb*. These knowledge bombs can contain complex understandings of scientific principles and information with a strong ecological and spiritual focus. These expressions also manifest through visual artwork and symbolism, through spontaneous vocal expressions in the form of languages of unknown origin, through well documented high sense abilities and altered perceptions, which allow the individual to perceive energy fields, thereby utilising this energy for healing and change. But finally, very tangible expressions can occur through dramatic life changes and physical and emotional healing within the individual.

It seems that even the most traumatic ET experiences do have some positive outcome or other, enhancing individual awareness and triggering some special ability. To understand why these expressions seem to manifest in this way, we have to look at the significant clues many experiencers mention, such as the space school phenomenon, when Aiden, age 5 said: "Mummy I learn more on the ship that I do at school". So could it be that these expressions and this new awareness is all part of a progressive and significant ET education programme? Numerous accounts have come in from experiencers who describe receiving education and learning on the ships, including being taught new scientific and philosophical concepts. Why we have Contact and whatever the reason is, we should acknowledge that it does seem to create some fascinating outcomes and intriguing human expressions, which I believe, can be a major chrysalis for change.

So what do these changes indicate and what do the experiencers themselves think this could mean for humanity as a whole?

Let's first of all summarise the expressions of ET Contact and look at how they may manifest within us:

Our consciousness

- HSA, High Sense Abilities
- Inter-dimensional interaction with other life forms
- Past lives with ET Contact
- Past lives as ETs
- Dual consciousness, feelings of having both a human and Et self
- Parallel lives, two aspects of the self co-existing at the same time.

Feelings and knowing

- Feelings of being visited by future selves
- Feelings of being part ET and human
- Awareness of being able to do more than this reality suggests
- Uncomfortable within the human body
- Feeling not connected to a human family, more with a galactic family
- Feeling very different to everyone else.

Spiritual and philosophical growth

- Major life changes in behaviour and beliefs
- Multidimensional exploration of our own consciousness, i.e. spiritual, astral or soul
- Awareness of other lifetimes.

Visual and vocal expressions

- The desire to speak unusual languages, (could this be the beginning of telepathy?)
- The desire to produce unusual writing or scripts
- The desire to produce art and symbolism.

Life changes and healing

- Awareness of energy healing of being healed through a Contact experience.
- A human/ET self observing healing being done on another extraterrestrial being.

Education, 'Homo Noeticus', the Star Kids

- Ecological and planetary awareness
- Downloading of information sometimes referred to as 'knowledge bombs'
- A sense of feeling of 'mission'.

Contact awakens a change in human consciousness, which not only manifests in terms of personal growth and philosophical values, but offers an awareness and knowledge of other realities, which are perceived as being past lives, giving us more understanding of the eternal nature of the human spirit or soul. With this we are granted an awareness of unlimited human reality, suggesting that we have the ability to exist and traverse through the dimensions of time and space. This kind of awareness can also incorporate concepts such as parallel universes and the possibility of parallel lives.

Julia says: "When you become aware of the other *yous*, the shock to the system is profound, both physically and mentally. Your life changes with this discovery, not only through the realisation, but with the people you meet and attract from there on.

The physical traumas experienced in past, parallel or multiple lives, give a bleed-through (awareness of these traumas), but at the same time it's possible that the higher self, or the more spiritually advanced aspect of ourselves is the reason. This aspect is unable to progress (spiritually), unless all the other parts do. The multiples, pasts and parallels need to be integrated somewhere."

These expressions can also manifest whereby an individual becomes aware of a 'dual consciousness', with strong ET connections. The dual consciousness suggests to them that one part, or one aspect of them, has this ET nature, whilst the other feels human. Some have said that their ET self can feel like a scientist or observer and that it struggles with the limits of the human self, particularly human emotions and relationships. Such people can feel deep emotional ties with what they believe to be their ET family, which can sometimes feel stronger than the connection they have with their own (human) family. Many experiencers also talk of incredible abilities they have that cannot manifest on earth, such as the ability to fly and they sense that this part of them is truly alien. The remarkable aspect to these kinds of expressions is that most of the individuals are amazed by their actual awareness of such concepts.

Contact awakens the individual, bringing the possibility of their multi-reality into their consciousness. These aspects can also show themselves through other expressions, such as visually and vocally, through fascinating artwork and scripts, or by being able to speak unusual languages. I have discovered that these expressions are far more commonplace than generally recognised. This was demonstrated to me through a series of events that let me and a group of special friends to produce a video (containing ACERN's visual and vocal data, called "Expressions of ET Contact, A Visual Blueprint").

A good friend, Bradley De Niese suggested the idea originally and helped me with its production. David Sandercock, a talented musician also volunteered and composed the music score, (which went on to win an award). Experiencers have said that David's music actually encapsulates the vibration, or energy of the various Et beings that are portrayed throughout the film. The main focus here was to bring a tangible, fascinating aspect of Contact to a much wider audience, informing them but also helping the experiencer understand and validate the unusual events in their lives. The video has been remarkably successful, as it demonstrates the more intriguing aspects of Contact. It has become a confirmatory resource for many experiencers and also demonstrates that these expressions are far more universal and not particularly unique.

Many individuals who have seen the video have told me that as they watched it they recognised behaviours, artwork, or a language that they too had expressed at some point in their lives, but previously dismissed them as being unimportant. Many have been amazed to see ET beings they recognised, finding that some of the drawings or symbols echoed their own. Some even recognised the strange languages spoken by Tracey Taylor and other experiencers.

Author, Dana Redfield commented: "When I saw the video I was stunned, not only by the art, but by certain pictures of ETs that were like drawings I had done myself. More links here in connecting in the spirit of *we are the message*. The video helped me in a special way. Feeling that my mother would enjoy the art, I invited her to watch "Expressions" with me. She saw my tears when the image of a particular lion man (drawn by Jane) came on the screen. At that moment I reached into a box and brought out the artwork I had drawn, to show her. For the first time she saw, she really saw, *finally, she got it*. She got that the UFO presence is real. She got *that something inexplicable is happening in consciousness* and she knew I had not been in contact with other Australian experiencers seven years ago, which is when I produced my artwork."

The DVD has been a validation of Contact for many experiencers who are continually questioning events in their lives. It has helped them to make sense of their own expressions and the unusual feelings and emotions that Contact can evoke. Many have told me that they were stunned, but relieved to see that other people had replicated the similar expressions of art, or scripts produced by themselves. For them, it evoked a deep, emotional response and these creative, visual expressions of art, symbology, writing and languages seem to act as a trigger for a whole new awareness and greater understanding.

Further, it would seem that the contents of the video proved to be a valuable tool for healing for many experiencers, because by watching it they gained more validation, giving integrity to their own experiences. For those who can produce the vocal and visual expressions, we offer further information and explore this process more deeply, looking through the eyes of others, examining their understanding, not only of why they are compelled to speak such unusual sounds, but also with regards to what it feels like and what they believe its purpose is. Many experiencers have told me that these languages feel very natural, that they enjoy speaking them and that it all seems very familiar in some way. Some have said that the languages flow easier than their native tongue and that there are several different kinds of language they have no trouble in speaking. One lady spoke dozens of them and used the 'tones' of the languages in her healing work, whereby she said that the individual would recognise the sounds on some deeper level. Tracey Taylor also speaks several of these languages (see Chapter 8) and she also feels that the Star Children have an awareness of them and if they try they will be able to speak them fluently. I have heard from experiencers in America and parts of Australia who have said they recognised and had an understanding of what was being said when they heard these languages spoken by Tracey (and others) in our video.

"When Tracey began to speak in the musical language, I spoke along with her, almost as if I was engaging in a two way conversation".

Dana Redfield

Tracey explains it this way: "The language is a more accurate representation of an individual *soul* vibration. It means that the language comes directly from the essence of the universal mind or God, which ultimately links all of existence together. The spoken sounds of a particular language tend to bypass much of the linear logical aspect of consciousness, as the interpretation is initially unknown by the conscious mind. Therefore there is no input from the analytical mind other than enabling the person to express the necessary sounds. There is no preconceived idea or concept about what a particular sound actually means because this type of language is not structured in the way the English language is. A particular sound or word is not related to a particular description or meaning. The language has no such structure and is therefore not related to the past in any way, therefore in its purest form, before it becomes vocal, it bypasses linear space-time. The language does not result in a reactive state of being as the language is expressed as creation. The language is a creation of the soul in a way that directly connects to the soul of another unconsciously. Therefore the languages cannot be interpreted over time in a way that we might interpret a language of another culture. There is no framework as the interpretation of the sound vibration is instantaneous and cannot be interpreted accurately into English, or another language spoken on earth at this time. It is teaching us to communicate with our soul and the souls of others.

This is one of the steps from words to telepathic communications. A person speaking the language to another may not comprehend what is being expressed consciously, although they do have a deeper sense and feeling of a deeper connection that is being achieved with another person. The other person often feels an urge to communicate back in a similar way as they feel deeply touched, with an understanding and equilibrium that extends and connects all of existence."

Researcher, Gary Anthony, in the United Kingdom is presently exploring and collating data about this aspect of the phenomenon and has several qualified linguists assisting him. But given Tracey's interpretation of these 'star languages' one wonders how successful they will be! Certainly Tracey's understanding of this language phenomenon is a very complex one, as she suggests that these languages are a beginning for us, an evolution of some form of telepathic communication.

Tracey also demonstrates her Contact through the writing of strange scripts and her geometric art, which incorporates complex symbolism. Some of the scripts look like hieroglyphs or shorthand and again, this process is automatic and fluid for her. As we have seen many times over, the experiencer does not have to instigate any of these processes, they just follow a natural desire to draw or write.

Tracey says: "The drawings are another aspect of a similar communication. Again, the instantaneous nature in which the drawings come through leave no room for conscious interference. As I have said before, I need to be distracted while bringing through the geometric designs. I believe I am in direct 'soul' communication, which cannot be interpreted or interfered with consciously. This form of pure creation leaves no room for a reaction to any part of the drawing I have previously drawn and again, the drawings communicate directly with the essence of the individual. The symbols contain more information than could ever be expressed using words. In the form of symbology, the soul or 'essence' of one's self can, on this level, comprehend the entirety of the message, or communication all at once. There is no relationship to the past as the communication is received instantly without the need for interpretation. This is the new way."

I also asked Tracey how long it took her do these drawings and she said that the coloured ones, because of their complicated nature took about four

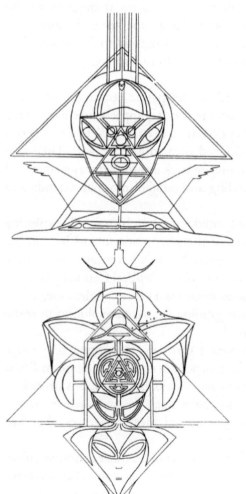

hours, whereas the simpler black and white ones just ten minutes. What's more, she did not use a ruler for any of the lines or angles she drew, which are not only symmetrical, but amazingly straight.

"I completed the symbols at different times over a two year period between 1997 and 1999. Some of the drawings are recollections of what I have seen during experiences, which involved ETs, their craft, or both. After each dream (experience), as I drew the symbol I remembered, my hand would take over, as though I had no conscious input with regards to which way the pen would go, or what shape I was drawing. When this happens, I just have the feeling that I am being guided. I am never in what I would call a trance, because I am completely aware of what's happening and of what's going on around me and I can always stop drawing if I want to. In fact, if I try to concentrate on which way the pen is supposed to go, then it becomes more and more difficult for me to complete the drawing.

"The drawings always ended up being much more detailed than any of my recollections and sometimes there would be this kind of hieroglyphic typescript aside, which I would complete after each symbol, or in some cases it's written into the symbol itself. I feel that the script is a description of their high meaning and is connected to where they (the ETs) originate.

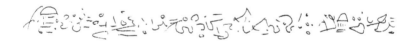

"As I write the script, I have a sense of its meaning and often key words will come into my mind giving me interpretations, (which I have written around the outside of the two larger coloured drawings). At one stage I became extremely irritated because I wanted to know exactly what the symbols meant, then I had an overwhelming feeling to put pen to paper and I completed a very complex, involved design, in colour. The message I received through my mind was that the true meaning of these symbols was far above anything I could comprehend at my present stage of evolution.

Were I to be given this information, it would be likely I'd *explode,* so I knew that from then on I would have to apply the art of patience.

"Initially, when I first started to draw, the symbols to me felt incomplete as only half of the drawing would be coloured and the other half left in black and white line. I asked about this and was told that the drawings are symbolic representations of humanity's evolution and that because our evolution is incomplete, (in our time and space), then so is the drawing - the uncoloured sections were symbolising our future. After completing each drawing I would always feel very alive and balanced, with a great feeling of exhilaration as I felt I had some knowledge, or that I knew something really important without really understanding what it was.

"Not all the symbols are completed from memories of dreams, most just come through at different times, usually when I am most distracted, like when I'm watching my favourite programme on TV, or talking to someone on the phone, or listening to information at talks and lectures. After completing seven of the black and white symbols at separate times over a two year period, I had an extremely vivid encounter with some beings who gave me a message and told me to photocopy all the symbols onto transparency material, because they would all fit together to form a larger symbol. Because of the intensity of the message, which kept coming to me over and over, I did what I was asked. To my amazement, they did fit together in many different ways. The triangles were at exactly the same angle and it wasn't until I went along to the support group meeting with other experiencers that it all came together for me. With the valuable input from the group, the symbols were put together in a way I had not previously tried. They all fitted together perfectly to form a backward L shape. Other symbols have been completed since then, which perfectly slot into this.

"The hieroglyphic-type writing, which comes through, is also completed in the same way as the drawings. I seem to be sidetracked from the writing, when it flows through, it feels as if it's being guided from somewhere else, or something else. It actually feels more natural to write in this way than it does for me to write in English, this also goes for speaking the language. I now feel I need to put all these images onto computer so that they can be seen multi- dimensionally, as this is how I am sure they are meant to be viewed. If this can happen, I think it will reveal much more to us about our reality and who we are."

Another woman, from another part of Australia (whose art I also included on the video), describes the process for her drawings, which depict many parallels to Tracey's description. She says: "When I do my drawings I feel a sense of purpose. I love, love and love doing them. And when the urge is gone I feel a sense of loss and abandonment. And then I feel like I am going through the motions of life and living, until this 'urge' starts again.

"I feel it hard to put my exact feelings into words; the urge (as I call it) is very strong when it happens. It's like nothing else matters or exists around me. It's like an unquestionable thirst and I can't get enough of it. I am aware of everything around me and have conversations, but I can still draw, so I am not in trance. I don't feel any entity taking me over or anything like that, but I do feel it is coming from me, whatever it all means. I feel it is embedded in my mind and it's a part of me that needs something in particular to trigger it off. I hope this all makes sense to you, as I am trying to put things I don't understand into words. I don't yet know the reason for the colours that I use, only that I sense the combinations."

Dana Redfield also relates her own experiences. In a letter to me she said: "While I did a lot of art and geometric drawings, such bliss, the focus of my work was the communications that resulted. However, the overall message coming from our related works is basically the same and that it all has to do with expanding our consciousness."

The fascinating insights that come from those who express their Contact in such a creative way suggests to me this could be another avenue of accessing the human psyche through visual and vocal expression. Certainly this creativity affects the person at a deep and profound level. Through this process they experience an expanded reality, access fascinating and complex information, which leaves them with a sense of awareness and a new understanding of our origins, our reality and ourselves. The awareness of human abilities and potential that can be accessed through these expressions also suggests that these expressions can act as a trigger for further Contact.

The ways in which Contact inspires such creativity, depicted through expressions such as these is not only tantalising but causes us to question further. Are these expressions given to us in this way to demonstrate to humanity, very graphically, that we are not alone? Or is it more than that? Is it a subtle, but powerful way of creating change within us? Through the use of 'unseen' energies, symbology, art and languages, are they put there to trigger some new awareness deep within our psyche? Certainly those who create these expressions believe that it could be.

From it, many begin to seek healthier lifestyles, develop a strong passion for healing themselves and the planet and demonstrate an awakened desire for understanding the soul and spiritual self, continually questioning through their expanding consciousness. The Star Children seem to be far more comfortable with this awareness, but still struggle to be 'human', living within the confines of what they see as being limited, human thinking. Their awareness seems to be way beyond their human years, with many role reversals, as they become our teachers and we the students. They already have much detailed information regarding our ET visitors, as well as an understanding of whom and what we are.

Tracey herself acknowledges that her drawings have been intricately woven with knowledge and information of our origins, showing her how these expressions have the ability to access the human psyche on a level relating to more subtle, intuitive awareness. She has confirmation of this also, from individuals who write to her after they have seen her artwork. Many say that they experienced a range of emotions as they saw it, including recognition and a deep resonance, which has become the catalyst to a new awareness of themselves and their reality.

So what is it about her work and others like her that creates this amazing recognition and response? Tracey believes that such material acts as a catalyst, or trigger, to open up the unconscious part of ourselves. We already know that such visual expressions offer us a 'window' into the psyche and there is no doubt that this is an amazing and very intriguing platform in which to view Contact.

I was contacted by Martin soon after I wrote Awakening. Martin was keen to connect with Tracey as he resonated to her art work and scripts. Martin's hieroglyphs are a wonderful example as is his process, of downloaded data through creative expression. His works demonstrate similar patterns to individuals having otherworldly experiences. Born in the UK, Martin has painted since childhood. He has worked in advertising, illustrated books and worked on an environmental magazine. He has lived and exhibited in various parts of Ireland since 1973. A self-taught musician, he plays improvised healing sounds on piano at Bantry House in Ireland.

Martin's authentic healing codes

Martin says of his complex scripts, "I am rather astonished at what "I" have done. I mean, the characters are totally consistent throughout and not only flawless but, to my senses written with the bold confidence and authenticity of a piece of Zen calligraphy. To be honest, I haven't a clue what I've written. But, I do know when I write only one character wrong, I throw it on the fire and start over. I can say for certain the script is an integral aspect of my work as a whole, which includes the painting, drawing, music, and writing. All of it is "received" in an inspirational sense, while simultaneously refined and perfected in all its minutest detail. I believe I am using both hemispheres of the brain in balance. Forty or so years of meditation have enabled me to empty the mind of all content, and be a receptive conduit, while still using the critical faculty which discerns the authenticity or otherwise of the minutest nuances. Whatever the source of the material it is all consciously attuned to transmitting a flow of images which spontaneously embody wholeness, harmony, balance, and beauty; a subliminally aesthetic healing code. I would say it comes from receptivity to "the wholeness" manifested into the here and now."

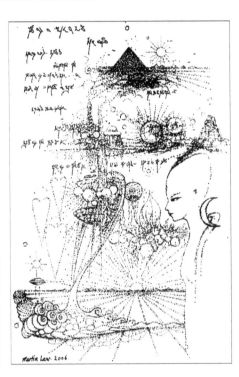

Martin Law. 2006

Martin Law's website is www.rainbowmaker.info

From trauma to understanding
The expressions of healing and transformation.
Discovering the optical illusion!

Throughout this book we have looked at how Contact can present itself as being a frightening experience for some people. We have also seen that as the individual understands more about their own experiences, this fear can often dissipate, change and become something far more positive, altering their perspective. So why is this, and what triggers this change?

It would seem that many experiences are often misinterpreted through the person's fears and lack of understanding. This creates a kind of 'optical illusion' of events. As the individual gains a deeper understanding of their experience, they discover that their fear has created this limited optical illusion and what they believed happened is more often than not completely different to what really did occur (see Ann Andrew's story, Chapter 10).

Even for those who haven't been able to yet uncover information regarding their traumatic experiences it still seems that they can find special abilities within themselves that are positive outcomes for these unusual and unexplained happenings. We have illustrated that some of these positive outcomes can manifest with heightened sense abilities, including healing, and although Contact would appear to instigate much of this, many have also said they have been physically healed through Contact. There is no doubt that for some, these positive outcomes have been seen initially through their 'self-made' optical illusion of fear. But with deeper exploration, what they find can give them a whole new understanding with the realisation that the encounters have been the catalyst for positive and dramatic life changes.

Two young men visited me (coincidentally), within a few weeks of each other. Both were of a similar age and both had almost identical life experiences, involving Contact encounters that were terrifying for them. Their initial understanding of their experiences was completely viewed through the optical illusion of fear. It was only later, when they delved deeper and explored these encounters more fully that they realised that the experiences had actually turned them around from living destructive and unhealthy lifestyles, to very positive, transformative ones.

Both these young men told me that they had experimented with a variety of drugs, (including 'hard' drugs, such a heroin). They indicated that they had done many things to support this habit, which they regretted. One of the men, who I shall call Mike said that it had been sheer good luck that had kept him out of trouble, which came in the form of a very sharp 'intuition' that guided him when danger of discovery was close. Mike said that as far as he was concerned, he was dead set on this road of self-destruction and would have continued this lifestyle had he not had a particularly terrifying Contact experience.

This experience was so horrifying for him that he stopped taking drugs immediately from that moment onwards. He did initially attribute this awful experience to drug abuse. He felt that the drugs he had taken had induced this state of mind and this is a reasonable supposition for anyone to make. However, there were dramatic physical changes that followed, which leads me to believe that there could have been more to it than that.

Mike told me how he had changed, not only in attitude and behaviour, but in many other ways that were new to him. He was keen to start a new life and was drawn to study many scientific and philosophical concepts. He wanted to understand a particularly frightening Contact encounter, which although had been life changing for him, it had puzzled him also. Regression would enable him to have a better understanding and would open up the discovery of what had happened and this is what he chose to do.

His conscious memory was limited, he remembered his terror as he woke up from a dream, the dog jumped up at him and bit him on the leg and then he remembers nothing after that. But through the regression he saw what he had initially interpreted as being his dog was in fact an ET being. The bite was not a bite from his dog at all, but was something given to tranquillise him. Mike saw himself being led out of the door into an 'energy vortex' and up into a spaceship, which he then described in great detail. He said he was shown many things whilst on the ship and also says that his body was purified and healed by the ETs. Again, he graphically described the process and said: "My liver had all this awful gunk in it, a brown, horrible mess was being removed from it". He described his body being put through a cleansing process, from the damage of the drug taking and alcohol abuse. Then he told me that he had woken up the next day feeling absolutely great for the first time in years.

To have this understanding was very helpful and he said that he now fully believes that his terrifying encounter was deliberately engineered to stop him taking drugs and to make him change his previous lifestyle. He believes that they made him so terrified and let him assume that the nightmare was drug induced. Certainly he said that the encounter terrified him so much that he stopped taking drugs from that day on and that he was compelled to totally change his destructive lifestyle.

It could be very easy to explain away this account as being a personal or 'drug induced' fantasy, even albeit a transformative one, but with this story we also had real and tangible evidence that something truly amazing had happened. Mike had been previously diagnosed with hepatitis C, due to his drug abuse. After this encounter, his latest blood analysis showed no evidence of the hepatitis C virus. He had apparently been completely healed.

Coincidentally at this time, another young man, who I shall call Steve, came to see me. As mentioned, Steve was of a similar age to Mike and had a similar history, his lifestyle also dramatically changed after Contact. Steve said that he had been on a cocktail of drugs since his early teens and then embarked on a methadone programme, which lasted a couple of years. He'd had a particular frightening encounter and after that he said he just knew he had to stop taking drugs. Soon after the experience, he said his perceptions were different, he could tune into peoples thoughts quite easily and he began to see energy fields around people and objects. Steve was very disturbed by it all, so much so he became a voluntary patient in a hospital and was put up for assessment by a mental health team.

After days of tests however, they failed to find anything psychologically wrong with him. He experienced amazing healing within himself and despite being on drugs for so many years, which destroy calcium in the teeth; he found that his teeth were in perfect health, with no evidence of decay. Also notwithstanding the sharing of needles when using drugs, his blood was healthy and totally clear of all infections and abnormalities. Steve regularly sees UFOs and he feels they are keeping an eye on him. He is slowly coping with his new awareness, his most difficult challenge being his family, who do not believe in the phenomenon and therefore attribute everything he tells them to the drugs he has taken in the past.

The Contact optical illusion of personal fear gives many experiencers a limited understanding. It is interesting though, that for both these young men it was the terrifying aspect of their Contact experiences that led to the very positive life changes. Dolores Cannon, a respected author and clinical hypnotherapist, has regressed many individuals who have experienced Contact. Her conclusions echo mine and she also believes that many of the so-called 'fearful' encounters are nothing but limited and distorted versions of the complete experience and when fully explored, can demonstrate a vastly different scenario. In her book, "The Custodians", she concludes that many of those who have had fearful encounters often reveal more positive perspectives once they have explored their experiences in depth.

- The optical illusion of fear suggests that the longer we abstain from judgements regarding our experiences, the more information and understanding we will have. It is inevitable for each individual to judge their experience based on what they feel has happened and how they are affecting them. But these conscious clues are hardly ever the full picture. We also know that our 'visitors' can utilize and use screen memories, and can make themselves appear in different guises, which all seem to fit with what we want to believe, thus reinforcing these optical illusions. Ironically, the ETs that may look the most frightening are the ones that mostly have demonstrated deep compassion, sympathy and wisdom. It seems that it may be a valuable lesson for us to learn that our appearance does not necessarily indicate good or bad, unless we judge it to be so and our conditioning both dictates and influences this. Perhaps the optical illusions are also used to teach us to look deeper into ourselves and see what the experience is really showing? Just like the small child that is taken to the doctors will believe that the doctor is a nasty person because he wants to stick a sharp needle into him. The child will not understand, not until his is older, when he is able to see that it was done to help him get better.

"Over time, I even started to view my involvement with the aliens and my relationship with the unknown as a valuable asset. What had once been only an annoying challenge, laced with nights of misery and emotional pain, gradually evolved to reveal the bright and friendly wrappings of a special gift? The gift was in the form of knowledge, or enlightenment and spiritual truth".

Excerpt from *"In The Presence of Aliens", Janet Bergmark*

Negative experiences can be seen differently once we have the understanding. It is not always possible to offer this deep 'inner work', but a new perspective can help the experiencer, whatever their level of awareness and understanding may be.

A few years ago, I was presenter and group therapist for an International UFO Congress in America. Attended by over a thousand people, workshops were also held for experiencers who exhibited a huge range of encounters, from the most loving experiences to the most terrifying. It can be very hard for some individuals who are having terrifying experiences to relate to those having the more positive ones. Understandably, those still traumatised feel very angry, perceiving themselves to be victims of these encounters. At the end of one workshop, I saw a mature lady, who I shall call Joan. She was very upset, so I went to talk with her. Joan said that she had felt very isolated in the group as it had seemed to her that no one else had experienced Contact in such a negative way as herself, or even if they had, they had moved through it enough to be able to adopt a more positive outlook.

Close to tears, Joan said that both she and her daughter were having very terrifying experiences. She was a very religious and spiritual person and said she had prayed constantly to God to be protected, but that nothing worked. She said she felt abandoned by God and that her religious beliefs were disintegrating before her. She was not only terrified by her experiences, (which included some fearful looking reptilian beings, that in themselves evoked fear and conjured up images of demons), she also felt that these encounters must mean on some level that she was a bad person. This was reinforced by her living in a very insular community, where she was perceived of as being different and regarded with suspicion.

There was no doubt that Joan was very traumatised, not only by her experiences with these beings, but through the loss of her religious beliefs and the way in which she had been ostracised by members of her community. For her to hear from some of the experiencers that she should welcome these experiences, only reinforced her feelings of isolation and doubled the fear that there must be something really wrong with her. In such a limited environment the only way in which I could support Joan was to reassure her, to tell her that it was okay and normal to feel the way she did and her fearful experiences in no way meant that she was a bad person. I did suggest that often there was more behind the conscious memory of the experiences than she may be aware of and when we looked at the facts, she realised that, despite the fearful experiences, both she and her daughter were always brought back.

I asked her if she had any special talents or strengths and she said she had a healing skill, which was in demand by people. She had apparently helped many who were suffering with the Aids virus. She told me her touch seemed to sooth them, although she didn't know why.

We talked about this gift of hers more. She said that she seemed to know intuitively what was going on with people because she picked up their feelings. Although Joan had struggled with the loss of her religious beliefs, whereby she felt that her prayers had not been answered, we explored what this meant for her and how these doubts had drawn her to the point whereby she had no alternative other than to rely on her own inner strengths.

It was very synchronous that three of the presenters at this congress shared their personal Contact stories with everyone and described how they too had learned to trust their own inner knowing and wisdom. They had moved from fear and it had proved to be their trigger for personal change and transformation.

Joan, (who was in such a *fear place* at the time) is such a special lady in my mind; she still continues to contact me and is actively pursuing her healing skills and exploring the meaning of her encounters. It seems that whatever our Contact experiences are, and the more we are able to come from a place of non-judgement and openness, the quicker we are able to realise that Contact does change us for the better.

James Walden, (author of "The Ultimate Alien Agenda") speaks about his issues with fear and said that at one point he had contemplated suicide. In a letter to me, he wrote: "I am much closer to the mastery of non-judgement. I don't feel qualified to judge anyone's thoughts and behaviours, (as long as they do no harm to others), especially after announcing *I was abducted by an alien*. Without judgement, my mind is free to select loving thoughts and responses, to reconnect with my spiritual awareness.

"When I healed my *victim* consciousness, my world shifted to a positive pole. I am now a full-time physical, emotional and spiritual healing practitioner, hypnotherapist and holistic educator. My primary goals are to help people learn how to take responsibility for their own health attitudes and awareness. This I think is what my abductors (teachers) were trying to help (force) me to accomplish."

Space education for terrestrials, what can this mean?

"I sometimes get a headache, my head's so small, I can't always take it all in so quickly, it's like knowledge bombs are being dropped on my head."

Jena – at ten years old

Are the Star Children's secret 'space schools' part of an extraterrestrial education programme?

"But mummy we learn more on the ships than we do at school".

Aiden – aged five

Whitley Strieber, author of many books about Contact, including "Communion" has also written about this 'secret' education. There is new research too, that shows how children are maturing much faster now, as opposed to how they were twenty years ago.

Many experiencers mention space schools, the encouragement of a multi-awareness and advanced maturity, knowledge bombs and a deep emotional connection to the 'galactic family' concept. Many of them are highly frustrated because they are not, as yet, consciously aware of what their 'mission' or purpose is. There is however, an awareness of being taught something, of being shown things through the mind and there is an increased consciousness regarding energy, frequencies and how to manage them.

A young man in his twenties told me that as a child he played games with his mind and could make a candle flame larger or smaller, just by thinking it. Unusual? Perhaps not, as a recently published book, *China's Super Psychics* also mentions children who display mind-telekinetic abilities, such as being able to make a flower bud open and bloom with mind power. So are all these accounts simple demonstrations of the new human?

Ann Andrews mentioned to me that her son Jason 'freaked her out' many times by demonstrating his mind-energy abilities. He could show her that he was unaffected by extreme heat, as he had picked eggs out of a boiling pan of water with is bare hands and taken a roast dinner out of the oven without the protection of oven gloves or a cloth.

The new humans are educated, have a respect for our living earth and they speak of being shown better and safer energy sources that will not continue to pollute the atmosphere. Interestingly, many of those who have this 'space education' become involved with organisations engaged in protecting the environment. With a heightened moral and spiritual awareness, they actively seek their life purpose. This heightened sensitivity and empathy for all creatures is combined with a strong desire to nurture and protect all forms of life. Many can become quite distraught with regards to any form of killing and there are feelings of deep sadness when any form of life is brutalised or destroyed. Some will say that many of the reasons for this are because they have been shown the horrific outcomes of war, nuclear disasters and biological warfare. These feelings expand and increase the cosmic connection to our space visitors, reinforcing a sense of mission and urgency. With huge, personal and often transformative lifestyle changes and beliefs, these people are drawn to a rural or more holistic life, with many engaged in healing and alternative practices. Some will opt out of materialist lifestyles altogether, propelled by the desire to lead simpler, more stress-free lives.

"But mummy, we are the aliens!"

Jena – at seven years old

Is there a multi-dimensional awakening with something incredible happening on a massive scale that most of the world has no 'open' consciousness of? There is no question that over recent years, many people are changing in ways that show an improvement in awareness, with the diminishing of human tendencies for aggression and destructive behaviour. Expanded awareness, a deep spirituality, sensitivity, creativity, healing, expressions of intuition, including the knowledge of new languages and writing, which reached the deepest parts of our awareness and psyche. All these experiences suggests that millions of people are not only changing, but being prepared, either by some new, genetic encoding (as some experiencers believe), or by the utilization of physical or energetic implants, triggering a greater awareness within, not only of their unusual abilities, but in a connection to the greater reality of all life. It all seems to be an indicator that something quite profound is happening. The individuals who are waking up to their multi-awareness do have some explanations to give. But whatever you or I choose to believe, there is no doubt that the many expressions of Contact are extremely fascinating and will tantalise us as we explore the Contact mystery for ourselves.

"Extraterrestrial? Inter-dimensional? Delusional? Chemical? To me, confirmation of the sources of alien encounters becomes less and less relevant. I am simply focused on the interface between human consciousness and other intelligences.

I sense that collective, human consciousness is being affected by the breakthroughs experienced by individuals like us. We are transporting information into the human dimension, which ripples into the consciousness of others. We are a pioneering world!"

James Walden

"I can only come to the conclusion that we are becoming conscious, co-participants in our own evolution. With that in mind, if we are going somewhere, then they had better give us a brochure, which I guess is what they're doing!"

Julia

"Your subconscious, I believe, will know the truth and if you ask it to reveal the truth of your encounters, the information will filter into your awareness."

James Walden – *The Ultimate Alien Agenda*

CHAPTER FIFTEEN
An Holistic Approach to Therapy and Support for Contact Experiences

This chapter looks at a holistic approach to Contact therapy and support, and what its value is for those with Contact experiences. We look at what is understood by holism and why this model is becoming more accepted as a preferred option for many, despite the fact that science has yet to quantify much of it. A holistic model may help us to discover *what we don't know* about Contact and with useful application we can see that through regression (for example) information about the mystery of contact can be obtained; information that offers individuals a new understanding, which resonates not just on a conscious level but on some deeper level of awareness as well.

Holism is a word coined from the Greek 'holos', meaning *whole* and is the word used to define the fundamental principle that the universe is a creation of 'wholes'. Therefore, as a living organism, we are mind, body and spirit. It is interesting that there has been a growing shift towards holistic principles throughout society, not only in such fields as medicine, but in psychology too, which demonstrates that we are starting to honour the non-quantifiable part of ourselves that is more than just body and mind.

But why is this holistic model so appropriate for Contact? Mainly because of the multilayered aspects of these experiences. If we can access the connection between mind, body and spirit, then it will help us to understand our multidimensional experiences from those other levels. This model does honour our holistic connection and the individual's inner wisdom and it demonstrates that by being open to the totality of our experiences, deeper understanding, healing and integration will naturally follow. The bonus for the researcher and therapist is that they also gain a greater understanding regarding the layers and different aspects that make up this multidimensional reality.

The holistic framework for Contact incorporates a recognised, traditional, therapeutic model, (i.e. the central truth being *the client knows best)*. This model of therapy has been pioneered by people such as Dr. Carl Rodgers. It is a non-directive approach, which fully honours the individual's personal reality, with a caring, non-judgemental acceptance. But the holistic model expands on this honouring of the individual and takes it to a deeper level of the person's 'personal' reality. To fully honour this personal reality, we must honour all aspects of an individual's experience, even though these experiences may conflict with present understanding and belief concepts.

Because *we don't know what we don't know,* some of these realities may no doubt appear to be incredibly bizarre, but then again, that is the nature of this phenomenon. In a multidimensional reality, we have no way of measuring or evaluating it, so to judge it without a 'yard stick', trying to define it is futile and unscientific. Until we have the proper data however, I do not believe we can afford to dismiss what it can offer. Thomas Khun, author of *The Structure of Scientific Revolutions.*

"Just observe, drop all your preconceived categories as best you can, put them aside and just collect raw information! Don't even worry about words like *happened,* or *didn't happen, exists* or *doesn't exist, inside* or *outside, real* or *unreal.* Put that all aside and just collect raw information (raw data)."

So how can we evaluate the data gathered, particularly when it may conflict with what we understand to be our reality? Do we draw a line at the conscious level and say that only information at this conscious level has credibility? Some believe that all information collected from people in altered states, or through regression is less reliable because the client is more suggestible at those levels. They argue that the therapist may consciously, or unconsciously, lead the client and that information gained could be just fantasy, coupled with suggestion through inexpert regression techniques. In such cases, if the therapist is inexperienced then this could happen. But for the more experienced practitioner this is doubtful. Further, research into 'altered states' is just in its infancy and we have no way of evaluating at what level of awareness information can be distorted, or if indeed it ever has been. Again, because *we don't know what we don't know,* if we dismiss all information gathered this way, we are in danger of 'throwing the baby out with the bath-water' and we could lose an important opportunity for understanding. All data should be classed as being valuable, even if at some later date some of it is found to be a symbolic representation of what the psyche offers us. So whatever the consciousness of the individual may be and whatever level it may be at, information and 'raw data' can provide clues (to the jigsaw) to our multilevel reality.

It must also be said at this point that most therapists are responsible, professional clinicians and they are fully aware of the danger of leading the client. As stated, before, sometimes this can be done deliberately by a skilled therapist, in order to try and check out what the client believes they are seeing. But I still maintain that information that surfaces from this technique has its value, even if we initially choose to see the material as a symbolic expression of what our psyche offers us.

For those who are critical of this approach and sceptical of what it reveals, because they feel the therapist has in some way influenced the material, then it is useful to remember that most clinicians are not deliberately seeking out this data, no more so than the client. Both parties are not harbouring any particular conscious desire to wade into this kind of multi-level experience. Remember also, that what is often revealed during these kinds of sessions can more often than not cause deep consternation within the clinician, as well as the client. It can be quite a daunting process when an individual spontaneously reveals information that the therapist has certainly not asked for, nor suggested.

Brian Weiss, American psychiatrist and former Chairman of Psychiatry at the Mount Sinai Medical Centre in Miami is a good example. He had the courage to write about a patient who regressed spontaneously into past lives. Many individuals have chosen to ignore this kind of information, but others have sought to verify it and have discovered, through their research, a high percentage of it to be valid. So, do we ignore the information because it challenges our present understanding, or do we allow it to surface in the attempt to quantify its validity and the source?

I also had a case where the last thing on my mind and my client's mind were UFOs. He came to me seeking information about a motor bike accident he'd had when he was a teenager. He explained that he had no memory of the accident and that all he remembered was arriving home severely concussed after being missing for five hours. He also said that although he had no operation in the hospital where he was taken after the accident, he had a strange scar on his abdomen he couldn't explain. Although I admitted to him I had no idea if I could help him regain missing memory after such a trauma, he still wanted to try.

The regression allowed information to surface not only about how the bike accident happened, but to his complete disbelief and amazement, (and mine, I hasten to add), he discovered he had also had an encounter with a space craft that same afternoon. He then went onto describe certain procedures that were carried out, which explained his scar. He discovered that the bike accident happened after the encounter. I wrote an article about this case called "Awakening to Contact", as I feel it clearly demonstrates how unsolicited information can surface, and at times when we least expect it.

There are many misconceptions about what happens in hypnosis, or altered states.

What is not known generally is that only a small percentage of individuals actually go into a deep trance state, where they are totally unaware of what they reveal. In most cases, the individual is only in a light state of relaxation and therefore conscious of what they are saying. In my experience, the client will actively block any suggestion which will conflict with what their inner exploration is showing them. This data can be so incredible, the client themselves will struggle with it and will often prefer not to own it. I never force any material on them, but I will ask sometimes if it makes any sense to them and often to my surprise and theirs, it does.

We know that just a few years ago, Contact data such as implants and 'hybrid children' were certainly viewed with suspicion by many ufologists, who thought they were far too bizarre or unrealistic to be true. In recent years, information has surfaced that has changed that general viewpoint. Data has revealed the reality of such things as implants, which were often viewed as a construct of a vivid imagination. We now have tangible proof that foreign objects have been found in the body exactly where the individuals have said they were. Some have even been removed. So, although we do not yet have that much concrete, physical evidence, many believe that anomalies such as implants, missing pregnancies and the very real, emotional trauma that goes with them, to be very convincing and it gives us reason to suspect there is some basis for these phenomena. It is only through exploring and honouring all information, gathered in as many different ways as possible that we can slowly build up a real picture of what Contact is showing us.

We know presently that many disciplines explore this holistic model, whether it is from a medical model or a psychological one. Holism in medicine is gaining in credibility, even though science still cannot prove how certain healing techniques work. But the positive effects of these kinds of treatments (such as acupuncture), have encouraged many medical doctors to explore them and even incorporate them within their own practice.

If we acknowledge the limits of conventional medicine and start to explore the complexity of the mind-body connection, we will gradually become aware of some thing far greater within ourselves that can both directly and indirectly affect our healing process. We are now beginning to see that our emotional and psychological health can affect our physical body, realising that individuals are healthier, not only through good diet, but by looking after their emotional, psychological and spiritual needs. In some circles it is generally understood that we need more than drugs and surgery to heal us. We need the desire, or the will to recover and heal and we may look to the part of ourselves we call the spirit or soul for this. A holistic framework acknowledges the spirit of our inner-self and accepts that if this aspect is unhappy or sick in some way, it can affect the more tangible, physical part of our being.

Finally, conventional medicine is beginning to acknowledge this. Medicine is starting to explore the 'science of the spirit' and it recognises that the healer/energy worker touches on this 'something' that helps us to heal and recover on all levels. This has proved to be very successful, so much so that holistically based hospitals now use healers because they have discovered that the benefits to the patient are very real and tangible. We may not yet scientifically understand this 'holistic soul process', but do we ignore what it has to offer us, until we can?

Psychological research has explored the mind and the mysteries of consciousness. As we discover more about human consciousness in general, we are forced to redefine what we have previously considered to be psychologically normal and address what is an actual valid, human experience. Up until a few years ago, many of these experiences would have been viewed as being abnormal in a traditional framework. Many experiences, such as astral travel and out of body experiences were considered, until recently, to be the bizarre fantasy of a mentally unbalanced person. Even today, many individuals experiencing multi-awareness are treated for mental illness due to lack of understanding on the part of the practitioner. This demonstrates once again the need to be open to the exploration of reality and the importance of such investigation and research. Psychiatrist Dr. John Mack pointed out that what we really need is a new discipline, 'the science of human experience'. We must research and redefine what we know as being 'real' because as we discover more aspects of our multidimensional selves, our reality and understanding will evolve and change.

Altered states of consciousness give us access to information not available to the wakened conscious mind; this can give us valuable insight into our psyche and reality. Very highly respected practitioners and researchers have already looked at some of these new areas of consciousness, such as:

- Out of body experiences (OBEs). Research suggests that 20% of the population spontaneously have these experiences.
- Near death experiences (NDEs). Thousands of individuals around the world have had this experience and have been changed dramatically as a result.
- Scientific remove viewing techniques (SRV) that allow us to access information from thousands of miles away suggests that we can use our consciousness to access information through time and space.
- Kundalini energy, which is a psychic energy at the base of our spine, is being explored by some of the medical/psychological fraternity. This energy (called 'kundalini') is said, by some, to cause mental

instability if activated too quickly, but can facilitate psi abilities and high sense perceptions. This and more, demonstrates that we are much more than complex biological machines.

Complementary therapists also demonstrate that they can access information from a cellular level. This is demonstrated by memories and flashbacks triggered by individuals seeking alternative healing therapies, such as body work that includes massage and kinesiology (muscle testing). Both work on a cellular level and the body can offer a range of information to the conscious mind in this way, as can relaxation techniques and meditation. It seems that these methods open up the psyche or 'body memory' to awareness, or to a range of experiences that our conscious, logical mind may be unaware of.

Again, many argue that the validity of information obtained and revealed through such alternative routes is less credible. But there is often so much unsolicited information that will take the practitioner and individual by surprise, so how do we explain this?

This in fact gives credibility to these processes, as well as the accompanying resonance within the individual in the form of deep feelings and emotions. Some describe this awareness as being intuition, giving us understanding of the multidimensional aspects of our nature. Again, although this is all less tangible, we cannot ignore what we intuitively sense, or feel, within this deep, knowing part of ourselves. To be able to explore this awareness however, we must honour its existence in the first place.

So if this knowing and awareness exists and we honour this wisdom within, how do we recognise it? For some, this soul/spirit understanding feels like a deep resonance in their inner being. Others just describe it as a gut feeling. Many lose this inner awareness through the belief that the brain and cognitive reasoning is the only thing to trust. But for those who honour their inner awareness, they do discover how accurate it can be even though it may conflict sometimes with their reasoning powers. When this intuitive side is trusted, it can offer a host of valuable information and be a wonderful tool helping us in our daily lives.

We really do need this intuitive awareness to help us sort out what is truth, as we are continually fed data that is distorted, or biased. It is this aspect of ourselves that helps us to discern between fact and fiction, truth and lies, basically it's what fits for us. Information revealed through regression work, or other alternative routes can be very bizarre and may conflict with what we understand cognitively about our reality. If this happens, it is the inner knowing of the individual that decides what resonates as being truth. If the data makes sense and helps the individual to understand their experiences, then it is a valid and useful tool, even if it is fairly unquantifiable. To assist individuals and to help them access this awareness, I use a technique called 'focused relaxation', which puts the client into a light 'alpha state' similar to what is experienced as they watch television or daydream. We have looked at some relaxation techniques already in this book and when a person is in this state, I am able to demonstrate the use of inner awareness as being a tool for understanding Contact experiences, on many different levels.

I used this model with Ellis Taylor (no relation to Tracey Taylor). He was one of the first people I met that said they were experiencing Contact. I demonstrated the different levels of his awareness and the process offered information and understanding about his experiences. Ellis was puzzled by many of his experiences, but there was one event in particular that bothered him, it had happened over forty years ago and he wanted to understand why, after so long, this event still intrigued him. Ellis said he was just seven years old, playing in a field with his friends, when he was offered a ride in a helicopter by two men. Ellis could never remember if he had actually taken the ride or not. More recently, he had met up with two of the boys that were with him at the time, now men, but strangely, although they could remember the incident, they couldn't remember what had happened either. It would have been a very significant event for them and for all of them not to remember is very odd indeed. So what did happen that day?

Ellis began the session by telling me everything that he could consciously remember, which was actually very little. He knew that at the time, he was living in Oxford, England at the time. Ellis told me that he was playing in a field with some of his friends, five or six of them. He said he was suddenly aware that a helicopter had landed and was very close to where they were playing, about 25 - 50 yards away. Two men got out of the helicopter, they were wearing flying suits and they came up to him and asked him if he wanted a ride. Ellis said that he had always thought it was strange that he couldn't remember what had happened there, as it was such a significant event in his life. Let's face it, it's not everyday you are offered a ride in a helicopter! He also said that when the men came out of the helicopter they never bent their heads, or crouched and only later did he wonder about that.

The notes that follow are a transcript of the regression session that we did. It was quite lengthy, so I have cut it down in parts and also added some of my own notes and thoughts on the way through *(see italics)*.

Ellis was in a mild state of relaxation when I began:

Mary: Go back to the experience and see yourself playing with your friends. What time of day was it?

Ellis: Morning, about 11 am.
          (Ellis is very clear and definite about the time.)

Mary: What was the day like?

Ellis: Nice day.

Mary: Look around; can you see all your friends?

Ellis: We are just playing.

Mary: Can you recognise and name your friends?
          (In this state, Ellis was able to name every child. He had however, been unable to do this while fully conscious, only moments before.)

Mary: Look at your clothing, what clothes are you wearing?

Ellis: Shoes and shorts.

Mary: What colour are your shorts?

Ellis: Brown.

Mary: What kind of a top are you wearing?

Ellis: A T-shirt.

Mary: Is it a warm or cold day?

Ellis: Warm day.

Mary: So you are all playing, okay. When did you first notice the helicopter? Who first saw it?

Ellis: Peter.

Mary: What did he say when he saw it?

Ellis: He didn't say anything, he just turned around and looked and it was there. *(Ellis doesn't mention any noise here. A helicopter would have been very noisy.)*

Mary: What was the first thing you saw when you looked at it?

Ellis: It was just a dim shape and then two men got out.
          (Again, 'a dim shape'. A helicopter at 25 - 50 yards away should have been seen clearly, especially on a bright, sunny day.)

Mary: Can you describe them?

Ellis: They both had blonde hair and they were tall with leather jackets and trousers.

Mary: What colour was the helicopter?

Ellis: Black, grey.

Mary: Has it got markings on it?

Ellis: Circle, with US on it.
            (This incident was approximately 38 years ago in the UK. It does seem very odd that an American helicopter would land to take small boys for a ride.)
Mary: Go back to the two men, what happened as they got out of the helicopter?
Ellis: They just stepped out and came towards us.
            (This was when Ellis consciously remembered that they got out of the helicopter upright, without ducking their heads.)
Mary: How close do they come?
Ellis: Right up to us.
Mary: So, very close?
Ellis: We were just standing there,
Mary: Who did they speak to first?
Ellis: To me.
Mary: As they are speaking to you, could you tell me the colour of their eyes?
Ellis: Blue eyes.
Mary: As you are looking at them, how do you feel about them?
Ellis: They looked like Americans.
Mary: Was that how they looked to you, or was it by their ac- cent?
Ellis: They called us something.
Mary: Go back to just before they spoke to you. You can see them coming towards you, tell me what they said?
Ellis: They said 'Howdy' . . . (chuckle),
Mary: So what did they say after that?
Ellis: How would you like to go for a ride?
Mary: What did you say?
Ellis: I felt a bit scared.
Mary: So you felt a bit scared, what happened next?
Ellis: We just walked up to them, me and Paul . . .

Ellis at this point became extremely agitated and very upset, he was breathing very fast and getting distressed. I spent some time calming him down and giving him reassurance. Several minutes later, Ellis was ready to continue, but I made it so that he could view this experience as though looking at a screen and I reminded him that this was all 'past' and that he was now safe. This reaction of fear and emotion wouldn't manifest this way, not unless something that he perceived as being traumatic had actually occurred.

Ellis: I feel all *buzzy* . . .
            (Ellis is still sounding quite disturbed and agitated).
Mary: *(More reassurance)* . . . View this experience as if looking at a
            television screen - you want to understand what happened?
Ellis: We got in and all the others just stayed there . . .they just looked at
            us and didn't do anything. *(Surprise exclamation from Ellis)*, it didn't
            have windows. I thought it had windows!
Mary: What happened next?
Ellis: We had a ride around and then came back.
Mary: They brought you back?
Ellis: Yes.
Mary: Nothing else happened?
Ellis: No.

Ellis said nothing more about this, which again, would be unusual for a
helicopter ride. One would expect him to give details regarding what it was
like, or how it felt and so on. In addition, the agitation that accompanied his
dialogue suggested to me that more had happened during this experience
than he was able to recall, even in a regressed state.

To access more information and to help him further, I enabled Ellis to
access another level of his inner knowing.

Mary: I am going to ask you, the part of you that knows *(subconscious)*, if
            anything else happened on that flight.
Ellis: *(Immediately)*, A bright light . . .*(mumbling)*.. Nothing to worry about,
            just a light.
            (Ellis sounded as if he was reassuring himself.)
Mary: What happened when you saw the light?
Ellis: Nothing to worry about.
            *(Ellis sounded as if he was repeating this and he spoke very quietly, it was
            difficult to hear him. I asked him how he knew there was nothing to worry
            about and he said that 'they' said there was nothing to worry about, that it
            was just a light.)*
Ellis: I am somewhere, round . . . curved sides.
Mary: Where?
Ellis: Paul is not talking . . .
            *(Ellis continued and said that he was in a room with Paul, there were seats
            there, but that he was standing and staring ahead, feeling unable to move. He
            said that he couldn't move his head and he then became very agitated again.)*

Ellis: There are two men . . . and the seats are coming up, I am paralysed, but standing up!

Mary: Why can't you move?

Ellis: Just can't.

(Ellis says he senses two presences behind him, wearing robes.)

Mary: Can you see them?

Ellis: Feel them there. . .

Mary: Is there anyone else there?

(Ellis sees a grotesque being in the corner of the room, doing 'something' but doesn't want to look. I ask if this being is involved, and he says no.)

Mary: Can you see your friend, Paul?

Ellis: He's lying down.

(Ellis becomes very upset and extremely agitated again, so I applied more calming techniques.)

Mary: Are you warm or cold?

Ellis: It's a bit stuffy *(hot and airless).*

Mary: Can you move?

Ellis: No, just lying. Two men are standing next to me, they are talking...

Mary: Can you hear their voices?

Ellis: No.

Mary: So how do you know they are talking?

Ellis: They are moving and making gestures, telepathic. . .

(Ellis sees a being coming up close to him.)

Ellis: One of them is coming and looking into my eyes, he's checking things, he can see who I am and put things into my mind and has seen where I've been and what I do. Now I am seeing space and stars, oh. . .it's lovely!

(Ellis describes this scene for a short time.)

Mary: What happens after this?

Ellis: I get off the table,

Mary: How are you feeling?

Ellis: Okay. Paul is standing there.

Mary: Do you see the other being?

Ellis: No, and then we are back with our friends.

Mary: So then you were back with your friends, are you playing?

Ellis: Yes.

For many clinicians the material, or information, would probably stop here. It certainly shows that something of an unusual nature occurred that day and it fits much of the classic Contact scenario. It also raises questions regarding the so-called 'black helicopters' that some individuals with Contact experiences say hover over their houses, or near to them and one could hypothesise that helicopters could be a screen illusion for a spacecraft.

These revelations left Ellis understandably very shaken and he needed to understand more about his experiences and make sense of them. I then moved his regression to a different level and I asked his inner wisdom to offer him some understanding of his experience.

Mary: Let us ask the part of you that understands, so that you can see this experience from a different space. What was being done to you on this craft?

Ellis: They can see everything in your mind, they, the ETs can put things there, do you know, they don't need to put solid things there?

Mary: Can you describe what you mean?

Ellis: Hard to describe, I've not got the words, they kind of read your thoughts, they do something to your brain, they can alter everything, they can trigger it, they take you to that space, they do not need to be with you to do it, they can see through your eyes, they can just do it. I can't explain it, it's when they do that, they have to send you somewhere else, that's why I'm drifting out in space, and they have to send part of you out to do that.

Mary: They have to send part of your consciousness out to do that?

Ellis: Yes.

(Ellis said that this procedure was done every so often, he said it was like a re-patterning and downloading of information, a procedure for realigning perhaps?)

Mary: So this was a check-up for you?

Ellis: Yes.

Mary: So is it to monitor and check-up on your movements and experiences?

Ellis: They can make you go places and do things and you don't remember any of it.

Mary: So, like, when you are given instructions and you do them without conscious awareness?

Ellis: Yes.

Mary: Why do they do this?

Ellis: You have to be in a place they can access you . . . and sometimes, someone else at the same time . . . but 'you' think you have done something else.

Mary: So you would have no recall of this?

Ellis: Yes.

Mary: Why do they do this and why don't they want you to know?

Ellis: Because of the fear.

Mary: So it's to stop you from getting frightened?

Ellis: Yes.

      (Ellis explains that the emotion of fear would get in the way of some of their procedures and so they sent his consciousness elsewhere for a short while, in this case into space. Ellis comments that it's so lovely there.)

Mary: With the part of you that knows, what about the being in the corner of the room? Who was it?

Ellis: No!

Mary: Do you wish to know?

Ellis: No!

I will always honour this kind of wisdom. In this instance, there was a part of Ellis that chose not to disclose certain information, so I naturally felt I must abide by this. I believe that the psyche/wisdom of the individual will reveal what can be understood and accepted at a particular time. So this approach is not only respectful and honours the individual's personal journey, but it honours their inner wisdom and allow them to reveal what they are able to deal with, when they are ready. To push for more information here, particularly for the sake of my agenda could be very damaging and highly inappropriate.

I now asked Ellis if he needed to understand more about this experience. He decided to look at the faces of the beings.

Ellis: White robes, convex forehead...protuberant eyes, they stand out....big chin.

Mary: What are your feelings about them?

Ellis: Good, yes. . .

Mary: Do you have a sense of their agenda?

Ellis: But they are not in charge.

      (I finally asked Ellis to look for some understanding for himself, through his inner wisdom.)

Mary: What is your understanding of your role, why are you having these experiences?

Ellis: To integrate what it's like to be human. They experience it through my eyes, they get a sense of what it's like, and they just want to know us.

(He also mentions that another member of the support group he belongs to, is part of 'the team'.)

Ellis had been quite traumatised as he had recalled some of these events, but the session ultimately progressed to give him his own personal understanding, not only of the events, but why they happened. All of this made complete sense to him. Ellis came out of the regression with a deep concern for his old friend who had been on the space craft with him all those years ago. He said to me that he knew his friend was having a difficult time and Ellis suspected that some of it could have been due to this encounter experience.

Note: Ellis has published an account of his own extraterrestrial and multi-dimensional experiences in his book "Dogged Days: The Strange life and times of a child from eternity. Paranormal experiences with Extraterrestrials, Humans, & Beings from other worlds and dimensions" www.ellisctaylor.com

So how can we validate the material uncovered through regression in this way?

- The recognisable Contact scenario
- Heightened emotions (the emotion displayed is often very dramatic and can only be sourced from real, perceived trauma)
- Often it is just too bizarre, even the client will question it
- Leading questions may be ignored by the client or even corrected
- The information resonates at a very deep gut level.

I would also like to point out that although it is important to get the corroborative information if possible, we can also access more about the experience and what it means, not just by asking the questions themselves, but by incorporating a different style of questioning. To corroborate and also validate his experience, Ellis could have located the other individuals who were with him at the time to see if they were receptive to his idea of what had happened. He said though, that at the moment it was enough for him to have an awareness of the event along with some personal understanding.

Ellis revealed through this process some intriguing information for us all, as well as offering himself some insight into what happened that day and why he was taken on board the spacecraft. The bonus here is that these kinds of procedures often reduce much of the fear, as integration and understanding of the experience is worked through.

I feel it may be relevant to point out that many experiencers feel that because of the multidimensional nature of the experience they are not asked appropriate questions from researchers. In the book *Direct Encounters* by Judith and Alan Gansberg, Mona, an experiencer said: "I feel that there could be so much more to learn from us, if they had different ways of questioning. If they let us tell everything in our minds about aliens, they would learn more." Mona said that the type and style of questioning limited the information the investigator gathered.

So what are the benefits of a holistic approach?

- To remove blocks from memories where there is the potential for trauma, which gives the individual some further insight.
- The holistic model offers information and understanding, healing and integration. Most people want to understand why this is happening to them as well as what it means. Are they just unlucky, a victim, or on some deep level, did they agree to participate? Accessing their inner wisdom will give them information about this; it will give them something that they can work with.

If Contact has been traumatic, on whatever level, I will ask the person if they have participated on some level, or agreed to have this experience. Up to this time, I have only had one client say they had not agreed. This was unusual, but then again, so was her regression, whereby she saw herself as a 'dual' entity, part human, part ET. When I asked her if she had consented, she said *no*, that it was a surprise. But I also knew that she saw herself through her regression as being part ET and part human. So I asked if the ET part of herself had consented and her answer was *yes*. She explained that she was upset that 'they' had not made her aware how much it would affect her human side.

Certainly this model challenges not only our clients, but also those working in this specialised area. But if we are to find out what this experience means and to look deeper into whom we are, we have to begin by asking different questions and honouring what our inner wisdom offers us.

What can we learn from this approach?

- Experiences of a 'dual' consciousness.
- A dual life, two aspects of the self living inter –dimensionally.

- Past lives with ET Contact.
- Past lives as ETs.
- Multidimensional exploration of our own consciousness i.e. spiritual, astral or soul body.
- Feelings of being visited by future selves.
- Healing performed on the ships.
- A human/ET self observing healing being done on another ET.
- Split souls, one in human form, another aspect of a soul living inter-dimensionally.

"Extraordinary experience is something profound and transforming. It penetrates your beliefs, values and attitudes, right to the core."

Janet Bergman – *In the Presence of Aliens*

Janet also says that when she tried to explain to her father about her Contact experiences, he said: "You sure live in a different world to the one I live in."

She explains: "In my world, even the laws of physics are no longer true. Walls become vapour, time flips on its side, locked doors are delusions of safety and sometimes I can fly. Even electrical appliances are unpredictable. I do live in a different world from my parents and most of my friends. But I am learning to cope with the extraordinary experiences in my life, as best I can. I have no other choice. I know now that living *in the presence of aliens* has always been my choice. My new understanding around my spiritual origins and my agreement to participate in an alien culture experiment also put my situation in a different light."

James Walden wrote to me and said: "I feel we must look at the enormous range of data available to us. It is through this openness to the more intuitive and multidimensional side of Contact experiences that we may get some answers."

Whatever your understanding or beliefs are about Contact phenomenon, it is here to stay. It is vital, as many more people 'wake up' to their Contact, that we find new ways of understanding what this phenomena is showing us. By using a total open framework of holism, as more evidence is revealed, we can discover the physical reality of this experience and other levels of consciousness. There is no doubt it can offer valuable insights into our multidimensional reality if we are prepared to honour the individual's unique understanding of it.

We all seek meaning through our experiences and our perceptions of them and we can only do this properly if our experiences are honoured. No matter what the life script may be, if we honour personal experience we are enabling integration, we are letting it happen through understanding. With this, healing can take place.

CHAPTER SIXTEEN
The ET Elephant

"The UFO presence is usually addressed from a religious, psychological, or scientific perspective because these form the platform for current thinking. This makes it difficult for the experiencer to communicate the truly alien ideas they have encountered. I write with a tension caused by the awareness that the meaning of what I share is lost. But that is my work, to try and mediate between two realms of consciousness."

Dana Redfield

"I didn't know what was going on, why was I having these experiences? The human part of me felt fear. The knowing, ET part of me realised exactly what was going on and why. There has always been an equal exchange between me and the Zetas (Greys). I helped them achieve their genetic goals and in return I received my healing/psychic abilities and my understanding of life on earth, extraterrestrials and the universe was enhanced. They also protect me when I ask for it. If I need the answer to a question they will answer telepathically. The knowing part of me had made the decision to assist the Greys. The understanding of this can be overpowered by the fear from limited human perceptions and reactions to the experience."

Tracey Taylor

I think that extraterrestrial Contact is similar to the story of the blind men and the elephant. Several blind men were asked to describe what an elephant looked like. One blind man touched the trunk and described something long and tubular, emitting warm air. Another man felt the tail, and described something narrow and pliable. Another felt the leg and said it was something like a tree trunk. Another felt the belly and described it as being massive but spongy. But not one of the blind men could step back and see the elephant as a whole.

I feel we are all like blind men, who think we can see the ET elephant, but due to our own personal limits we can only see parts of it. The only way we will be able to see more of the whole will be when we are open to each other's perspective and awareness.

I can offer my personal interpretation with regards to what I understand this ET elephant to be, but again, this interpretation will be limited because of the complexity and range of the phenomena. For those who already believe they do know, they will find they are on an ice flow that quickly melts as they learn more. For you to learn more, you must honour the perspective of all the individuals who have stepped out of their box of blind and limiting beliefs and taken ownership of what they are experiencing, because as they bravely share their stories, it helps the rest of us make better sense of the whole. Some of this material will inevitably challenge you, your beliefs and perceptions, as it has challenged mine. My personal ET elephant has changed so much that I have no idea what it is I am looking at, but I do acknowledge how little I know. Socrates said: "Wisdom is knowing how little we know."

Well, *we don't know what we don't know*, but if we can open ourselves up to value everything that our reality is showing us, it may lead us to another important part of the elephant and help us to understand the whole. So if we want to find out more of the whole, we should start with what we already know.

The parts of the ET elephant, what do we know?

- We know that most individuals are returned after their experiences because they are here to talk about it.
- We know that there are a variety of experiences, from very painful to very loving.
- We know that many of those who have experiences have often had lifelong and loving interactions with these beings and have connected with some of the beings intimately.
- We know that some experiencers have strong emotions and feelings for the beings, so much so they feel like family to them.
- We know that a variety of procedures are performed, which are sometimes very intrusive and can involve human, biological material.
- We know that healing of the physical, human body is performed and there is documented evidence to substantiate this.
- We know that secret schools suggest an education programme could be in operation and experiencers are taught, often experiencing a 'downloading' of information that can be way beyond their own conscious knowledge or learning.
- We know that there is transformation. People change, not just because they are surviving these challenging experiences but because this change is far more fundamental in terms of awakening consciousness.
- We know that Contact also manifests through human expressions of creativity, through art, language and writing, as well as the understanding of energy, vibration and frequencies.

- We know that those with Contact experiences seek a metaphysical or more universal spirituality, as well as having an ecological passion for harmony and a nurturing of themselves and the planet.
- We know that special human senses appear to be enhanced and individuals become aware of a new 'super-reality', of a multidimensional nature.
- We know there is evidence that supports the theory of 'Homo Noeticus', a new generation of human children.

"All truth passes through three stages. First it is ridiculed, second it is violently opposed, and third it is accepted as being self-evident."

Schopenhuer

Making sense of the whole ET elephant

The previous list denotes a microcosm of what is known about this enigma. It is not meant to be comprehensive, but it can help us explore certain thoughts or ideas about the mystery. We should remember that even the most enlightened, informed and scientific sources can only offer us a limited view. Although it is natural for us to look for answers, we must try to separate fact from what *may be* fiction and discern what data has integrity for ourselves, especially as this phenomenon attracts more than its fair share of disinformation. It is important to sift through this 'muddy' data, to discern the truth through our own, personal inner resonance. Although the hardest thing in the world sometimes is for us to trust our inner knowing, it only by trusting this intuitive awareness that we can make sense of the information we have. It is interesting that the nature of these experiences only offer this understanding when we choose to recognise and honour our inner resonance.

This phenomenon gives us so many different interpretations that we have to trust the part of us that intuitively guides and understands. We have to be aware at the same time that our personal attitudes and perceptions will frame this understanding, as our life experiences and judgement create personal 'colouring'. Because of the complexity of the experiences and the myriad of ways they can be perceived, it is important that we are aware that this personal colouring will reflect what we choose to believe and focus on. The more aware we are of this, the more open our 'frame' becomes and the more opportunity we have, granting ourselves a clearer understanding of what the ET elephant looks like.

Exploring your personal ET reality

Your personal ET reality will reflect your beliefs and philosophy and the more aware you are of how your beliefs and attitudes affect your focus, the more clearly you can explore your experiences and your judgement of it. Your attitude reflects how you view any life experiences, an example analogy being *is the cup half full or half empty?* So we can say: "Isn't the ET elephant an amazing creature?" Or we could say: "This ET elephant may kill me!" Ultimately, every interpretation is your choice, but the choice you make will affect what you decide to believe and ultimately how you cope.

Those who explore this from a philosophical soul/spirit perspective and choose to see all life experiences as being their soul's desire to expand its 'human' limits and physical horizons, may view the ET experience as being another challenge to the human spirit, here to aid them on their human/soul journey. This could be interpreted as a 'shamanic-like journey', a soul's opportunity to transcend fear limitations, to explore the university of higher consciousness. But if you decide to perceive this experience through a very human reality, then Contact suggests that numerous kinds of extraterrestrial beings are interacting with us in a variety of ways and with a myriad of agendas. There are as many interpretations of ET agendas as there are ET beings, so you must determine what your experiences are showing you and decide what resonates well for you.

The extraterrestrial elephant is so multifaceted, offering so many kinds of experiences that whatever you choose will come from your focus as you explore the multitude of differing views. For those of you who feel the ET agenda is a malevolent one, there are just as many people, if not more, who feel that *the aliens are out to get us* scenario is far too simplistic and they argue that, despite the individuals who have been traumatised, there are just as many others who have been helped. So what can you make of such diverse and conflicting information?

One fact is clear; this experience certainly changes people, but what those changes are for, or about, is still up for debate. The hypotheses range from the sublime to the ridiculous, such as: intelligent ET species are here to awaken our superior, perceptive abilities in order to help us evolve, or that they are here to enslave us for their own purposes! Personally, I find the latter to be rather nonsensical. Given the superior technologies they demonstrate, if this were really their intention then they have had ample opportunity to do so, not only in the past, but also right now in the present. Despite our technological advances, reports of their capabilities suggest that they could easily take us apart and put us back together again, (and indeed, they possibly have!).

The biblical scholar, Zecharia Sitchin suggests in his "Earth Chronicles" that the ETs are creator gods. He calls them the 'Annunaki' and says that we were created by them using a mixture of terrestrial and alien biological material. That we are derived from 'seedlings', products of a continuous, genetic manipulation of ET and terrestrial genes. He proposes that the Annunaki have continuously monitored us and encouraged our development right up to the present day. So, if what he suggests is correct, then why would they continue to assist us in raising human consciousness if their ultimate goal is to create human slaves, or biological fodder?

We may have to accept that, compared to alien intelligence, human thinking could be, and most probably is, extremely limited and we cannot possibly hope to understand the minds of our visitors. Because their intelligence may be so far removed from our own, (as is the ape and the grasshopper), it is highly possible that we may never know. But logically, as humans, we can relate to an advanced species wanting to populate and expand their territory, because as human beings we have already done this throughout our own planet. Our advances in technology and such things as genetic engineering make such a hypothesis very credible.

Sooner, rather than later, we could be exploring new worlds in true 'Star Trek' fashion! If this happens we may want to make our human, creative mark on habitable planets by seeing them ourselves. Hypothetically, if we were to be human progenitors of a planet, it is reasonable to assume that we would want to assist with its evolution.

But over time, how would we react to 'our seedlings' when they reach their age of technological maturity, acquiring many diverse ways in which they were able to destroy themselves and their home world, especially if they still had their human, aggressive mindset? What would we do?

As the ancestor, or progenitor of such a planet it is plausible to admit that we would need to facilitate a 'higher consciousness education programme' within the mind/consciousness of our seedlings, to encourage them to protect and preserve each other and their world. It would make sense perhaps to apply some genetic reprogramming to limit the more aggressive and destructive traits in their nature. Awakening them to new potentials would be necessary first, then the triggering of desire for spiritual understanding regarding the nature of energy and creativity, so that the seedlings could use their abilities wisely and with respect for all life. Wisdom would suggest that this would be a process whereby the change would have to be gradual, so that the 'new seeds' were not too different as to be seen as a threat by previous 'models'.

They would need to have abilities that would slowly allow for the old mind seedlings to understand and grow, to welcome the healthy changes to their planet. The new seeds would have to learn patience and rely on the trust of their inner knowing, because for a time they would be very isolated as well as feeling different and alone .But when enough new seedlings are introduced, the gentle process of awareness and change will begin.

Through sensitivity and healing awareness they would intuitively know how to integrate and change this consciousness, without the need for aggression. These seedlings would therefore be a tribute to their creators.

The Fruits of Contact

"By their fruits you will know them."

Matthew 7:20

To come to any conclusions as to the purposes of ET interaction, we can only look at the effects of Contact. The effects have been discussed in this book and you must decide how you wish to interpret them. Multidimensional reality and high sense perceptions - they are *the fruits of Contact*. Are they here for our ultimate benefit, or are they being established for some unknowable and malevolent ET agenda? I know that my own understanding of the ET elephant changes constantly and I can only share with you what I understand at this moment in time. For the most part, I have tried to avoid suggesting any hypothesis as to the ET agenda because of this complexity. I believe that interpretations of alien agenda may not come from what we know, but from what we fear and don't know. We know from those who are having this experience that what they believed has happened is not always what actually did happen. The experience has layers, like an onion, but whichever layer of the onion you peel away, one fact remains constant - that Contact awakens us to our multi -reality and through this super reality, we have a better understanding of our experiences and our human potential. So are the transformations and changes in human consciousness the penultimate purpose of Contact?

We can only guess at the purpose and agenda because for all we know there could be a multitude of reasons as well as multitudes of alien species. There are many who think that we are being duped, or programmed to believe what they want us to believe and this itself is a programme, or some kind of *ET take-over bid*. It does seem rather illogical, I think. Why would they facilitate greater awareness and understanding within us, enhancing our abilities and so on, only to precede a take over? If you look at how we are progressively destroying our earth and each other, through materialism, violence and greed, then in all honesty, if they left us alone for a few more years, judging by the rate we are going we would probably do this job for them!

If you like the world the way it is then you could easily see 'them' as being a distinct threat to all you know. But they are waking us up to a higher consciousness, perhaps assisting us with the evolution of mankind, and we have the Star Children and a renewed passion for healing. Are we honestly to believe that these traits are a manipulation of ET malevolence?

Whatever you choose to believe as being the purpose of Contact, there is no doubt they have changed what we understand as being the human reality barrier. Contact demonstrates new human potential and abilities, which suggest we are only limited by what we believe. Now it seems that human consciousness is beginning to awaken and it is open to exploring our multi-universes. We know that such things as remote viewing, sensing, out of body experiences, teleportation, levitation and travelling through solid objects during Contact, clearly demonstrate that what we think is impossible, is in fact possible and it suggests that human potential is far in excess of what we presently believe.

We are now beginning to question the reality constructs of time and space. Are they consciousness constructs, reality limits that human beings have imposed upon themselves? Humans need to evolve and they do this by challenging traditional mindsets, as we did several hundred years ago when we challenged the beliefs of a flat earth, (although there are some people in the world today that do still believe the earth is flat!). Human curiosity continually encourages us to transcend our limited belief systems *and to go where no one has gone before*. If some people challenge our present limits then we are all changed ultimately and we are transformed from who we once were. Contact experience presents just such a challenge, because those who live it find that they have to challenge the most fundamental human mindset of all, our present third-dimensional reality.

As Schopenhauer said: "All truth passes through three stages, first it is ridiculed." Contact experience shows us that we all have a unique window to reality and those who are more open to their experiences discover that reality can be fluid, with many faces. It suggests that what we perceive as being 'limits', may well be choice and how far we choose to expand our own reality boundaries. The question is, what if this experience is part of an unconscious choosing, to experience an expanded awareness, as the 'aware', unconscious part encourages the limited conscious part to expand and grow? Is this Contact experience a trigger that we unconsciously provide ourselves with to assist us in this process of expansion? Is the ET Contact experience just another part of our soul/spirit's journey in getting us to wake up? And, if we want to wake up, we have to make a choice and that choice means we have to face our fears.

One of these fears maybe that we will be perceived as being different and we have seen, or experienced what it is like to be different. Even as a child, many people are bullied because they look, or appear different. Adult human society honours conformity and acceptance of the mindset and most religions demand it. But Contact will throw us this 'wild card', it challenges us to be different and makes us acknowledge and face up to our uniqueness, through our reality and experiences. Its multifaceted nature forces us to look at our differentness. It takes us out of the conventional mode with a feeling of *I don't think I belong.* So what is the purpose, unless it is to force us to honour and accept these differences, because the concept of being different may offer us a greater understanding of our reality, through our personal, unique window?

By acknowledging differences we can celebrate each unique view and we can share in one another's. This process can expand human reality horizons beyond the limits and boundaries that we have created, to achieve a more holistic and complete understanding of who we are. So Contact, with its variety of faces, forces us to break the conspiracy of silence about the limits of present reality, as it makes it increasingly difficult to live within accepted beliefs. It entices us through a doorway, which can awaken the desire for human expansion and what it can offer us.

Whatever personal journey we are on, whatever the many challenges we face, this phenomenon gives us a reason to look at the bigger picture. We are living in a world, which on the surface looks as if we may be heading for destruction, due to carelessness and juvenile treatment of our earth home. However, I believe this enigma gives us reason for hope, because despite the challenges and fear brought about through the seemingly intrusive side of this phenomenon, the ultimate effect for those that can integrate and accept it, is one of change and hope, as it shows us new ways to explore and change our reality and make us find out what we are capable of. That is why it is even more vital that we support and honour those with Contact, as they may well be the pioneers of human evolution and a new future for humankind.

AFTERWORD
The Alien Lady

A few years ago, I was at a local shopping centre and it was one of those times when I was in a hurry and my hunger had persuaded me to buy a snack. I proceeded to eat rapidly, walking towards the escalator. Suddenly from behind me I heard a loud shout: "Hey! Aren't you the Alien Lady?" For a brief moment my heart stopped and my stomach curdled. I looked up in disbelief, my *fight or flight* instincts deserting me, and I just nodded my head.

A young woman came hurrying over with a small child in tow. She rapidly began to tell me about her young son who she said had been having alien experiences. As I stood there, silently listening, I wondered how many people might be listening in, or overhearing this interchange. She seemed to be oblivious to just how bizarre this situation was and as a part of me answered her; I became acutely aware that with this dialogue, my life had changed forever.

I realised perhaps, not so consciously that my life had changed irrevocably when I seriously began to explore this phenomenon. The term 'Alien Lady' is as good as any I suppose, as I sometimes feel like I'm a bit of an alien, on a planet where the majority of the population still dismiss the ET reality. But I would like to think of myself as being more of a *cosmic Agatha Christy*, a space detective, who wants to investigate the ET elephant and find out what it is truly made up of.

I once said this to Julia (an experiencer) and she said: "So what does that make me? A cosmic reporter?" Well, in a way, I think that it does. The experiencers are in a sense, the cosmic reporters of this phenomenon and whether I am the cosmic detective or not, I am continuously seeking new clues as to the reality of this 'drama', its suspects and motives and who may have done it and why. Perhaps my hunches will prove to be correct one day, or will it be a never-ending mystery? For me personally, this mystery is likely to be unfolding for the rest of my life. A journey of discovery, which begets more questions than answers and the answers that are received, beget even more questions, as I learn more about myself and my reality in the process.

Certainly what I have been shown through my clients multi-reality is far beyond the tools available to measure. I now have a passion, a fascination with the mysteries of life; I am and have always been an avid reader of the inexplicable, weird, wonderful and strange. I had already read books by Dr. John Mack and Whitley Strieber before I met my first experiencer, but, fascinating as they were, none of this reading material had made any kind of impact on me in any real way. I just added this information to my jigsaw of knowledge, like a jackdaw that collects bright objects because they are attracted to them, without necessarily understanding why.

But when the first client came to see me, it was like I woke up! This was a reality. It had to be because it impacted so much on people's lives and in such a powerful way. I became even more fascinated and intrigued, as I was confronted with one mystery, one tantalising enigma after another. However, throughout my own professional and personal process, I have continually tried to evaluate how real this is.

I was once asked on a live TV breakfast show the inevitable question: "Do you believe your client's stories?" I said: "If enough people tell you they have been to Alaska and describe what they experienced, even though you have never been to Alaska yourself and probably never will, does that mean that Alaska doesn't exist?" In truth, I would love to go to *Alaska* and I am quite disappointed with our visitors because it's okay having this proof through my clients, but what about me? I am one of their most vocal, public relations agents, you know, it would be nice of them to give me a buzz and invite me on board. They must know where I live by now! Well, if they have been to visit me, then they haven't told me about it yet!

Meanwhile, because I haven't been to *Alaska*, I continually search for new evidence that this place exists, so that I'm not just taking other people's word for it. My personal search has taken me across many scientific, psychological, historical and spiritual divides. My curiosity inspires a deep desire to understand, as well as offering support to those who have been touched by this phenomenon. This journey has inextricably changed me, not experientially (as far as I'm aware), but in my role as the conscious observer and recorder of Contact accounts. As I strive to support and honour my clients' unique journeys, I am always going to be called to explore and understand my own.

As Contact challenges the people who directly experience it, it also challenges me, my understanding of reality, my beliefs and my truth. I have found more and more that I would question 'reality' mindsets, from every corner of human knowledge. This has been very difficult, as I do not pretend to be any form of authority in many of the areas that I have sought to question. But I have discovered that much of what we are taught has many interpretations and not all of it is based on solid facts, as we are often led to believe. The bookworm part of me, the part that loved to read eclectically, discovered awhile ago just how much of what we believe is fluid. Even in my ignorance, through exploring reference material from many fields of human understanding, I have been able to discern clearly that there is much that we don't know about our reality and ourselves. It was through this process I realised that we are all seeking to understand the 'unknowable' and that each personal reality is extremely flexible. It was a revelation to me as I processed this fact, because it freed me up and enabled me to really explore for myself 'my world'. Now, I am no longer prepared to accept blindly all I read, or am told, just because it comes from a purported 'respectable' source. I continue to question it all and will always do so.

The Australian UFO International Symposium I attended in Brisbane in 1997 was another catalyst event for me. It was *mind blowing* and it traumatised my increasingly fragile world even more. As I listened to eloquent speakers, such as Bob Dean and Joe Lewels, (*The God Hypotheses*), it seemed to me that their personal journeys and understanding encapsulated much of my own. They managed to convey it to me in a way that I could draw my disintegrating paradigm together and make some sense of it. It proved to be the glue for my fragile world and it laid fresh foundations for an emerging new paradigm. I left with more knowledge of not just the physical and scientific evidence of the reality, but I saw how it provided so many fascinating, potential answers to many of our historical and spiritual mysteries. So finally, I was able to build a new picture of my world that made a great deal more sense to me than the old one did. I could see how the mystery of this phenomenon has shaped our lives.

I have often wondered why I chose to be so passionate about a subject that I had no personal experience of, one which has led me such a merry dance throughout my personal, professional and spiritual life. This has always been a mystery to me, one part of me being horrified that I could throw away my old reality 'coat' so willingly, another part celebrating the new person who no longer minded what I said, or thought, which wasn't in line with the conditioned framework, or mindset of others. It wasn't arrogance on my part, more of a feeling that I needed to be true to myself and my genuine, growing need for understanding. By accepting my inner resonance as my guide, it gave me a freedom and a renewed sense of self. I wondered if this was what the experiencer gained when they were finally able to let go of the need to prove what they feel and know is true and begin to integrate their new awareness?

But as a clinician, as I honoured these experiences, helping me to let go of outmoded beliefs, my whole professional (as well as personal) paradigm certainly began to lose its distinct reality boundaries. It challenged me, as I asked myself how far could I step into the river of this experience, without being dragged headlong down the rapids, being pulled out of the 'reality' I had previously known and accepted?

Fortunately, I had some understanding and personal experience of the non-physical world, which gave me some parameters that I could hold onto. This vision of a multi-reality exposing a bewildering and complex array of possibilities became at times, a terrifying concept for me, but despite all of this, I still wonder if this is what the experiencer feels?

My friend Julia, an experiencer herself, has had significant input in my work because I have always valued her perspective, as I have with all the wonderful and courageous individuals I have included throughout this book. Their insight and awareness has helped me to understand a little of what they experience and I believe that if you really want to understand what something is like, then who better to ask than those who personally experience it? Contact is a living and unique reference to this phenomenon, as Dr. John Mack says: "People *know* their experiences".

Julia once said to me that her personal exploration was like joining up the dots to an ever-unfolding mystery and the dots seem to encompass a universe. I found that particularly apt, as it fitted for me too. I feel that this work has offered me so many unique opportunities to understand what my reality consists of and as I begin to make up a new jigsaw of reality for myself, I will continue to explore this complex paradigm with my clients. I realise, as I give them permission to explore what their experiences may be showing them, I am also giving myself permission. Despite the incredible nature of some of the material I receive, I am continually finding that, far from creating confusion through this process of openness we are able to discover a new depth of understanding, feel more integrated and become more complete.

As I have let go of trying to conform to an outdated reality and instead, trust in my own inner resonance, I have become at peace with the information just as many experiencers do. I can see how it is societal judgement of the experiences that cause the conflict.

I am a therapist and healer before researcher and to meet my client's needs I have no choice other than to dip my toe in *the river of the unknown*. Through it, I too have been irretrievably changed. Through honouring the clients reality I have been taken into realms that I did not even suspect existed. My interpretation of that particular therapeutic model was even more liberal than the originator may have intended, but it created a framework that allowed for true openness and non-judgement, to accept that *I don't know what I don't know*. I feel it unlikely that I will ever know more than a miniscule part of what the ET elephant looks like. But like the blind man who explored the elephant, I still grab a hold of the trunk wanting to believe that I do actually know what it is. Always I get the feeling that the elephant could lift me up with his trunk, put me on his huge back and turn my world completely upside down again. It is exhilarating, but deeply confronting, and part of me would like to be back in my safe, ordered world of a few years ago, where there were answers, irrespective of whether they were the right ones or not!

But the other part of me knows that I would never be satisfied with that now and how boring that would be, compared to sitting high up on the back of the elephant, where I am able to see the amazing and fascinating new world that surrounds me. With that comes profound humility, for this exploration shows how little we do know. I do feel humbled when I listen to the incredible journeys of my clients, whose lives have been touched irretrievably by this experience. They demonstrate amazing resilience and courage that is encompassed within the human spirit and, when people ask me what it is that I do, I say I am blessed with the most fascinating work in the world. I get to meet some of the most interesting, multi-aware individuals on the planet, who are teaching me how little I know.

END

ADDENDUM

This article discusses the evidence and implications of a possible human upgrade program orchestrated by extraterrestrial contact. First published in 2006 it has been featured on many web sites and in magazines such as UFO Magazine in the USA.

The New Human
5th Root race, Indigos, China's Super Psychics & Star Children.

'A new race of human beings has emerged. Whilst superficially they are undistinguishable however, they are the part of the next wave of the bringers of light, to assist humanity with the awakening of terrestrial consciousness. Human beings are awakening to their innate connection to the Universe. This is the primary role for all the NEW CHILDREN, coming to planet earth'

Tracey Taylor, experiencer (2000)

A seven-year old boy called Boriska from the Volgograd region began to tell his family of his life on Mars, its inhabitants and civilisation. He said he knew of Earth and Lemuria in very specific detail. He possessed profound knowledge and a high intellect (*Pravda*, Sept 2004, Russia). Boriska displayed signs of extraordinary behaviour. At two weeks of age he was able to raise his head, spoke his first word at four months and as a one-year-old, Boriska could read the large print of a newspaper. With precision and clarity, he recounted his knowledge of Mars, planetary systems and their inhabitants. He spoke about the gifted kids which he referred to as 'indigos' and of their essential role in assisting humanity during the anticipated Earth Changes.

Is humanity changing as a species?
The new kids on the block: A global phenomenon.

Renowned prophet and healer Edgar Cayce (1877-1945) not only spoke of a new humanity and referred to it as the 5th Root race but he also predicted that it would appear in the years 1998 to 2010. Metaphysicians and other gurus also share the belief and the anticipation of this recent emergence of the new type of human they call Indigos. They are also referred to as Children of the New Millennium, Crystal Children, Children of Light, Rainbow and Golden Children, to mention a few.

The ufology community is conducting research into the extraterrestrial phenomenon experienced by children. Their explorations thus far have produced such terms as the New Humans or, more commonly, Star Children.

The profiles of the Indigo children share the same attributes as Star Children or are strikingly similar. They are highly intelligent, creative, psychic, telepathic and posses healing and clairvoyant abilities. The Indigo children also share an inherent capacity to articulately express knowledge and awareness of deep spiritual concepts, historical, anthropological and scientific data, far beyond the capacity of even the most learned scholars, regardless of their age, level of cognitive development, education and numerous other pertinent factors.

This confronting evidence has even captured the attention and interest of the Chinese government who are researching children who possess 'exceptional human functioning' (EHF), more commonly referred to as 'China's Super Psychics'

Through this article I explore the extraordinary qualities and states of consciousness demonstrated by such children and the inference of the emerging New Humans. Despite the plethora of information and supporting evidence, this phenomenon still manages to defy our logic and challenges our beliefs and yet it is scientifically supported. Everything seems to suggest that humanity is on the verge of an evolutionary quantum leap. If we accept this premise, is it not plausible that the phenomenon related to extraterrestrial experience is equally valid and could offer a reasonable explanation for these developments?

Metaphysicians who speak about the emerging New Humans have professional, psychological and medical science backgrounds. Doreen Virtue, (*The Crystal Children*) has a PhD, and an MA and BA degree in Counselling Psychology. The publication *The Indigo Children* (1999) by Lee Carroll and Jan Tober took information from psychologists and therapists. The research in China is sponsored by the government and suggests that the phenomenon is taken seriously. Ufology researchers, too, have credible science, medical and psychological backgrounds.

If we are changing as a species, ufology offers a reasonable explanation. Scientific, biological and anthropological anomalies certainly suggest some form of intervention in the evolution of Homo sapiens. The missing link in our evolutionary tree certainly indicates a primary intervention in our genetic make-up. If this is the case, then the New Humans may well have been orchestrated in a similar way with genetic upgrades in our DNA. But the present upgrade is so radical that it appears like an evolutionary jump start, hence the name the New Humans.

If humanity is experiencing a quantum leap in its evolution, why is it happening now? Star Children believe they are here to 'guide the awakening of terrestrial consciousness' (Tracey Taylor). But how will this be achieved?

New scientific research could provide us with some of those answers and may qualify what the Star Children seem to understand, such as their role in the awakening of human consciousness. It may also explain why our connections to extraterrestrials could be far more intimate than we have previously suspected, as well as why they are currently so interested in us.

Extraterrestrial contact and genetic manipulation?

UFOs and their appearance in our airspace have been systematically ridiculed as pure nonsense by governments for years. This has been an effective strategy, despite the evidence that one in ten people see such craft. Ridicule and disinformation has meant that most people will hesitate to speak of what they have seen, let alone admit they had any interactions with such craft. Evidence in the form of photographs, hours of video footage and credible testimony from airline pilots and military personnel seems to mean nothing. Even the radar sightings which confirm this reality are hidden from public view.

A medical practitioner, Dr Stephen Greer, supports a disclosure program and owns videotape of hundreds of hours of testimony from high ranking military personal. They all confirm that UFOs are real and that there is a systemic and deliberate cover up by government agencies. Retired American Army and NATO Command Sergeant-Major Robert O. Dean in the 1960s and 70s guarded COSMIC-classified files, which showed that government agencies were fully aware that extraterrestrials and UFOs regularly penetrated our airspace.

Compelling as this is, the evidence of such craft in our skies is really a very small part of this phenomenon. Surely we have to ask who is controlling these craft and why are they here? Robert Dean believes that we are very closely connected to aliens, both spiritually and physically, and suggests that they are responsible for the Star Child phenomenon. The development of a new humanity called Homo Noeticus is a term coined by John White who studied parapsychology and noetics (the investigation of consciousness). Many well-known researchers such as English author and UFO investigator Jenny Randles agree. She wrote about this in *Star Children: The True Story of Alien Offspring Among Us*.

It has been shown that contact experience is an inter-generational one and that such children appear to be more intelligent, exhibit extraordinary psychic and intuitive abilities and have knowledge that they have not consciously learnt. Ufology research shows that consistent genetic lines play an important factor in this phenomenon.

Podiatry surgeon, Dr Roger Leir, is renowned in ufology for his pioneering surgery removing alleged alien implants and his autobiographical book *The Aliens and the Scalpel*. Dr Leir included the phenomenon of Star Children in his research. He writes:

"I believe that any mother that looks at her recently born child, in comparison with children born twenty years ago, will testify that there is a tremendous difference. Some look upon the differences in the New Humans and say they have to do with better prenatal care etc. In my opinion this supposition is nonsense and in light of my more recent studies and exposure to the abduction phenomenon I have come to the conclusion that the rapid advancement of our human species is due to alien intervention in our bodies and minds."

Dr Roger Leir

Dr Leir has based his statement not only on research into alien implants but from his observations of children. Comparing today's statistics on the developmental stages in young children to forty years ago (when such records and studies began) he discovered that the level of higher psychological functioning in some cases was increased by as much as much as 80%. The question is, how could this happen?
Dr Leir: 'I suggest that the answer involves alien manipulation of human genetics' (*The Aliens and the Scalpel*, p.192).
Recent genetic research could qualify this starling revelation. There are unexplainable anomalies in our genetic history and in 2003 it was discovered that 223 genes do not have the required predecessors on our genomic evolutionary tree. These extra genes are completely missing in the invertebrate phrase. Therefore scientists can only explain their presence as recent in evolutionary time scale, and comment that this was not through gradual evolution, vertically on the tree of life, but horizontally as a *'side ways insertion of genetic material'*. Significantly these 223 genes are two-thirds the difference between the chimpanzee and Homo sapiens and include important psychological and psychiatric functions. How did humanity acquire such enigmatic genes? Dr Leir and other researchers believe the answer may well be extraterrestrial genetic intervention!

Dr Richard Boylan, a behavioural scientist, anthropologist and clinical hypnotherapist, has studied Star Children phenomenon and their connection to close encounter experience. He offers a precise profile of the New Humans and our intimate connection to extraterrestrials, or Star Visitors as he calls them. The Star Child may be defined as a child of both human and extraterrestrial origin. The ET contribution to the child's make-up may come from genetic engineering, from biomedical technology and from telepathic consciousness linking." *Star Kids are psychically and metaphysically changed as a result of their own contacts with the 'visitors' or ETs modifying their parent's reproductive DNA.'*

Both, Dr Boylan and Doreen Virtue believe that these children are often misdiagnosed with syndromes as questionable as ADD. Boylan suggests is that 'these kids are just crushingly bored with the slow, pedestrian way they are being educated' and that is why they often misbehave. Doreen Virtue believes that Indigo and Crystal children can be also diagnosed as autistic or having Aspergers syndrome. More research is warranted to explore such possibilities.

There are numerous accounts where the contactee or experiencer recalls details of their genetic material being harvested. Dr John Mack, former Professor of Psychiatry at Harvard Medical School wrote about the subject of genetic material being taken in his book *Abduction*. I have covered this important fact in my book *Awakening,* in the chapter on missing pregnancies. Many of my clients, both male and female recall experiences when this procedure occurred. Some women also believe that their genetic material has been taken and altered in some way prior to their pregnancy. They say they knew the child was different or special because of this. What I found astonishing was that many of these children seemed to have an awareness that they were different. A letter to ACERN states:

'Yes I have always believed I was from elsewhere, and, like I said, I used to speak and write in a strange language in private. Sometimes, even in front of my mum, I used to cry because I felt so different. I would tell her not to touch me, as it was dangerous, and I am not yours. I am one of them. When the greys used to leave, I would get upset and believe they had left me behind, which made me angry and upset. I have memories of planets with golden buildings'

James Basil (UK)

What are these differences, apart from higher physical and psychological functioning? Generally they are enhanced psychic and intuitive abilities, with an awareness of universal knowledge and even their true genetic origins. '*I am not yours'* implies that some Star Children are aware they are connected in some way to the extraterrestrial beings who visit them.

From a letter (USA): *'I started walking at 8 months, talking in sentences by 10 months, and how to read at 2 years; no one taught me. I had friends who walked through walls, became invisible, and we spoke telepathically. I desperately wanted to go home.'*

David from Perth, Western Australia shared his childhood psychic and telepathic abilities with me: 'I would have telepathic conversations with my sister until she told me to stop being lazy and start talking. I could turn street lights on and off with my mind"

Ann Andrews, author of *Abducted*, wrote about her family's extraterrestrial contacts. Jason, her youngest son, exhibits many of these higher senses, regularly astral travels and even heals individuals in this dream state.

Jason told his mother how the Star Child profile fitted him. Jason, like many other Star Children, complains about the bulkiness of his human body, saying how limited it is. He was tight lipped about his experiences for a long time because he said it was hard to trust anyone because you never know who they are working for. He was very serious when he asked Ann if I thought it was very strange that after hundreds of years of slow progress we had suddenly come on in leaps and bounds in just fifty years. According to Jason, 'they' (including himself) gave us the relevant knowledge. They showed us how to split the atom and harness nuclear power so that we might finally meet them as equals. However, he says angrily that we have turned all this knowledge into power over others less fortunate than ourselves, for example with atomic weapons. But when asked about genetic engineering, Jason said *'it is the ETs who choose the parents'*. The children are genetically altered before they are born. *'They are given extraterrestrial DNA.'*

Again it appears that many of the children know about their mixed human and ET gene pool. This was demonstrated to me quite graphically when a confused young mother told me about her ten-year-old son. She said that whilst out walking with him one day, her son very casually told her the *actual percentage of ET genes in every person they passed!*

Extraterrestrial education program, telepathic communication.

Five-year-old Aiden from Western Australia says *'I don't mind going through the walls, and they teach me more on the ships than I learn at school. They come through walls, float not walk, become invisible, but are still around!'* His mother writes, 'This astounds me. He is very blasé about it and says he will introduce them to me one day! Aiden knows what I am thinking, finishes my sentences for me, and feels pain when I do' *(see chapter 9 Awakening).*

Star Children can be aware of extraterrestrial educational programs when information is downloaded on a subconscious or super-conscious level. Jena is an eight-year-old girl in Perth who described this process as 'knowledge bombs' in her head, which sometimes hurt. They can have strange dreams where they know they are on-board spacecraft. They are taught to use their higher sense abilities and they know when they have done well at such tests.

Whitley Strieber, experiencer and author of *The Secret School,* also experienced such lessons on spacecraft. This testimony certainly suggests that the New Humans are not only upgraded physically and psychologically, but are also taught to operate on a broader multi-dimensional frequency which helps them access information and knowledge not available to others.

Tracey Taylor, who intuitively draws complex artwork and symbols related to her ET experiences, wrote 'As for my own contact experiences, I have become very compassionate towards ET beings, there is much that humans can learn and benefit by interacting with them. Initially I didn't know what was going on or why, but there has always been an equal exchange.

I helped them to achieve their genetic goals and, in return, developed my healing and psychic abilities, plus my understanding of life on earth. Star children are born with greater wisdom and awareness, and are also gifted creatively. They have a great feeling of being connected to nature and all that exists. They are the bringers of the new, the bringers of light, they are here to guide the awakening of terrestrial consciousness.'

Tracey Taylor

So, if the new humanity is already here, whatever we choose to call them, how is this awakening of terrestrial consciousness orchestrated? The answer may well be contained in the creative expressions and data connected to contact experience.

Breaking down the barriers. The limits of traditional ufology research.

Traditional ufology attempts to convince the general public of UFO reality with research focused primarily on UFO sightings and other such scientific data. Although this approach is important, I believe it is far too limited a perspective for such a complex phenomenon. Some ufologists still exhibit ambivalence towards the abduction or contact phenomenon. This is despite the many thousands of credible people and families who experience such a reality, and tangible data such as unusual marks the body, missing time and implants, which are the anomalies that can verify this reality. It seems that no matter how profound the evidence, some will still argue that it is far too insubstantial to be taken seriously. Likewise, they ignore any mixture of spiritual or metaphysical interpretations, or psychological and emotional evidence, despite the degree to which these experiences can dramatically change an individual's personal paradigm. Such information may just convince sceptical researchers that the experiencer is psychologically impaired. This is especially true of any information that experiencers receive telepathically or express in other ways.

I disagree totally with such a limited perspective and believe that if we are to understand contact more fully we have to be receptive to any physical, emotional, psychological or spiritual data that is linked to this phenomenon.

'Wisdom is knowing how little we know' – Socrates

Since 1996 I have received volumes of data and personal testimony that have convinced me of contact reality. But I was particularly intrigued to find that, despite the enormous fear some people experienced (and this is by no means standard), many were more traumatised by isolation and judgement than their experiences. What I discovered was that such experiences were eventually life changing and transformational.

Are these experiences transformational because such individuals are exposed to a broader spectrum of reality, or is it more than that?

I found that individuals who received support regained their equilibrium and accepted a broader frame of reality, which obviously changed their perspectives in many ways, both psychologically and spiritually. This integration meant that they now became more peaceful and open to their contact experiences. But I also felt it was their new openness to the extraordinary data they received which made their changes so profound.

Although such extraordinary data is treated with ambivalence, if not disinterest, by some researchers, it is common knowledge that creativity and artistic expression is one way that human beings express human experience. There is no doubt that contact experience can inspire some individuals to draw the extraterrestrial life forms they interact with, and that many of them look identical, which I believe is further testament to this reality. Likewise, they may draw unusual landscapes of planets, with which they can have a deep emotional connection. The landscapes may sometimes be strikingly similar, as are some of the artwork, symbols and written scripts. Sometimes they vocalise strange languages without conscious thought, and articulate them more fluidly than their normal human language.

In researching these matters we need to recognise our own limits and that we are unaware of what we don't know. I felt that, no matter how unusual or challenging this material was, if it is part of the contact experience then we cannot afford to ignore it.

Researching a broader paradigm requires an open mind, and by that I mean being open to all data. Thorough researcher seeks to reconcile this data with science fact as much as possible. It is always profound and exciting for me when conventional science comes to the rescue and offers a possible explanation. But what is even more fascinating is when the scientific explanations are so similar to what experiencers themselves have intuitively understood.

Expressions of ET contact: a visual communication and healing blueprint?

The strange expressions of contact; stunning images, symbols, drawings of strange planets, languages and unusual scripts is a fascinating enigma. I initially collated such data so experiencers could compare notes. I found that, when shared with other experiencers, the material was extraordinarily helpful in assisting them to honour and validate their own contact.

The ACERN DVD, *Expressions of ET Contact: A Visual Blueprint?* was an attempt to share this information with the ufology community and experiencers. What we discovered was that our lack of expertise in film making did not detract from the material or the stories. I am certain that the two film awards presented at the International UFO Congress in the USA came from the impact of these images, because they seemed to connect with individuals at some deep level, whether they were experiencers or not! The 2004 sequel video *Expressions of ET Contact: A Communication and Healing Blueprint?* similarly explored the subject from a more global perspective. Again, the combination of languages, art, scripts and personal stories touched a deep chord with people, creating strong emotional reactions and resonance.

The average experiencer believes such expressions are contact communications, containing complex holographic data which helps us to connect with who and what we are. Energetic signatures, perhaps containing blocks of coding, like holographic blueprints which we absorb on many levels.

'It should be born in mind that the nature of extraterrestrial communications is that, in a majority of instances, star visitors communicate with humans by telepathic transfer of mental images and concepts, rather than by words and speech'

Marie

In his review of the Expressions series, Duncan Roads, editor of *Nexus* Magazine wrote:

'These Expressions of ET Contact DVD's are two of the most amazing documentaries you will ever watch. I don't count myself as being a "sensitive" person at all, but I can assure you that I felt things "shifting inside of me" as I watched the videos. In fact, at least 15 minutes of one video that I watched I don't remember a thing about! I am sure viewers will also be surprised at the large number and variety of different life-forms visiting and interacting with us. It becomes clear that as contacts between "us" and "them" progresses, more and more information is being transmitted. Amongst the many people featured by Mary Rodwell in these documentaries, most are currently of the opinion that there are many life forms "out there" that are trying to assist humanity - now, more than ever. This assistance can take many forms; however, it is obvious that most of the assistance is via information packets transmitted to us.

Yet obviously it is still early days in the "getting to know you" process, so a lot of the information relayed to humans is still very basic, i.e., what "they" look like, what "they" are like and how our "reality" is but one of zillions of valid but different realities. The interviews are most interesting and compelling. And the artwork "does things to you" when you look at it. The paintings of the ETs or aliens ("beings" is probably a better word) are just riveting. One gets the "feeling" of what the being is "like" just by looking at these paintings — a result of the extra information packets transmitted by the artist, perhaps? ... These videos are more in the category of "spiritual awakening", but this is a result of the content and (probably) not the intention of the producers.'

Duncan Roads *(video review, Nexus, Aug-Sept 2004, p.78).*

Communication and reprogramming of our DNA, by language, and frequencies?

Are telepathic transfers of mental images and concepts communication from aliens. SETI (the official search for extraterrestrial intelligence) still argues that they have not received any anomalous radio signals to suggest extraterrestrial life exists. Whether this is the truth or not, that is their official line. But perhaps extraterrestrials would find radio transmissions a very primitive way to communicate. If we listen to experiencers, they say it is more likely to happen through multi-dimensional levels of human consciousness.

'This communication happens because everything is made up of the same matter resonating at different harmonics, so that the ETs are able to communicate with us, directing thought on subatomic levels, and so activate subconscious interaction. This is interpreted by the

conscious mind as a simplified form of communication, such as symbology. Symbols are meant to communicate the nature of the macrocosm.'

Tracey Taylor – Experiencer (WA).

There is no doubt that such expressions although not yet consciously quantifiable, certainly connect to a deep resonance within people, in the same way as crop circles do. Interestingly, some of the crop circle symbols are actually contained within some of the symbols the experiencers create and it's possible both phenomena may well be connected. Certainly we know that by viewing or standing in the crop circles many people feel something, as they also do with viewing the videos. Duncan Roads admits that, although he believes he is not particularly sensitive, he also felt something by seeing these images.

In the eastern states of Australia, a male hypnotherapist told me he felt that one particular symbol had affected his third eye centre, feeling a strange buzzing (interestingly this is the spot in the middle of the forehead through which some psychic abilities supposedly manifest). This certainly suggests that these expressions act as a trigger or catalyst for something within us. Some experiencers believe this data has frequencies that affect us energetically on a subconscious level, acting like a holographic program.

Is there a scientific basis to support the hypotheses that such communications or expressions can actually affect or talk to us, even to our DNA?

Recent Russian research offers support for such a possibility, and demonstrates that reliable scientific investigations could explain what experiencers have intuitively known all along. Russian DNA discoveries documented by Grazyna Fosar and Franz Bludorf in their book *Vernetzte Intelligenz* have been summarised by Baerbel. 'The human DNA is a biological Internet' with evidence that DNA can be *'influenced and reprogrammed by words and frequencies.'* This suggests that 'our DNA is not only responsible for the construction of our body, but also serves as data storage and communication.' The Russian scientists and linguists have found that the genetic code 'follows the same rules as all our human languages.' In effect, human language did not appear coincidentally but is a reflection of our DNA.

The Russian researchers believe that 'Living chromosomes function just like a holographic computer using endogenous DNA laser radiation. This means that they managed to modulate certain frequency patterns (sound) onto a laser-like ray which influence DNA frequency and thus the genetic information itself. Since the basic structure of DNA-alkaline pairs and language is of the same structure, no DNA decoding is necessary. One can simply use words and sentences of the human language! This, too, was experimentally proven!' Of course the frequency has to be correct. (I recommend that the article be read in full.) But for the purposes of this article, the Russian research shows how science now can demonstrate a way to reprogram DNA *through language and frequencies*.

Experiencers who manifest unusual languages, such as Rochelle (see the DVD *Expressions of ET Contact: A Communication and Healing Blueprint?*) call these 'soul languages'. Rochelle vocalises them when doing energy work and healing. Healing with sound and frequencies takes on a new meaning in this context. It could mean that Rochelle and others like her may well intuitively be able to change or reprogram DNA though such frequencies while healing. We already know that our subconscious is affected by subliminal frequencies and hypnosis, and the Russian research may have given us a scientific explanation why such techniques work so well. The question is whether the specific frequencies of these languages are designed to affect or reprogram our human DNA? This may well give us grounds for reviewing ancient texts in regards to our origins.

The bible quote below may be more than just symbolic rhetoric. In the Book of John (chapter 1: verse 1) it is written: *'In the beginning was the Word, and the Word was with God, and the Word was God. The same was in the beginning with God'* and verse 14 states: *'And the Word was made flesh, and dwelt amongst us'.*

The Russian DNA research article coincidentally mentions the changes in our children in terms of group consciousness. They comment that 'if humans with full individuality would regain group consciousness they would have a godlike power to create, alter and shape things on Earth and humanity is collectively moving towards a group consciousness of a new kind.' They state that 'fifty percent of children will become a problem as soon as they go to school, since the system lumps everyone together and demands adjustment. But the individuality of today's children is so strong that they refuse this adjustment and resist giving up their idiosyncrasies. ... At the same time more and more clairvoyant children are being born. Something in those children is striving more towards group consciousness of a new kind and it can no longer be suppressed. "

Are the Russian researchers in fact referring to what is now called the ADD (attention deficit disorder) child? Unfortunately, because there is no funded global research it's hard to gain accurate statistics. But, if the process of labelling children as ADD is an indicator of this phenomenon, then we are indeed evolving at an astounding rate.

The global perspective and more pieces fit the puzzle: Science, anthropology, theology, archaeology and the kids.

This short article entitled 'Learning to communicate with extraterrestrials: young children in India-China Himalaya use strange sign language' appeared on the website of *India Daily* (29 Jan 2005) by a staff reporter:

'In the deep region of Himalayas, people are reporting strange behaviours in children. The children are using sign languages which are unknown to their families and anyone around. Many of the children draw pictures of triangular objects flying in the sky. Many of them do not know what they saw and how they learnt these sign languages. Some in the region of Aksai Chin believe that these children regularly communicate with the extraterrestrials who are only visible to these children and communicate via telepathy. The children learn the sign language to communicate back to these beings. According to UFO research materials, some Mexican children also manifest similar behaviour, when many in the area reported for a long time UFO sightings. … According to some teachers in the schools in that area, young children are extra agile and extra talented these days. Their problem solving skills have increased and they are much more disciplined. They continually use a strange sign language among themselves. However they cannot teach this language to adults! The locals in the area believe UFOs have been visiting the area for thousands of years. It stopped for a while and now it has started again.'

Families have contacted me from all over the globe, not only from Australia, Europe, North and South America, but Asia and Russia, and all describe children advanced from the norm in psychological and physical development and with exceptional psychic abilities.

In Mexico City these same New Humans have begun to emerge, and it is said that over 1000 children are able to 'see' with various parts of their bodies. In some countries, government agencies interested in such children are actively researching the phenomenon. China has a program for investigating children with similar abilities, which is taken very seriously by the Chinese Government in Beijing. The book *China's Super Psychics* by Paul Dong and Thomas Raffill describes children with exceptional human functioning (EHF) who display similar patterns to Indigo or Star Children. They, too, are very psychic and intuitive, for example some have the ability to open flower buds by thought alone. And like the Mexican children, many have shown an ability to see with other parts of their bodies. They display telekinetic abilities as well as other fascinating multi-dimensional skills, such as sensing another's thoughts (telepathy). It has also been reported that the Chinese government has observed these children changing the human DNA molecule in a petri-dish before cameras and scientific equipment to record this supposedly impossible feat. We have no evidence to prove that these abilities are the result of extraterrestrial interventions. But, given the fact that the Chinese government is very secretive, this may well be something they do not feel ready to share. However, I am told that the Chinese are extremely interested in the UFO phenomenon and take it very seriously.

More pieces of the puzzle.

Although I can't cover all my research in this article, I can give the reader some points to ponder. The late Francis Crick, Nobel Prize winner, co-discoverer of the shape of the DNA molecule and author of *Life Itself,* made the astounding claim 'that an advanced civilisation transported the seeds of life in a spacecraft'! One wonders what led him to such an incredible conclusion. References in religious and biblical texts certainly raise questions as to our real origins. Anthropology still can't explain how we changed or morphed so dramatically from Neanderthal to Homo sapiens and the missing link has not been discovered or explanations given on how the developmental gap was bridged. Biblical scholar, Zecharia Sitchin, author of the *Earth Chronicles* suggests such answers could lie in ancient religious texts, such as the Bible. According to Sitchen, the Bible is a condensed rendering of ancient Sumerian and Akkadian texts. From his research he believes that Homo sapiens was a genetic upgrade of existing hominids which was undertaken by extraterrestrial beings called the Nephilim who came to Earth 450,000 years ago.

Indigenous tribes worldwide have within their oral history that they are visited by sky beings and are being genetically upgraded. The Dogan tribe (African Mali Tribe) call the star visitors the Nummo, an alien species which came from Sirius and genetically upgraded humans when they came to Earth. The Aborigines of Australia also talk of the sky beings Wandjina, who made them and gave them laws to live by.

Many sacred texts apart from the Bible raise similar questions. Will Hart, author of *The Dawn of the Genesis Race* notes references to God in *'plurality'.* Genesis, verse 26, states 'Then God said, and now we will make human beings, they will be like us and resemble us.' The question is who is **'us'**?

For those who seek to explore, there are many such anomalies in archaeological, anthropological, religious and spiritual texts that must guide the thinking person to question what we are educated to believe in terms of our origins and genetic heritage. But, the most compelling evidence comes from the testimony of children, many of them not old enough to read. Its information so profound one has to wonder how and where they obtained it.

Mike Oram resides in the United Kingdom. He told me that he was only 4 years old when he told his mother that there was no such thing as death. His mother disagreed, but Mike said:

'The Universe goes on for eternity and it's not true that we no longer play a part in the Universe. We come back.' 'I was too young to know the word reincarnation', he said. 'I then shocked her by saying "You are not my real parents, my parents are in space, and something of incredible importance will happen in this planet and it will affect all levels of consciousness, it will not happen in your life time but it will in mine." My poor mother never forgot that conversation.'

Mike Oram – Author *Does it Rain in Other Dimensions*

Colin Wilson in *Alien Dawn* (1998) wrote that not long before Andrija Puharich's death he asked him what he was working on. 'Paranormal children', he said: 'You wouldn't believe how many of these kids are out there, they seem to be at genius level. I know dozens, and there are probably thousands.' Wilson concludes, 'and this, I suspect is the beginning of the change that the UFOs are working on' (p.309).

Unfortunately many such phenomena are only recognised through a particular discipline's limited field of study, and this sadly narrows the perspective. There is no doubt that, for some, the extraterrestrial hypothesis is a hard one to swallow. But even if (for now) we interpret this data from a desire to understand why we may be evolving so rapidly, as this research suggests, we need to be open to all possibilities. Even if the puzzle is just perceived as another way of understanding ourselves, the question remains that, if we are evolving at an accelerated rate than cannot be explained in normal evolutionary terms, how and why is it happening?

Are Star Children, New Humans, Indigos and smart kids, etc, one and the same phenomenon? If they are, then the extraterrestrial hypothesis makes more sense. After all, it is ludicrous for the thinking person to believe we are the only intelligent life in the universe, given the vastness of space. And it is logical to believe that some of those other life forms may have evolved sufficiently to be able to visit us, even if how they travel here may be beyond our current scientific understanding.

The hypothesis of extraterrestrial reality is not only possible but also probable and explains many anomalies in our origins, our mythology and religions. Certainly, if what experiencers and indigenous people tell us is true, we have a very intimate and on-going relationship with the visitors, in addition to a common gene pool. This would certainly explain their continuing interest and participation in our evolutionary development.

The primitive and aggressive nature of Homo sapiens, armed with technology to destroy not only each other but also our beautiful planet, may well be why these ET ancestors have decided to accelerate humanity's evolutionary upgrade program. A New Human with multi-level awareness of our cosmic connection to all that is, may well be the only way we will finally appreciate what we have, change our behaviour, and grow up to take full responsibility for ourselves and this beautiful planet. The Star Children could be an integral part of this wake up call and it may be that through them we are being led to an understanding of this profound connection.

'Human beings are here to remember themselves, with conscious awareness and with complete understanding of their innate connection to the Universe.'

Tracey Taylor

If quantum theory is correct, science can't disagree that we are indeed connected to everything, including our extraterrestrial visitors!

'To them we are the aliens!'

Jess – 8 years old

What can I say: 'Out of the mouths of babes!'

ACKNOWLEDGEMENTS

Where can I begin . . . so many wonderful souls that have helped me on this journey . . .

Firstly, a huge thank you to all those beautiful people who *woke me up* and taught me "*how little I know.*" The members past and present of the ACERN Support group in Perth. Especially those who courageously allowed me to use their personal accounts in this book.

Julia, my friend, what can I say to one of my best *cosmic* reporters and artists, you are amazing, and as usual, just very modest and matter of fact about all your incredible experiences, your cosmic understanding I find awesome!

Ellis Taylor, you have a lot to answer for! Without your story I might have stayed with my knitting! And this is so much more fun, you are an inspiration, a special and dear friend.

Elle, we began a special journey together, and it was your courage and integrity which has been an inspiration to me, and so many others who you have helped, also a big thanks to daughter Jena for sharing her amazing awareness. Thank you both.

Jacqueline Tuffnell, Tia and Adam a true *Star Family* and extension of mine. You are all so special and priceless, love you heaps!

David, thank you for sharing your experiences so articulately, and displaying so well what the Awakening process is like for so many, and for your kindness in allowing me to share your story.

Tracey Taylor, for her generosity in sharing her amazing story with us all, and also for allowing me the privilege of sharing her incredible artwork with everyone. A courageous and gentle soul, a true *Star Child* who is a pleasure to know.

Sandra, a brave young woman in every sense, and one who has experienced the most difficult challenges of this experience with integrity, courage and humour. You are just one amazing young woman.

Dana Redfield, fellow author, and dear friend, your wisdom and experiences, supported me throughout the writing of *Awakening*. I cannot find words to express my thanks and appreciation.

The Andrews family for allowing me to share your story. Thanks to Headline Publishers for allowing me to use excerpts from Abducted:

Also thank you to Rochelle, Louise and Aiden, Chloe and Miranda, Mark, Margaret, Melanie, Jenny, Mike, Steve.

Thank you to Heather Pedley, publisher and friend - for the gift of your support and help with my book, it is through your wonderful openness and encouragement I have had the opportunity to share what I have learned. For that boundless gift I cannot thank you enough.

To Bradley De Niese (sadly deceased), and David Sandercock, *the team* who have continuously offered their creative skills and expertise, to help offer resources to so many. I cannot thank you enough.

Wendy Meynert, dear friend, thank you for being such a loving and supportive friend throughout my journey with this.

Jacinta Goerke, daughter number 15, another special friend and beautiful soul, who generously shares her many talents to help me in my work. You have been such a real blessing, and support in so many areas in my life thank you, beautiful!

Barbara Ingham, teacher and friend, whose wisdom, insight and love, has been of inestimable, thank you for offering me your encouragement and skills to be all I could be. You have much to answer for!

Penny Mackeague, one of my beautiful, soul sisters, we have shared a special journey and throughout it all, you have shown me love, humour and continuous encouragement.

To all these dear and beautiful friends, Baljeet, Michelle, Julia, Kim, Gillian and Patsy, very special souls from Centrecare, for all your continuing support and love, you are all so dear to my heart!

Blessings and thanks to another very special friend, Sharon Jones, a pioneering soul, your insight and many talents will be of such value to all who resource you.

Wendy Burnham, a very special lady, and dear friend, who works tirelessly to support and help all those she can in this time of awakening thank you for your continued dedication to help research and promote these phenomena.

As well as all the amazing and special people researchers and therapeutic support here in Australia, Sheryl and Martin Gottishall, Bryan Dickeson, Peter Khoury, and the many more, their invaluable work stretches across Australia.

Susan Hansen UFOCUSNZ for her friendship and courage in sharing her Contact story, and for her insight and the support she offers to those who resource her.

Donna and family, thank you for your contribution to raise awareness of this phenomenon.

Penny, and John, Bianca and Jess, for sharing so much.

Rob Townshend, who is responsible for the artwork on the cover of *Awakening*, for his dedication, and commitment to make sure that *they are shown as they really are!*

The ASPR/UFORUM committee, of WA Professor John Frodsham, Mike Jordan, Simon Harvey-Wilson, Steve Boak, Marianne Batternberg, Morley Legg, Judith Andrews, Andrew Milani and Brian Richards, and Julie Underwood my personal computer expert, for your love, support and generosity.

Dolores Cannon, a lady I truly admire for her willingness to explore beyond conventional boundaries with integrity, may you continue to move our horizons with your books.

Richard Boylan PhD and Ruth McKinley, Hoover of the pioneering organisation ACCET, which originally inspired me to create ACERN. With your encouragement and support ACERN has become a reality thank you.

Special thanks to authors James Walden and Janet Bergmark and Whitley Strieber for allowing me to use information from their books and for their encouragement and sharing.

Also many thanks to Lori Cordini, and Simon Chrystal for their contribution.

And finally, a very special thanks to Doctor Roger Leir for writing the foreword for Awakening and for using his professional expertise to show the evidence for a *reality* of this phenomenon.

My special thanks to Jane Milligan Melkior for her wonderful artwork of the Lion Being and the Gray being: see images (Chapter 8.)

Danielle Johnson for her generosity in sharing her wonderful talent, a very special person whom I treasure in my life always.

To all the rest of my beautiful and special friends, who know who they are and what gifts they have brought me. Thank you.

Since Awakening was first published some special people have moved to the spirit world: Their contribution to this phenomenon has been unique:

Dr John Mack, Simon Harvey Wilson, Dana Redfield, Bradley De Niese Laurie Campbell, Ernie Sears, Tony Dodd, and Adrian Dvir.

AUTHOR NOTES

The symptoms for Post Traumatic Stress Disorder are:

1. Confusion, immobilization and disorientation.
2. Denial of events - and this may manifest in such ways as poor or blocked memory of the events. If the person does not receive support it can become a chronic condition.

Chronic Post Traumatic Stress Disorder:

1. Extreme anxiety, i.e. panic attacks.
2. Fear and anger.
3. Confusion.
4. Insomnia and nightmares, with sleep disturbances and remembering or dreaming of the 'event' or events.
5. Flashbacks to events when triggered by similar scenes.
6. Phobias.
7. Intrusive, obsessive thoughts.
8. Denial.
9. Addiction to drugs or alcohol (another form of coping).
10. Depression.
11. Poor concentration.
12. Suicidal Feelings.

REFERENCES

Reference material, listed in chapter order:

INTRODUCTION

Hopkins, Budd. "Missing Time" (1981). A Documented Study of UFO Abductions. *Richard Marek Publishers, USA,* p 20.

Harvey-Wilson, Simon, Brian. "Shamanism and Alien Abductions A Comparative Study" (2000). Thesis, *Edith Cowen University Western Australia.* (www.ecu.edu.au) p 25.

Mack, John. "Abduction: Human Encounters with Aliens" (1994). *Simon &Schuster, London, p 26*

Mack, John. "Passport To The Cosmos Human Transformation and Alien Encounters"(1999). *Crown Publishers*, p 26.

CHAPTER ONE

Andrews, Ann & Richie, Jean. "Abducted: The True Tale Of Alien Abduction in Rural England" (1998*). London, Headline*, p 30.

CHAPTER TWO

Hynek, J.Allen. "The UFO Experience" (1972). *Regnery,* p 43

CHAPTER THREE

Redfield, Dana. "Summoned" (1999) & "The Et-Human link, We Are The Message"(2001). *Hampton Roads Publishing,* pp 54-56.

Downing, Barry H. "The Bible and Flying Saucers" (1968). Philadelphia, PA: *J.B. Lippencott Co,* p 55.

Strieber, Whitley. "Confirmation The Hard Evidence" (1998). *Simon & Schuster,* p 55.

Hesemann, Michael. "UFOs A Secret History" *Marlow & Co,* p55.

Hesemann, Michael Editor-in-chief Magazin 2000, p 55.

Mack, John "Abduction: Human Encounters with Aliens" (1994). *Simon & Schuster. London,* p 56.

Mack, John. "Passport to The Cosmos, Human Transformation and Alien Encounters"(1999) *Crown Publishers*, pp56-57.

Strieber, Whitley. "Communion" (1987). *Century,* p 59.

Chalker, Bill. "The OZ Files" (1996). *Duffy and Snelgrove,* p 62.

Leir, Roger "The Aliens and the Scalpel (1998). *Granite Publishing,* p 61.

Andrews, Ann & Richie, Jean. "Abducted: The True Tale of Alien Abduction in Rural England" (1998). *London, Headline,* p 62.

Walden, James."The Ultimate Alien Agenda, the Re-Engineering of Humankind". *Llewellyn Books USA,* p 67.

CHAPTER FOUR

Andrews, Ann & Richie, Jean. "Abducted: The True Tale of Alien Abduction in Rural England" (1998). *London, Headline,* p 70.

CHAPTER FIVE

Walden, James "The Ultimate Alien Agenda, The Re-Engineering Of Humankind". *Llewellyn Books. USA,* pp 83 & 96-97.

Redfield, Dana. "Summoned" (1999) & "The Et-Human link, We Are The Message"(2001). *Hampton Roads Publishing,* p 97.

Mack, John "Abduction: Human Encounters with Aliens" (1994). *Simon & Schuster. London,* p 93.

Mack, John. "Passport To The Cosmos, Human Transformation and Alien Encounters" (1999), p 92.

Wilde, Stuart. "Sixth Sense" *Hay House Australia Pty* (2000) p 96.

CHAPTER SIX

Redfield, Dana. "Summoned" (1999) & "The Et-Human link, We Are The Message"(2001) *Hampton Roads Publishing,* p 100.

Rogers, Carl. "Client-Centered Therapy: Its current practice implications and theory" (1951) Boston: *Houghton Mifflin,* p 106.

Mearns, Dave & Thorne, Brian. "Person-Centred Counselling In Action" (1988). *Sage,* p 106.

CHAPTER SEVEN

America: Support and resources - **ACCET** Academy Of Clinical Close Encounter Therapists, PO BOX 22310, Sacramento, California, 95822 USA (916) 422-7400, p 313.

Australia: **ACERN** The Australian Close Encounter Resource Network, . Email: starline@iinet.net.au *See "RESOURCES" a Comprehensive list: 313*

CHAPTER EIGHT

Taylor Tracey www.universalblueprints.com

CHAPTER NINE

Leir, Roger. "The Aliens and the Scalpel (1998) Scientific proof of Extraterrestrial Implants in Humans" *Granite Publishing USA*, p 140.

Wilson, Colin. "Alien Dawn, An Investigation into the Contact Experience" (1998).*London Virgin Publishing*, p 140.

Boylan, Richard. "Star kids benefit from Special schooling" (1999) *Academy of Clinical Close Encounter Therapists (ACCET Newsletter), USA*, pp 142-143. www3.eu.spiritweb.org/spirit/richard-boylan.html

Pope, Nick. "The Uninvited, An Expose Of the Alien Abduction Phenomenon"(1997). *Simon & Schuster London*, p 156.

Carroll, Lee & Tober. Jan "The Indigo Children" (1999) *Hay House*, p 141.

Randles, Jenny. "Star Children The True Story Of Alien Offspring among Us"(1995) *Sterling Publishing New York*, p 166.

Boylan, Richard. "Winter Academy of Clinical Close Encounter Therapists (ACCET) Newsletter" (1999), p 160.

Cannon, Dolores. "The Custodians, Beyond Abductions" (1998) & "The Convoluted Universe Book 1" (2002) *Ozark Mountain Publishers*, p 149.

Dong, Paul. "The Four Major Mysteries of Mainland China" (1984). *Prentice Hall*, p 166.

Dong, Paul & Thomas E Raffill. "China's Super Psychics" (1997). *Marlow and Company*, p 166.

Redfield, Dana. "Summoned" (1999) & 'The ET-Human link, We Are The Message" (2001). *Hampton Roads Publishing*, pp 165 & 167.

Pritchard, Andrea & David E. Mack, J. Kasey, Pam. Yapp, Claudia. Editors: "Alien Discussions, Proceedings of the Abduction Study Conference". Cambridge MA (1994). Page 116 "Alien experiences in Children" D. Bruce Truncale. *North Cambridge Press USA*, p 164.

Strieber, Whitley. "The Secret School" (1997) "Preparation for Contact" *New YorkHarper Collins*, p 167.

Andrews, Ann and & Jean Ritchie. "Abducted: The True Tale of Alien Abduction in Rural England" (1998). London: *Headline*, p 143.

Rodwell, Mary & Bradley De Niese. Sandercock David. "Expressions of ET Contact, a visual Blueprint?" Revised 2002. *ACERN West Australia*, p 156.

To Contact Dr Roger Leir and His A&S project: "The New Human" 253, Lombard Street, Suite B, Thousand Oaks, California 91360 USA, p 166.

CHAPTER TEN

Andrews, Ann & Richie, Jean. (1998) "Abducted: The True Tale Of Alien Abduction in Rural England" London, *Headline,* pp 170, 173, 177-185.

Bolton, Iris, "My Son My Son" (1983) *Atlanta GA Bolton Press* p 165.

CHAPTER ELEVEN

Redfield, Dana. "Summoned" (1999) & "The Et-Human link, We Are The Message" (2001) *Hampton Roads Publishing,* p 189.

Leir, Roger. "The Aliens and the Scalpel", *Granite Publishing USA,* pp186 & 189.

Strieber, Whitley. "Confirmation" (1998) *Simon & Schuster,* p 189.

Lawlor, Robert. "Voices of the First Day", p 191.

Mack, John. "Abduction: Human Encounters with Aliens" (1994) *Simon & Schuster. London,* p 191.

Mack, John. "Passport To The Cosmos Human Transformation and Alien Encounters"(1999). *Crown Publishers,* p 191.

Harvey-Wilson, Simon. Brian. "Shamanism and Alien Abductions A Comparative Study" (2000) Thesis. *Edith Cowen University Western Australia.* www.ecu.edu.au, p 192.

Weiss, Brian. "Many Lives Many Masters & Through Time Into Healing" (1992).*Simon & Schuster,* p 202.

Woolger, Roger J. "Other Lives, Other Selves" (1987). *Aquarian Press,* p 202.

Cannon, Dolores. "The Custodians, Beyond Abduction" (1999). *Ozark Mountain Publishing,* p 193-194.

Cannon, Dolores. "Keepers of the Garden" (1993). *Ozark Press,* p 193.

Cannon, Dolores. "The Convoluted Universe Book 1" (2002). *Ozark Mountain Publishing,* p 202.

CHAPTER TWELVE

Pellegrino-Estrich, Robert. "The Miracle Man. The Life Story of Joao De Deus" *Traid Publishing,* p 208.

Brennan, Barbara Ann. "Hands OF Light" (1988) *Bantam books,* p 208.

Monroe, Robert. "Journeys Out Of Body" (1974) *Corgi,* p 213.

Mack, John. "Abduction: Human Encounters with Aliens" (1994). Simon & Schuster. London, p 208.

Rodwell, Mary. De Niese, Bradley. Sandercock, David. "Expressions Of ET Contact, A visual Blueprint?"(2000). *Video produced by ACERN,* p 212.

Klimo, Jon. "Channelling, Investigations On Receiving Information From Paranormal Sources" (1987). *Aquarian Press,* p 212.

LeShan, Lawrence. "The Mystic and The Physicist: Toward A General Theory Of The Paranormal" (1974). *Viking Press,* p 216.

Thompson Smith, Angela. "Remote Perceptions" (1998) *Hampton Roads,* p 218.

Andrews, Ann & Richie, Jean. "Abducted: The True Tale Of Alien Abduction in Rural England" (1998). *Headline,* pp 211-220.

Panati, Charles. "The Geller Papers Scientific Observations On The Paranormal Powers Of Uri Geller" (1976). *Houghton & Miffin,* p 220.

Wilson, Colin. "Alien Dawn" (1998) *Virgin,* p 220.

CHAPTER FOURTEEN

Walden, James. "The Ultimate Alien Agenda. The Re-engineering Of Humankind" *Llewellyn Books USA,* pp 244 & 246

Cannon, Dolores. "The Custodians" & "Beyond Abduction" (1999). Ozark Mountain Publishing, p 241.

Redfield, Dana. "Summoned" (1999) & "The Et-Human link, We Are The Message" (2001). *Hampton Roads Publishing,* pp 230-231 & 236.

Rodwell, Mary. De Niese, Bradley. Sandercock, David. "Expressions Of ET Contact, A visual Blueprint?" (2000). *Video produced by ACERN,* p 230.

For Scripts, and symbols contact researcher Mr Gary Anthony, 39, Barnetby Road, First Lane, Hessle, East Yorkshire, UK, HU13 9HE Email: garyant@mithrand.karoo.co.uk, p 230.

Dennet, Preston. "UFO Healings. True accounts of people healed by Extraterrestrials"(1996). *Wildflower Press,* p 232.

Bergmark, Janet. "In The Presence Of Aliens" (1997). *Llewellyn Publications USA,* p 234.

Dong, Paul & Raffill T.E. "China's Super Psychics" (1997) Marlow & Co. p 237.

CHAPTER FIFTEEN

Rogers, Carl. "Client-Centered Therapy: Its current practice implications and theory" (1951). *Houghton Mifflin,* p 249.

Mack, John. "Abduction: Human Encounters with Aliens" (1994) *Simon & Schuster. London,* p 253.

Moody, Raymond. "Life after Life" (1979). *Bantam Books,* p 254.

Kuhn, Thomas. "The Structure of Scientific Revolutions" (1962). *2nd Edition University of Chicago Press,* p 250.

Weiss, Brian. "Many Lives, Many Masters" *Simon & Schuster New York,* p 251.

Kason, Yvonne. "A Farther Shore" p 254.

Grof, Stanislav. "Spiritual Emergencies", p 254.

Gansberg, Judith & Alan. "Direct Encounters" (1980) *Walker Publishing Inc UK,* p 263.

Bergmark, Janet. "In The Presence Of Aliens" (1997). *Llewellyn Publications USA,* p 264.

Walden, James. "The Ultimate Alien Agenda. The Re Engineering Of Humankind" *Llewellyn Books USA,* p 239.

Monroe, Robert. "Far Journeys" p 254.

CHAPTER SIXTEEN

Redfield, Dana. "The ET-Human Link. We Are the Message" (2001). *Hampton Roads Publishing Co,* p 266.

Dennet, Preston. "UFO Healings. True accounts of people healed by Extraterrestrials" (1996). *Wildflower Press,* p 267.

Sitchin, Zecharia. "The Earth Chronicles" Avon. *New York,* p 270.

AFTERWORD

Mack, John. "Abduction: Human Encounters with Aliens" (Page 272) (1994). *Simon & Schuster, London*

Lewels, Joe. "The God Hypothesis" (1997). *Wildflower Press USA,* p 276.

USEFUL RESOURCES

Books related to the UFO, abduction and Contact Phenomenon

There are a huge range of books about the ET Contact phenomenon available through most large bookshops. Listed below are just a few of the many you can choose from. I have listed the specific areas that certain books focus on and in the Science section of a bookstore you will find reference books, featuring the hard *physical* evidence of the reality of Extraterrestrial presence in our skies, particularly those documenting sightings of UFOs with photographs. You will find the more esoteric, or spiritual aspects of this experience to be in the self-help or New Age/Metaphysical sections.

The 'nuts and bolts' scientific evidence for Extraterrestrial life visiting Earth:

"The complete book of UFOs" Jenny Randles/P.Hough
"The Oz Files" Bill Chalker
"Witnessed" Budd Hopkins
"An Alien Harvest" Linda Moulton Howe
"Glimpses of Other Realities, Vol 1 & 2"
"Alien Base" Timothy Good
"Alien Liason"
"The UFO Experience, A Scientific Inquiry" Dr J Allen Hyn
"Close Encounters of the Fourth Kind" C. D. B. Bryan
"Unconventional Flying Objects" P.R. Hill
"UFO Quest" Alan Watts
"UFO Visitation" Alan Watts
"UFOs (Reports of Australian Encounters)" Keith Basterfield
"The Aliens and the Scalpel" Dr. Roger Leir

Abductions by therapists and researchers, which focus on the case studies of those with abductee/Contact experiences

"Abduction" Dr. J. Mack
"Passport to the Cosmos" Dr J.Mack
"Close Extraterrestrial Encounters" Richard Boylan & L.Boylan
"Encounters" Edith Fiore PhD
"Intruders" Budd Hopkins
"Missing Time"
"The Watchers" R.Fowler
"The Allagash Abductions"
"The Tujunga Canyon Contacts" Ann Druffel and Scott Rogo
"Alien Dawn" Colin Wilson
"Oz Files" Bill Chalker
"Alien Investigator" Tony Dodd

"The Andreasson Affair" Raymond Fowler
"Direct Encounters" Judith Gansberg & Alan Gansberg
"The Janos People" Frank Johnson
"UFOs and Abductions in Brazil" Irene Granchi
"Shamanism and Alien Abductions" Simon Harvey-Wilson
"The Interrupted Journey" John Fuller
"Secret Life" David Jacobs PhD
"Without Consent" Carl Nagaitis & Philip Mantle

Books on government conspiracies, cover up's etc:

"Extraterrestrial Contact: The Evidence and Implications" Stephen Greer M.D
"Above Top Secret" Timothy Good
"The F.B.I. Files" Nicholas Redfern
"The Truth about the UFO crash at Roswell" K. Basterfield.
"Left at the East Gate" Larry Warren
"Psychic Warrior" David Morehouse
"The Philadelphia Experiment" B. Steiger & S. Hanson Steiger
"Open Skies Closed Minds" Nick Pope
"Top Secret" Stanton Friedman
"In These Signs Conquer" Ellis C. Taylor

Books that show some different types of Extraterrestrials that have been seen, and what they look like:

"The Field guide to Extraterrestrials" Patrick Huyghe
"Faces Of The Visitors" K. Randle & R. Estes

Psychology and therapeutic understanding of the experience:

"Alien Discussions" Andrea Pritchard
"Spiritual Emergencies" S. Grof
"A Farther Shore" Y. Kason, M.D. and T. Degler.
"The Omega Project" Kenneth Ring
"Close Extraterrestrial Encounters" R. J. Boylan, & L. Boylan
"Laboured Journey to the Stars"
"Encounter" Edith Fiore "Reaching for Reality" Constance Clear. M.S.W.

Metaphysical/spiritual understanding of these phenomena often found under the spiritual/personal growth sections:

"Healing Shattered Reality" Alice Bryant and Linda Seebach

Scientific Remote viewing gives further evidence, as well as an understanding of the general purpose of the Extraterrestrials:

"Cosmic Voyage" Courtney Brown
"Psychic Warrior" David Morehouse
"Remote Perceptions" Angela Thompson Smith
Past life references and regression information:
"Legacy from the Stars" Dolores Cannon
"Starcrash"
"Keepers Of The Garden"
"The Custodians" & " Beyond abduction" Dolores Cannon
"The Convoluted Universe Book 1"
"Abduction" Dr J. Mack.
"Passport to the Cosmos" Dr J.Mack
"A Beginner's Guide to Life After Death" Peter Shires

Books written by those having Contact experiences:

"Dogged Days" Ellis Taylor
"Does It Rain In Other Dimensions?" Mike Oram
"Walking Between Worlds, Belonging to None" Ann Andrews
"Communion" Whitley Strieber
"Transformation" Whitley Strieber
"Breakthrough" Whitley Strieber
"The Secret School" Whitley Strieber
"The Communion Letters" Whitley Strieber
"In The Presence Of Aliens" Janet Bergmark.
"Abducted" Ann Andrews and Jean Ritchie
"Connections" B. Collings & Anna Jamerson
"The Ultimate Alien Agenda" James Walden
"Summoned" Dana Redfield
"ET-Human Link" Dana Redfield
"Abducted" Debbie Jordan & Kathy Mitchell
"Searchers" Ron Felber
"Intruders in the Night" Christopher Martin
"Beyond my Wildest Dreams" Kim Carlsberg
"Lost was the Key" Leah A. Haley
"The Excyles" Mia Adams
"Into the Fringe" Karla Turner PhD
"Alien Jigsaw" Katharina Wilson
"A Time to Remember" Joy S.Gilbert
"Uri Geller, My Story" Uri Geller

Books by Contactees:

"Co-Evolution" Alec Newold
"Abduction to the Ninth Planet" M. Desmarquet
"Link-An Extraterrestrial Odyssey" Dr.J.Reed & R.Raith
The Star Child Phenomenon:
"Star Children: The True Story of Alien Offspring Among Us." Jenny Randles
"The Millennium Children" Caryl Dennis, with Parker Whitma
"The Indigo Children" Jan Tober & Lee Carroll
"ET/Human Link, We Are The Message" Dana Redfield
"Star Kids: The Emerging Cosmic Generation" Richard Boylan (2005)
"China's Super Psychics" Dong, Paul, and Raffill, Thomas E. (1997)
"The Crystal Children" Doreen Virtue

Positive physical/spiritual outcomes from ET Contact:

"UFO Healings" Preston Dennett
"We come as friends" Peter Michaels

Channelled information/metaphysical information that may give you understanding of the purpose or agenda of ETs:

"Prism of Lyra" Lyssa Royal & K. Priest
"Visitors from Within" Lyssa Royal & K.Priest
"Preparing for Contact" Lyssa Royal & K.Priest
"ETs and the Explorer Race" Robert Shapiro
"Journey into The New Millenium" Wendy Munroe
"The Books of Enoch" Joseph Milik
"The Only Planet of Choice" P. Schlemmer
"The Other" Brad Steiger
"Sixth Sense" Stuart Wilde

If you are looking for answers from a historical/archaeological base then such material will be found under science/archaeological:

"Fingerprints of The Gods" Graham Hancock
"The Monuments of Mars" Richard C. Hoagland.
"The Earth Chronicles" Zechariah Sitchin
"The Holographic Universe" Michael Talbot
"The Holotrophic Mind" Stanislav Grof.
"Beyond Supernature" Lyle Watson.
"Architects of the Underworld" Bruce Rux
"The Genesis of the Grail Kings" Laurence Gardner
"The Spaceships of Ezekiel" J.F.Blumrich
"The Super Gods" Maurice Cotterell
"The Dawn of the Genesis Race" Will Hart

Because this Phenomena has a very real paranormal/psychic aspect to it then some information on this is useful:

"The Encyclopedia of Mystical and Paranormal Experience" R.E. Guiley.
"Channelling" Jon Klimo
"Journeys Out Of The Body" Robert Monroe
"Aliens Among Us" Ruth Montgomery

If you want information from a religious, spiritual and philosophical perspective:

"The God Hypotheses" Joe Lewels PhD
"The Bible"
"The Bible and Flying Saucers" Barry H. Downing
"Flying Saucers: A Modern Myth of Things Seen in The Skies" Carl Jung
"The Gnostic Gospels" E. Pagels

Anomalous Phenomena e.g. Crop circles:

Crop Circle Connector
Circular Site

Genetic science

"Vernetzte Intelligenz" Fosar, Grazyna & Bludorf, Franz.
"Summary of 'Russian DNA Discoveries" Baerbel

Magazines

Large newsagents stock magazines that cover many topics on ufology and Contact phenomena, and most will list resources for those with experiences. These magazines will sometimes be seen in the science section or alternative/New Age sections.
These magazines also list Ufology/Contact organisations for you to resource.
Just ask your newsagent what is available!

Alternative/ New Age magazines

You can get further insight about this phenomenon through some of the more alternative healing and spiritual magazines; they will often cover the more paranormal aspects to this experience and channelled explanations.

Newspapers

National and local newspapers are also another resource. Sightings of UFOs are news. Often the newspaper will include resources.

National and Local Radio

If you enjoy listening to the radio you may find this will give you information. Researchers, therapists, and experiencers will use the radio to go public. I have often been asked to do radio interviews, and find it is a valuable way of advertising the support available, as well as generally raising awareness in the community. This provides unusual synchronicity sometimes. For example: I was doing an interview on a local radio show when a lady phoned to the radio station and told me that her son had just been woken up by his clock radio, which was *coincidentally* tuned to the radio channel at the precise time I was talking about my work with experiencers. He listened and then called out for his mother to come and listen. He then told her that he had been having Contact experiences since he was three years old. Synchronicity, or co-incidence? Certainly the universe acts beautifully sometimes!

Television

This is perhaps one of the most valuable resources for information. A growing interest in Ufology and the abduction/Contact phenomenon means there are numer233 ous talk shows, documentaries and many news stories featuring sightings, researchers, therapists and sceptics. It is useful to read the television magazines, which advertise these programmes beforehand to see if there is anything relevant to UFO phenomena.

DVDs

DVDs are another valuable resource. Some cover the more tangible physical evidence, government cover-ups, archaeological and religious evidence, UFO sightings, and Contact experiences. The support group and my work has been featured on a documentary called "OZ Encounters, UFOs in Australia". It was a good overview of the phenomena, including sightings by many credible and reliable witnesses, and illustrates the trauma it can cause for some. The documentary shows photographic evidence of UFOs and the physical evidence, such as marks and scars. But there are many good quality videos on this subject available. The UFO magazines have numerous videos on this topic. You might also try video stores under the special interest section; ask the store manager if you can't find them; alternatively try some of the larger department stores. For example, the video of "OZ Encounters, UFOs in Australia" is being sold in many of the bigger stores throughout Australia.

The Internet
This is a vast resource for information on ufology and Contact experiences. Contact details for therapists, researchers and other experiencers are often to be found on subject associated websites and web forums.

Shopping for help
New Age shops and alternative bookstores have many books on these subjects, and may advertise talks and seminars too.

Lectures, workshops and conferences
Look for posters, advertisements in shops, magazines and local papers. Ufology groups usually advertise their conferences through the internet.

Organisations
It would be impossible to list all the organizations worldwide that offer information and support for those with Contact. But, if you resource any of these organisations below they can offer you information or referrals for you: A few organisations I have personally connected with.

AUSTRALIA
ACERN (Australian Close Encounter Resource Network).
Principal: Mary Rodwell R.N. Counsellor, Hypnotherapist
Email starline@iinet.net.au
Web address: www.acern.com.au

UFOR Sydney
UFO-PRSA. UFO and Paranormal Research Society of Australia
UFORQ UFO organisation Queensland

UK
CONCERN UK
BUFORA (British UFO research society)

USA
ACCET (Academy of Clinical Close Encounter Therapists)

NEW ZEALAND
UFOCUS NZ (Suzanne Hansen)

HONG KONG
HONG KONG UFO society

There are too many organisations to list, check for more with the Internet

What kinds of extraterrestrial beings do people see? What kind of art, symbols do they draw?

Scripts and strange language, what do they look and sound like?

Mary Rodwell, therapist and researcher, Principal of ACERN, introduces the best audio visual material from ACERN's data base.

Incredible art work, drawings of Et beings, symbols and scripts drawn by experiencers themselves show an integrity of experiences and visual expressions of Contact. How and why do "experiencers' feel impelled to create such artwork and symbolism?

Tracey Taylor, an experience briefly narrates her story and the process that guides and inspires her drawing of these unusual intricate designs. She explains the symbolism of them and why she feels they act as a 'trigger' to awaken us to further understanding of our origins.

Expressions of ET Contact, like the "Crop Circles' may offer another piece of the puzzle in understanding this enigma.

This DVD is a fascinating record of Contact in Australia.

Expressions of ET Contact a Communication and Healing Blueprint?

Mary Rodwell Author of Awakening and Principal of ACERN guides you through this unique data with personal accounts from the UK, and Australia share their stories and explain how their artistic abilities are used to draw the ' star visitors' as they really are. American author, Dana Redfield translates "contact communication" through geometric concepts and codes she believes act as a Universal language with energetic triggers to 'awaken us.'

Adrian Dvir, computer engineer, heals with the help of 'extraterrestrial doctors.' Rochelle D 'Elia feels she has a dual –consciousness through her extraterrestrial heritage and uses sound and energy to heal on many levels.

Whatever you choose to believe, Contact experiences demonstrate a global phenomenon, with transformative outcomes   from healing to unusual forms of communication. These "Expressions' offer us a tantalizing glimpse into this fascinating enigma.

Expressions of ET Contact are two of the most amazing documentaries you will ever watch. I don't count myself as being a "sensitive" person at all, but I can assure you that I felt things "shifting inside of me. The artwork "does things to you" when you look at it. Expressions are more in the category of "spiritual awakening."

Duncan Roads – Editor *review, Nexus Magazine 2004*

New Mind Records presents a range of relaxation and meditation Cds
to suit everyone. Whether you're a novice or advanced, these
Cds will enable you to reach a more relaxed and peaceful state
of being. Combined with the latest audio technology,
stunning music, subliminal positive affirmations and
creative imagery this is the whole package.

cds to expand your mind

Inner Alchemy is for those individuals who wish to
expand their creative and intuitive abilities.

FOR HEALTHY MIND, BODY AND SPIRIT

Mind Medicine is created for stress related illnesses,
and changing old negative programs.

Take Ten

10 Minute Meditations for Busy People

Take Ten is designed for the busy person, who wishes
to refresh and rebalance with limited time.

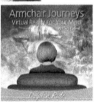

Armchair journey is a virtual reality for the mind.
Have fun as your explore your imagination.

Natural Mother

Natural Mother is a new way for women to approach relaxation
and connect to their baby in pregnancy
and motherhood.

retune your mind, body & spirit

Sound healing for those individuals who wish to try sound
frequencies for mind body spirit healing.

New Mind Records | E contact@newmindrecords.com | www.newmindrecords.com

Lightning Source UK Ltd.
Milton Keynes UK
UKHW021836200422
401802UK00008B/2016